TEXTUAL CONVERSATIONS
IN THE RENAISSANCE

For Anne Lake Prescott

Textual Conversations
in the Renaissance

Ethics, Authors, Technologies

Edited by

ZACHARY LESSER
University of Pennsylvania, USA

and

BENEDICT S. ROBINSON
SUNY-Stony Brook, USA

ASHGATE

Published by
Ashgate Publishing Limited
Gower House
Croft Road
Aldershot
Hampshire GU11 3HR
England

Ashgate Publishing Company
Suite 420
101 Cherry Street
Burlington, VT 05401-4405
USA

Ashgate website: http://www.ashgate.com

British Library Cataloguing in Publication Data
Textual conversations in the Renaissance : ethics, authors, technologies
    1.English literature – Early modern, 1500-1700 – History and criticism 2.Conversation
    in literature 3.Renaissance – England I.Lesser, Zachary II.Robinson, Benedict
    820.9'003

Library of Congress Cataloging-in-Publication Data
    Textual conversations in the Renaissance : ethics, authors, technologies / edited by Zachary Lesser and Benedict Robinson.
    p. cm.
Includes bibliographical references and index.
ISBN-13: 978-0-7546-5685-2 (alk. paper)
ISBN-10: 0-7546-5685-3 (alk. paper)
    1. Conversation analysis. 2. Renaissance. 3. Literature, Modern—16th century—History and criticism. 4. Language and culture. 5. Ethics. I. Lesser, Zachary. II. Robinson, Benedict.

    P95.45.T46 2006
    302.3'4609409031--dc22

                                                                                2006016416
ISBN-10: 0-7546-5685-3
ISBN-13: 978-0-7546-5685-2

Printed and bound in Great Britain by Antony Rowe Ltd, Chippenham, Wiltshire.

Contents

Part 3   Technologies of Conversation

Notes on Contributors

JUDITH H. ANDERSON is Chancellor's Professor of English at Indiana University. Her books include *The Growth of a Personal Voice: "Piers Plowman" and "The Faerie Queene"* (Yale University Press, 1976), *Biographical Truth: The Representation of Historical Persons in Tudor-Stuart Writing* (Yale University Press, 1984), *Words That Matter: Linguistic Perception in Renaissance English* (Stanford University Press, 1996), and *Translating Investments: Metaphor and the Dynamic of Cultural Change* (Fordham University Press, 2005). She edited, with Elizabeth Kirk, *Will's Vision of Piers Plowman*, by William Langland (Norton, 1990) and, with Donald Cheney and David A. Richardson, *Spenser's Life and the Subject of Biography* (University of Massachusetts Press, 1996). Her collection of essays *Integrating Literature and Writing Instruction: First-Year English, Humanities Core Courses, Seminars*, edited with Christine R. Farris, is forthcoming from the Modern Language Association. Her current book project is *Reading the Intertext: Chaucer, Shakespeare, Spenser, Milton*.

DOUGLAS A. BROOKS is Associate Professor of English at Texas A&M University and the editor of *Shakespeare Yearbook*. He is the author of *From Playhouse to Printing House: Drama and Authorship in Early Modern England* (Cambridge University Press, 2000) and editor of *Printing and Parenting in Early Modern England* (Ashgate, 2006). His articles have appeared in *Studies in English Literature*, *Renaissance Drama*, *Medieval and Renaissance Drama in England*, *Ben Jonson Journal*, *English Literary Renaissance*, and *Poetics Today*. He is currently completing a second monograph, *"In Such a Questionable Shape": The Imprint of Paternity in Early Modern England*, and editing a collection of essays, *Milton and the Jews*.

PATRICK CHENEY is Professor of English and Comparative Literature at Pennsylvania State University. He is the author of *Shakespeare, National Poet-Playwright* (Cambridge University Press, 2004) and editor of *The Cambridge Companion to Shakespeare's Poetry* (Cambridge University Press, 2006). With Anne Lake Prescott, he has edited *Approaches to Teaching Shorter Elizabethan Poetry* (MLA, 2000). He is currently at work on *Marlowe's Republican Authorship: Early Modern Political Representation* (Palgrave Macmillan, 2007).

MARGARET P. HANNAY, Professor of English at Siena College, is the author of *Philip's Phoenix: Mary Sidney, Countess of Pembroke* (Oxford University Press, 1990). With Suzanne Woods, she edited *Teaching Tudor and Stuart Women Writers* (MLA, 2000). She has also edited, with Noel Kinnamon and Michael Brennan, *The Collected Works of Mary Sidney Herbert, Countess of Pembroke* (Oxford University Press, 1998); a modern spelling edition for students of *Selected Works of Mary Sidney Herbert, Countess of Pembroke* (MRTS, 2005); and *Domestic Politics and Family Absence: The Correspondence (1588-1621) of Robert Sidney, first Earl of Leicester, and Barbara Gamage Sidney* (Ashgate, 2005). She is currently writing a biography of Lady Mary Wroth.

WILLIAM J. KENNEDY is Professor of Comparative Literature at Cornell University. He is the author of *Rhetorical Norms in Renaissance Literature* (Yale University Press, 1978); *Jacopo Sannazaro and the Uses of Pastoral* (University Press of New England, 1983), for which he was awarded the Howard R. Marraro MLA Prize; *Authorizing Petrarch* (Cornell University Press, 1994); and *The Site of Petrarchism: National Sentiment in Early Modern Italy, France, and England* (Johns Hopkins University Press, 2003). He co-edited *Writing in the Disciplines* (Prentice-Hall, 1986) and guest-edited two issues of *Annals of Scholarship: Art Practices and the Human Sciences in a Global Culture*, one on *Cosmopolitan Crossings* and the other on *Transactions and Exchanges in the European Renaissance*.

ARTHUR F. KINNEY is Thomas W. Copeland Professor of Literary History and Director of the Center for Renaissance Studies at the University of Massachusetts, Amherst. He has written or edited more than thirty books, including *Humanist Poetics: Thought, Rhetoric, and Fiction in Sixteenth-Century England* (University of Massachusetts Press, 1986), *John Skelton, Priest as Poet: Seasons of Discovery* (University of North Carolina Press, 1987), and *Continental Humanist Poetics: Studies in Erasmus, Castiglione, Marguerite de Navarre, Rabelais, and Cervantes* (University of Massachusetts Press, 1989). He is the founding editor of *English Literary History* and is currently editing the series *Studies in Early Modern Culture* for the University of Massachusetts Press. His most recent books are *Shakespeare's Webs* (2004) and *Shakespeare and Cognition* (2006), both published by Routledge.

ROGER KUIN is Professor of English at York University. He is the editor of Robert Langham's *Letter (1575)* (Brill, 1983), and author of *Chamber Music: Elizabethan Sonnet-Sequences and the Pleasure of Criticism* (University of Toronto Press, 1998) as well as numerous articles in *Criticism*, *English Literary Renaissance*, *Renaissance Quarterly*, *Sidney Journal*, and *Spenser Studies*. He is on the editorial board of *Sidney Journal*, is Secretary of the International Sidney Society, and is currently preparing an edition of Sir Philip Sidney's correspondence.

ZACHARY LESSER is Assistant Professor of English at the University of Pennsylvania. He is the author of *Renaissance Drama and the Politics of Publication: Readings in the English Book Trade* (Cambridge University Press, 2004) and articles in *ELH, English Literary Renaissance, Shakespeare Quarterly*, and elsewhere. He is currently working on two books, *Structures of Popularity in the Early Modern Book Trade: Publishers, Readers, and Printed Drama* (co-written with Alan B. Farmer), and *The Birth of Tragicomedy: Mixed Form, Mixed Politics in Renaissance Drama.*

PETER G. PLATT is Associate Professor of English and chair of the Medieval and Renaissance Studies Program at Barnard College. He is the author of *Reason Diminished: Shakespeare and the Marvelous* (University of Nebraska Press, 1997) and the editor of *Wonders, Marvels, and Monsters in Early Modern Culture* (University of Delaware Press, 1999). His articles have appeared in *Renaissance Quarterly, Review of English Studies*, and *Sidney Newsletter and Journal*. He is currently finishing a book on Shakespeare and the paradoxes of Renaissance culture.

BENEDICT S. ROBINSON is Assistant Professor of English at the State University of New York at Stony Brook. He is the author of *Islam and Early Modern English Literature: The Politics of Romance from Spenser to Milton*, forthcoming from Palgrave Macmillan, and has published articles in *SEL, Spenser Studies, Sixteenth Century Journal*, and elsewhere. He is currently at work on a project tentatively titled *Heterodoxy: Religious Identities in Transit in the Early Modern World.*

BETTY S. TRAVITSKY is the author of articles that have appeared in *Medieval and Renaissance Drama in England, English Literary Renaissance, Renaissance Quarterly*, and *Women's Studies*. She has edited numerous books, including *Subordination and Authorship in Early Modern England: The Case of Elizabeth Cavendish Egerton and Her 'Loose Papers'* (Arizona Center for Medieval and Renaissance Studies, 1999), *Female and Male Voices in Early Modern England: An Anthology of Renaissance Writing* (Columbia University Press, 2000), with Anne Lake Prescott, and *The Renaissance Englishwoman in Print: Counterbalancing the Canon* (University of Massachusetts Press, 1990), with Anne M. Haselkorn.

Preface

These essays on Renaissance conversation are themselves offered as the record of a particular series of contemporary dialogues: the conversations that all of us, editors and contributors alike, have enjoyed over many years with Anne Lake Prescott.

Anne's own work might be said to center on the concept of conversation: conversations between people, texts, and nations. Her two monographs both address the literary dialogue between Renaissance England and France: *French Poets and the English Renaissance: Studies in Fame and Transformation* (New Haven, 1978) takes as its subject English poetic relations with Ronsard, Du Bellay, Du Bartas, and others; and *Imagining Rabelais in Renaissance England* (New Haven, 1998) reads England's complex and ambivalent responses to sixteenth-century France's most iconoclastic, unruly, yet also enabling author—at least to his name, if not always to his actual texts. Her work has even at times taken the form of a humanist dialogue: "Divided State," which appeared in *English Literary Renaissance* in 1995, projected two seemingly contradictory readings of the current "state" of Renaissance studies, in which Anne's own position, rather like More's in *Utopia* or Spenser's in the *View of the Present State of Ireland*, must be interpreted dialogically. *Female and Male Voices in Early Modern England: An Anthology of Renaissance Writing* (New York, 2000), which Anne co-edited with Betty Travitsky, is likewise structured as a conversation: texts on similar themes by early modern women and men are paired as a strategy for foregrounding questions of gender and authorship in the early modern period. And throughout her work, the question of dialogue and conversation recurs: in the poetics and politics of coteries, in literary dialogues across national and gender lines, in generic transformations expressed as forms of dialogue with the past. This dialogic sensibility enables her to present complex and nuanced accounts of the cultural formations she studies, and to remain skeptical about all received orthodoxies, always aware of the exception or the dissonant voice in the conversation.

Some of the contributors to this volume are former students of Anne's; some are her co-authors or co-editors; others are longtime colleagues. All of us are her friends, in the full sense of that important humanist word, and all of us have learned from her, both from the substance of her scholarship and from the poise, wit, and generosity with which she has entered what is at times a turbulent discussion. Her knowledge and the obvious enjoyment with which she pursues and shares that knowledge are clear to anyone who has studied with her in the classroom, worked with her on a conference panel, or received one of her long, informative, and seriously witty e-mails (a familiar epistle whose form she has mastered). As two of her former students, we can say that the range of her learning is both inspiring and, at times, a little daunting. And yet anyone who has spoken with her will remember how effortlessly she carries that learning, as well as her clear enjoyment of all aspects of Renaissance culture, from the highest to (and perhaps especially) the lowest: in Anne, an elegance of thought and expression goes hand in hand with a real appreciation for the "low" or obscene aspects of Renaissance texts, an enjoyment that manifests itself in part in her love of Rabelais. With her knowledge, her ecumenical sensibility, her healthy skepticism, and her love of crossing disciplinary and aesthetic boundaries, Anne has been a treasured teacher and colleague for all of us, and we join in honoring and celebrating her work as a key voice in the conversation of Renaissance studies.

Zachary Lesser
Benedict S. Robinson

Introduction

Zachary Lesser
Benedict S. Robinson

"Conversation," Stephano Guazzo writes in the book translated into English in 1581 as *Civile Conversation*, "is the beginning and end of knowledge."[1] Tellingly, the remark itself makes up part of a conversation between the characters of "Guazzo" and "Anniball," and it is voiced not by the author's own fictional persona but by his interlocutor: the philosophy of conversation expresses itself through conversation, and through the literary effort to imagine voices in dialogue.

Like Guazzo's, this is a book dedicated to the Renaissance concept of conversation, a concept that functioned simultaneously as a privileged literary form (the dialogue), an intellectual and artistic program (Petrarch's letters to the ancients), an exercise in rhetoric (the argument *in utramque partem*), and a political possibility (the king's council, or the republican concept of mixed government). Conversation served the early modern period simultaneously as form, method, and practice. In its varieties of knowledge production, the Renaissance was centrally concerned with debate and dialogue, not only among scholars, but also, and perhaps more importantly, among and with texts. In a letter to his friend Francesco Vettori, Machiavelli famously describes his "little work," *The Prince*, as deriving from his "conversation" with the writers of antiquity: "I enter into the ancient courts of ancient men and am welcomed by them kindly ... and there I am not ashamed to speak to them, to ask them the reasons for their actions; and they, in their humanity, answer me."[2] Renaissance reading practices were active and engaged, and such conversations were two-way: the humanists did not merely read the ancients, they responded to them—sometimes, as in Petrarch's case, quite literally. And, as anyone who has glanced at the margins of early modern books sees immediately, Petrarch was far from the only reader who "wrote back" to his authors; indeed, humanist educational principles and philological

---

[1] Stephano Guazzo, *The Civile Conuersation of M. Steeuen Guazzo* (1581), trans. George Pettie, sig. B6ʳ.

[2] Letter to Francesco Vettori, 10 December 1513, quoted from *The Portable Machiavelli*, trans and eds Peter Bondanella and Mark Musa (New York, 1979), p. 69.

techniques provided readers with a complex set of tools—annotation, commonplacing, glossing, cross-referencing—for enabling conversations with texts.

Such conversations were meant as preparation for an active political and civic life, and the political itself was conceived as fundamentally conversational: education enabled the courtier to offer political counsel; humanist writing presented itself as advice to princes; and, through their engagement with the works of Aristotle, Polybius, Livy, Lucan, and others, Renaissance writers began to reimagine the state and sovereignty itself as an ongoing dialogue among multiple political forces and factions. And with its close connections to Renaissance ideas about friendship, sociability, and hospitality—ideas transmitted partly through a conversation with Cicero—the dialogue form could at times transform even highly charged topics into material for "politic" communication and negotiation. At these moments, conversation enabled the temporary production of a safe social space within which questions could be explored that otherwise might lead to the collapse of sociability in a reversion to mutually antagonistic identities.

This is perhaps nowhere clearer than in Jean Bodin's notorious *Colloquium Heptaplomeres*, a text that remained in manuscript throughout the period but that nevertheless circulated widely and became the subject of a conversation about religion whose participants included John Milton. In the *Colloquium*, seven speakers from across the globe—identified as a Catholic, a philosopher, a skeptic, a Lutheran, a Calvinist, a Catholic convert to Islam, and a Jew—meet in Venice at the house of Paulus Coronaeus, the Catholic speaker, where they hold a series of after-dinner conversations stretching over six days. For the first three days, they range through various learned topics, from demonology to Egyptian mummies to the causes of storms. On the fourth, the question of religion is broached, and at this point the conversation almost breaks down. Several of the speakers question whether it would be conversationally appropriate and doctrinally acceptable for them to proceed: as Salomon, the Jewish scholar, puts it,

> ... since I am already old, I could scarcely uproot from my heart my religion of long standing. Indeed the decrees of your priests and ours forbid me to lead you away from your religion. What then will be the fruit of this discussion?[3]

Nevertheless, conversation continues—in fact, the bulk of it is yet to come—because here, in this house, the speakers are "among friends and acquaintances" (p. 193), and because Coronaeus has worked hard to gather together "the most scholarly men in an intimate society," a gathering of strangers who nevertheless are united in Coronaeus's "incredible desire to understand the languages,

---

[3] Jean Bodin, *Colloquium of the Seven about Secrets of the Sublime: Colloquium Heptaplomeres de Rerum Sublimium Arcanis Abditis*, trans. Marion Leathers Daniels Kuntz (Princeton, 1975), p. 166; further references will be given parenthetically in the text.

inclinations, activities, customs, and virtues of different peoples" (p. 3). The speakers proceed to debate the truth and value of the world's religions and to explore the possibility that all the revealed religions in fact compose one universal natural religion, from which they vary only in indifferent ceremonies and practices. The conversation about religion, in other words, proceeds beyond comparative religion or religious polemic to a radical reconsideration of the basis of religion itself. This is a text with which philosophers would continue to be in dialogue throughout the seventeenth and eighteenth centuries.

At the end of the last day, Coronaeus concludes by singing a song that metaphorizes the conversation itself, imagining how friendly and learned conversation enables these seven to negotiate even the most controversial questions: "Lo, how good and pleasing it is for brothers to live in unity, arranged not in common diatonics or chromatics, but in enharmonics with a certain, more divine modulation." Musical harmony, which depends on different voices singing different parts, accommodates even antithetical perspectives into a single conversation: in fact, it *requires* difference, and cannot exist without it. And yet, there are limits, moments when the speakers allow a particularly uncomfortable point to be passed over in silence. More than this, the question of religion, as the final sentence of the manuscript informs us, is a topic to which they will never attempt to return: "afterwards they held no other conversation about religions, although each one defended his own religion with the supreme sanctity of his life" (p. 471). And, of course, from the very beginning we are reminded of the exclusiveness of this conversation: it includes only "brothers" and only scholars; it takes place in the private space of a wealthy house; it can only occur, we are explicitly told, in cosmopolitan and tolerant Venice (p. 3); and its record, the written text that purports to be expanded from shorthand notes taken down at the occasion itself, remains within the restricted ambit of manuscript circulation. Finally, the whole work of the conversation is to produce a kind of consensus that excludes even some of this restricted circle of speakers: if the idea of a universal natural religion is adumbrated by Salomon, Toralba the philosopher, Senamus the skeptic, and Octavius the Muslim convert, it is refused by both of the Protestant speakers, and gets only a qualified assent from Coronaeus; at other moments in the text, we see the emergence of a social constellation that includes the Christians, the philosophers, and the Jewish scholar, but in which the Muslim convert's claims for his religion are met with silent embarrassment. If conversation announces certain social and political possibilities, Bodin's text also reminds us of the limits of those possibilities, reminds us that conversation produces arrangements of social power and forms of exclusion.

The conversations on which we will focus in this volume are fundamentally *textual* conversations, practices of writing and reading conceived as dialogue, or the dialogue itself as a literary form. This is not to deny the importance of oral conversation in the period, nor to suggest any opposition or even firm boundary between orality and literacy.[4] We have chosen to concentrate on textual conversations not only to limit a vast topic but also because, as J.G.A. Pocock has argued, it was through such textual conversations that crucial early modern transformations in literature, history, and politics came to pass. Pocock notes that the humanists' eschewing of logic for grammar and philology was seen as enabling a classical author's "mind to communicate direct with his reader's," a scholarly shift with huge "epistemological and, ultimately, … philosophical consequences":

> The more it was stressed that an author long dead was speaking to us in the present, and the less we made of any structure of timeless universals through which his voice was mediated, the more conscious we must be of communication across time and of the time-space separating him from us; and the more carefully we facilitated this communication by studying the text and the context in which he had spoken or written, the more conscious we must become of the temporal, social, and historical circumstances in which he had expressed his thought and which, in shaping the language and the content of it, had shaped the thought itself.[5]

Textual conversation, in other words, offered the Renaissance its preeminent model of historicism. This historical consciousness, this idea of knowledge itself as intrinsically conversational—as a dialogue between individuals located in historical particularity, rather than an apprehension of universals—has something "ineradicably social or even political about it," and, in Pocock's argument, perhaps even something republican about it.[6] Whether or not we accept this strong claim, however, what is clear is that the humanist idea of textual conversation went far beyond the scholarly endeavors of philology or grammar to reach into the most basic aspects of social life, of art, of government. As an early modern historicist method that brought texts, genres, and authors into contact with the "the temporal, social, and historical circumstances" that shape them, conversation, we believe, still has much to tell us in the current scholarly moment.

The essays in *Textual Conversations in the Renaissance* approach the question of textual conversation from a variety of perspectives, but the contributors are linked in their desire to push the concept beyond its traditional domain of

---

[4] See, for example, Adam Fox, *Oral and Literate Culture in England, 1500–1700* (Oxford, 2000); Adam Fox and Daniel Woolf (eds), *The Spoken Word: Oral Culture in Britain, 1500–1850* (New York, 2002); Tessa Watt, *Cheap Print and Popular Piety, 1550–1640* (Cambridge, 1991); and, of course, Walter J. Ong, *Orality and Literacy: The Technologizing of the Word* (New York, 1982).

[5] J.G.A. Pocock, *The Machiavellian Moment: Florentine Political Thought and the Atlantic Republican Tradition* (Princeton, 1975), p. 61; on humanism and the consciousness of historical, cultural, and linguistic change, see also Thomas M. Greene, *The Light in Troy: Imitation and Discovery in Renaissance Poetry* (New Haven, 1982).

[6] Pocock, *The Machiavellian Moment*, p. 62.

sixteenth-century humanism.[7] Rather than pursuing a history of the humanist idea of conversation, the essays investigate the varied ways in which the Renaissance incorporated conversation and dialogue into its literary, political, juridical, religious, and social practices. While the essays intersect at numerous points, and while they can be productively read in multiple combinations, they seem to us to fall into three broad areas, each of which is concerned with a fundamental aspect of Renaissance textual conversations: ethics, authors, and technologies.

Part 1, "Conversational Ethics," considers the ramifications of dialogue, debate, and dialectic on early modern understandings of justice, ethics, and politics. As Arthur Kinney stresses in his wide-ranging contribution, "The Art of *Conversazioni*," Renaissance court culture was preeminently rhetorical, and, Kinney suggests, we (both citizens of the twenty-first century and contemporary academics) still have much to learn from early modern ideas of rhetorical dialogue. Beginning with the writings of Guazzo, and especially Castiglione, whose *Courtier* is "rooted in dialectic, an ongoing intricate interplay in fashioning the ideal courtier," Kinney articulates the humanist concept of conversation with twentieth-century literary and linguistic theories—including those of Wittgenstein, Bakhtin, and Austin—showing how the concerns of sixteenth-century humanist texts can be seen to dovetail with and illuminate the preoccupations of recent critical theory. At the heart of his essay is a detailed close reading of a crucial passage in *The Courtier*, the debate between Count Ludovico Canossa and Giovan Cristoforo Romano over the relative merits of painting and sculpture. Drawing on Lynne Magnusson's understanding of "social dialogue," Kinney's reading reveals how this sort of polite conversation, on a topic seemingly far removed from political and ethical concerns, in fact functions as a conduit for expressing aggression, hierarchy, and enmity.[8] At the same time, Kinney argues, such antagonisms never become so open that they prevent the continuation of dialogue because *sprezzatura*, in this context indicating an elegant conversational style, maintains the delicate dialectic between the antagonistic renegotiation of social relations and their harmonious reinforcement. For Kinney, style—so at the heart of Castiglione's text and of humanist rhetorical and educational programs more generally—opens up complex ethical questions about language and meaning that speak both to our

---

[7] Recent critical work on conversation in the early modern period seems similarly engaged in an attempt to think beyond both idealizing accounts of Renaissance humanism and its investment in conversation, and new historicism's nearly exclusive focus on forms of power centered on the court. See Lynne Magnusson, *Shakespeare and Social Dialogue: Dramatic Language and Elizabethan Letters* (Cambridge, 1999); Jennifer Richards, *Rhetoric and Courtliness in Early Modern Literature* (Cambridge, 2002); and Dorothea Heitsch and Jean-François Vallée (eds), *Printed Voices: The Renaissance Culture of Dialogue* (Toronto, 2004).

[8] Magnusson, *Shakespeare and Social Dialogue*.

reading of Renaissance texts and to our own social and institutional practices as academics.

The next two essays move from court culture to wider questions of justice in the early modern state, and from conversational theory to political practice. Jennifer Richards has recently urged critics to rethink the place of conversation in early modern politics by "consider[ing] what a recovery of a sixteenth-century conception of the 'social sphere' might mean for our understanding of the period's political idiom"; both of these essays do just that.[9] In "'Defend his freedom 'gainst a monarchy," Patrick Cheney reads Marlowe's partial translation of Lucan and the first part of *Tamburlaine* in the context of what he describes as an ongoing republican "cultural conversation." Cheney quotes Pocock's argument that, before 1649, English republicanism was "a language, not a programme," but he agrees with David Norbrook and other recent scholars that such republican language was in fact far more widespread than has been supposed. If this period constitutes, in Cheney's words, "a phase of English republicanism that we might call *imaginative* and *linguistic*," then English literary production provides a fertile site for tracing oblique English engagements with republicanism before the republic. Such an approach fruitfully opens up the definition of republicanism, considering it less as an activist political program and more as a way of thinking and writing: in David Norbrook's words, republicanism is a "politics of open speech and dialogue," that is, a politics of conversation—one that Norbrook, nevertheless, traces back only to the 1620s, despite the place of humanism in his analysis.[10] In his reading of *1 Tamburlaine*, and particularly in his close focus on the repeated use of the word *friend*, Cheney pursues this "politics of open speech," contrasting it with the more monologic nature of monarchy, in a play that strangely and paradoxically offers us a hero who is a republican tyrant. By examining Marlowe's paradoxical politics, Cheney seeks to explain why Marlowe's creation of an English republican language, of English "republican representation," has been almost wholly neglected, and why Marlowe has been erased from England's republican conversation, both by seventeenth-century republicans like Thomas May and by modern critics.

Peter Platt's "Much More the Better for Being a Little Bad" focuses centrally on the ethics of what Platt calls "Shakespearean paradox," that is, "an astonished expression of the encounter with double or multiple perspectives that usually accompanies epistemological change in Shakespeare's plays." Platt links this mode of paradox—which reveals connections with the formal dialogue in its insistence on the limits or inconsistencies of our knowledge—to a kind of juridical conversation: equity. The legal concept of equity is itself both paradoxical and

---

[9]   Richards, *Rhetoric and Courtliness in Early Modern Literature*, p. 2.

[10]   J.G.A. Pocock (ed.), *The Political Works of James Harrington* (Cambridge, 1977), p. 15; David Norbrook, *Writing the English Republic: Poetry, Rhetoric, and Politics, 1627–1660* (Cambridge, 1999), p. 20.

dialogic in its negotiation between strict justice and particular circumstance, and, like Cheney, Platt opposes this conversational discourse to single-minded and absolute perspectives, embodied for Platt by Duke Solinus at the start of *Comedy of Errors*. But the key text for Platt is *Measure for Measure*: perhaps more than any other Shakespearean drama, this play participates in equity, which seeks to refigure the demands of reason and justice in favor of "interpretive possibility and legal flexibility." The play ultimately interrogates and challenges the double perspective that equity embodies, however, revealing how and why it too can lead not to dialogic openness but to absolutism. Finally, Platt speculates on the special relation of equity to fiction and to dramatic fiction in particular, which may help to explain why drama functions as a privileged site for the investigation of this legal principle: equity, as Platt shows, itself requires imaginative textual conversation, because the judge must move from his reading of the letter of the law to the legal fiction of conversation with the law's creator, imagining how to legislate beyond the space of the law's specific provisions and how to recreate the law from its intent, not its content.

As Petrarch's letters show, Renaissance writers often thought of literary history itself as an ongoing conversation, and this dialogue is the subject of Part 2, "Authors in Conversation." These essays take such authorial conversations as their starting points, but they do so not from the relatively narrow perspective of allusion hunting. Rather, they seek out more complex, broader interactions between literary authors as well as the social, cultural, and historical ramifications of such dialogue. In "Allegory, Irony, Despair," Judith Anderson examines Spenser's conversation with Chaucer in *The Faerie Queene*, Books I and III, which Anderson interprets as offering sustained and compelling rereadings of the Pardoner's and the Franklin's tales. Beginning with local verbal echoes, Anderson pursues the close relations between these texts to a broader study of the relation of Chaucerian to Spenserian allegorical form. Anderson details how Spenser typically revises a Chaucerian character or motif by dividing or refracting it across an entire book, thereby reinterpreting it within his more abstract allegory. In her analysis, allegory itself becomes a conversational literary form, as she traces the fractured relationships among Spenser's allegorical elements and the dialogic relationship in allegory between the "deictic" and the "nondeictic" elements, the "real" (realistic, particular) and the "Real" (universal, essential).

William Kennedy's essay on "Shakespeare, French Poetry, and Alien Tongues" traces an international dialogue within Shakespeare's plays and poems, one that links English literature to other sites of textual production, including Italy, France, Spain, Portugal, and the Netherlands, and seeks to recover—as far as possible—the multilingual and multicultural dialogues that must have been ongoing in early modern London itself. Kennedy demonstrates Shakespeare's knowledge of and indebtedness to Continental literatures and languages, a knowledge acquired not only through his virtual conversations with the books of Florio, Du Bellay, or Ronsard, but also through his physical conversations with Huguenot refugees, foreign merchants, and other "aliens" settled in London. Like Anderson, Kennedy begins with verbal echoes but moves to larger thematic concerns, and like Kinney, he shows how dialogue can mask or even facilitate aggression, focusing particularly on the antagonistic game of one-upmanship that Shakespeare played against the "University Wits" precisely through his deployment of French poetry.

In "Joining the Conversation," Margaret Hannay addresses the role of early modern women in these literary conversations. Religious poetry, Hannay argues, provided a "culturally acceptable way [for women] to enter the English poetic tradition." She traces the Countess of Pembroke's dialogue with "the discourses that clustered around the authorizing voices of Petrarch and of David," analyzing her work in completing the metrical *Psalmes* begun by her brother Philip Sidney and her entrance into an otherwise male-dominated literary conversation, the English lyric tradition conventionally associated with Wyatt, Sidney, and Spenser. Pembroke finds in the psalms a literary form that can express the same lyric subjectivity that these male authors elaborated in the sonnet sequence, although both Pembroke's gender and her religious subject matter work to shape this subjectivity in ways that are significantly different from, for instance, her brother's in *Astrophil and Stella*; her psalms both refer to and overgo the lyric mode with which her brother became virtually synonymous, establishing Pembroke's own authority through a complex dialogue with her literary predecessors. As Pembroke revises her psalms, she moves further from her brother's translations and develops a more independent voice and poetic subjectivity. Ultimately, Hannay argues, Pembroke affirms her own poetic vocation in her psalms, joining a typically male conversation with a characteristic combination of humility and self-assertion.

Part 3, "Technologies of Conversation," turns to the material tools that enabled early modern textual conversations. The section begins with an ancient form, the familiar letter, a form that was foundational to the Renaissance; indeed, the literary origins of the Renaissance might with only some exaggeration be dated to Petrarch's 1345 discovery of the manuscripts of Cicero's letters. But the section ends with a thoroughly modern form, the printed book, famously part of the triumvirate (along with the compass and gunpowder) of modern inventions that, according to Francis Bacon, "have changed the whole face and state of things throughout the world."[11]

Betty Travistky's study of "The Puzzling Letters of Sister Elizabeth Sa[u]nder[s]" begins the section by continuing Hannay's investigation of the writing practices of early modern women. Starting from Erasmus' and Madeleine de Scudéry's comments that letters should be the material form of "conversations

---

[11] Francis Bacon, *Novum Organum, With Other Parts of The Great Instauration*, trans and eds Peter Urbach and John Gibson (Chicago, 1994), Book 1, aphorism 129, p. 131; Bacon was hardly the first to make such a claim for this triumvirate, however; see Elizabeth L. Eisenstein, *The Printing Press as an Agent of Change: Communications and Cultural Transformations in Early-Modern Europe* (2 vols, Cambridge, 1979), vol. 1, p. 21.

between absent friends," Travitsky reads the remarkable letters of this Bridgettine nun and reconstructs the eventful story that lay behind them and behind the experience of many English Catholics. In a series of letters to her aristocratic patron, the Catholic Sir Francis Englefield, Sanders describes her residence in hiding in England, her capture, her six-year imprisonment in Bridewell, her several attempts to escape, and her eventual return to Sion Abbey in Louvain. As texts written by a recusant woman, these letters represent important and vastly under-examined documents of early modern life and a crucial contribution to early modern women's history. At the same time, they illustrate the historiographic and archival challenges that scholars face when dealing with such a doubly marginalized group as early modern Catholic women. Importantly, Travitsky also traces the afterlife of Sanders's letters. In Robert Persons's 1590 printing of Sanders's letters as part of a propaganda campaign to publicize the dire situation of English Catholics, we can see the blurry boundaries between manuscript and print, and between private and public conversations.

The paradoxical relationship of private and public is precisely the impetus for Roger Kuin's "A Civil Conversation: Letters and the Edge of Form," a study of the theory and practice of the familiar epistle as a literary form, and of what Kuin calls the "edge" of this form: the familiar letter is a private conversation between absent friends, but it is also written with the awareness and often the intention of a more public reception. As such, Renaissance theories and manuals of letter-writing mingle injunctions to familiarity with injunctions to formality, recommendations to tailor each letter to its particular addressee with recommendations to maintain the style and decorum suited to the textual productions of a cultured and educated man or woman. Kuin begins with Montaigne's reminder that even his essays should in effect be construed as letters to a dead addressee, Étienne de la Boétie, and proceeds to an "epistolography" that encompasses Cicero, Petrarch, and Erasmus and concludes with an extensive examination of five letters from Philip Sidney's correspondence. Kuin's reading of Sidney and his correspondents seeks to displace the usual critical discussion of letters exclusively within the context of relationships of power and patronage and to offer instead a discussion of letter-writing in terms of this "edge," the "narrow line, the arête, between private and public, between today's Friend and someday's Reader, between the ephemeral and the enduring, between familiar chat and pride in one's mastery." The letter is a "meeting-place in absence," a border-zone between public and private, and a site of personal and political anxiety and possibility. As Kuin shows, even in the most personal and pressing of letters, Sidney's scrawled note telling his doctor to "hurry" to his deathbed, a public and communal set of conditioning expectations—that is, *form*—intervenes.

The final essay, Douglas Brooks's "The Imprint of Paternity in Spenser's *Faerie Queene*," shares the concern with politics, gender, authorial conversations, and literary form shown in the preceding essays and sets these issues alongside an investigation of the period's most crucial new technology of textual conversation:

print. Brooks describes what he calls "a transhistorical discussion of sorts between Ancient Greece and Elizabethan England," a conversation that centers on the relation of paternity and patriarchal authority to new modes of textuality—the invention of the alphabet in antiquity and the movable-type printing press in the early modern period. Brooks locates part of this conversation in *The Faerie Queene*, focusing on the episode of Error in Book I and on the haunting of Book VI by the names of various Renaissance printers to argue that Spenser's text seeks to negotiate competing matriarchal and patriarchal models of textual and biological reproduction—an especially urgent question for a poet writing in the last years of Elizabeth's reign. *The Faerie Queene* in effect seizes control of the technologies of literary and cultural productivity from a threatening maternal presence. In so doing, Spenser seeks to come to terms at once with the still-recent emergence of print culture and with specifically Elizabethan anxieties about inheritance, succession, and parentage. Here Brooks returns us again to the question of the political, neither in the republican sense discussed by Cheney nor in the juridical sense explored by Platt, but in a wider and more diffuse effort to think through the political implications of the cultural impact of print.

Our three sections—on ethics, authors, and technologies—can of course make no claim to exhausting the subject of Renaissance textual conversations; given our emphasis on the expansive or proliferative function of dialogue, such a claim would turn the book into a kind of self-consuming artifact. We want to encourage conversational readings of these essays across the inevitably somewhat arbitrary barriers of organizational division. Cheney's work on Marlowe and republicanism, for instance, proceeds by way of a meditation on "authorial conversations": Marlowe's reception and revision of Lucan, Shakespeare's and others' reception of Marlowe's reception of Lucan. Platt's essay suggests that drama functions as a crucial "technology of conversation" for testing the paradoxical merits of equity. Hannay's and Travitsky's analyses of the gendered and religious dynamics of such conversations certainly offer insights into important questions of "conversational ethics," for both early moderns and contemporary academics. This collaborative and dialogic study of Renaissance textual conversations can thus be considered neither exhaustive nor definitive, but then that is itself one of the first lessons of such a study. Our goals (and by that first-person plural we mean not only the editors but all the contributors) will have been accomplished if the essays succeed in producing further conversation.

PART 1
Conversational Ethics

Chapter 1

The Art of *Conversazioni*
Practices in Renaissance Rhetoric

Arthur F. Kinney

Life begins only at the point where utterance crosses utterance.

V.N. Vološinov[1]

People construct the social world using language, they deliberately and continually formulate reality through reference, description, and a variety of other speech functions .... More than just a tool for describing the world, language, no less than perception and bodily mobility, is a means of access to the world.

William F. Hanks[2]

Publicke affaires are rockes, private conversacions are whirlepooles and quickesandes. It is a like perilous to doe well and to doe ill.

Sir Walter Ralegh[3]

Asked to compose an essay on the state of Renaissance studies at the close of the twentieth century, Anne Lake Prescott, in her characteristically witty way, saw the pun inherent in the word "state" and, like humanists of the sixteenth century, found her model in Erasmus' Moria, Sir Thomas More. She begins this way:

> Εὔφρων [Happy]: Here in this garden—planted not in Antwerp this time, but in the State of Renaissance Studies—and seated on our grassy bench shall we imagine a Utopia? There is only a single person here, but since she is of at least two minds we could have a dialogue of one.
> Δυσχερής [Grumpy]: Certainly the stern traveler whose bench we have borrowed would

---

[1] V.N. Vološinov, *Marxism and the Philosophy of Language*, trans. Ladislav Matejka and I.R. Titunik (Cambridge, 1986), p. 145.

[2] William F. Hanks, "Notes on Semantics in Linguistic Practice," in Craig Calhoun, Edward LiPuma, and Moishe Postone (eds), *Bourdieu: Critical Perspectives* (Cambridge, 1993), p. 139.

[3] British Library MS Additional 22587, as cited by Agnes M.C. Latham, "Sir Walter Raleigh's *Instructions to his Son*," in *Elizabethan and Jacobean Studies Presented to Frank Percy Wilson in Honour of His Seventieth Birthday* (Oxford, 1959), pp. 207–8.

say that, like Tudor England, the SRS suffers from vanity, greed, a more punitive than persuasive way with criminals (humanists, formalists, liberals, essentialists), subservience to authorities, and pride in (critical) ancestry.

Eulfrwn: In my gloomy mood I would agree.

Dnsxerh/j: You forget—I *am* your gloomy mood. *Our dialogue's real point is this very division.*[4]

and she transported this pun-turned-paradox into her very title: "Divided State."

But writing coherently about potential incoherencies—or at least the multiplicities of meaning harbored in language—was nothing new for Prescott. She was then completing a book on "how early modern English writers read, cited, judged, enjoyed, reviled, imagined, and appropriated François Rabelais—or, often, the *name* Rabelais—before Thomas Urquhart's obstreperous 1653 translation made him part of English literature," and had found, because of these disparate responses, that Rabelais himself had become not one person (or writer) but at least three: "Rabelais the atheist scoffer, Rabelais the dirty-minded drunk, Rabelais the maker of silly stories."[5] If the subject, Rabelais, had initially seemed focused, the situation grew increasingly complex, her study resonating with her earlier book on Marot, Du Bellay, Ronsard, Desportes, and Du Bartas. That book, she declared, "attempts to explore what intelligent or at least literate Englishmen during the sixteenth and much of the seventeenth centuries thought of the major French Renaissance poets and what they made of them—'made of' both in the sense of understanding or interpreting and in the sense of refashioning or reworking." As with the book on Rabelais, transporting these poets into new surroundings meant divided focus: the poets and their works, and then the English readers and English reception. "Just as the image on the retina does not merely reproduce what is really 'out there' so our response to a friend, a poem, a public figure, is in part a 'feigning,' an act of the imagination. And the very fantasies we create, the sometimes astonishing distortions and selectivity of our perceptions, show in part who and what we are."[6] She had begun with the idea of *conversation*, of placing the French and English in *dialogue*, and she wound up exploring—and in time writing—dialectic, a kind of advanced dialectic with infinite regress. It was as if practicing Renaissance rhetoric, she became a participant in it, her own readings of Rabelais and Ronsard caught in a web of other people's responses. This, in turn, might not have surprised her own subjects. The Renaissance reveled in conversation. In large part, that was because it reveled in rhetoric, too.

---

[4] Anne Lake Prescott, "Divided State," *English Literary Renaissance* 25 (1995): 445.

[5] Anne Lake Prescott, *Imagining Rabelais in Renaissance England* (New Haven, 1998), pp. vii, xi.

[6] Anne Lake Prescott, *French Poets and the English Renaissance* (New Haven, 1978), p. xi.

Dialogue, Dialectic, Disparity

We know that Tudor England viewed conversation rhetorically. Their chief testament—the *Conversazioni civile* of Stephano Guazzo—had been Italian (for the Tudors, the cradle of civilization), but it had been translated into French, the language of Rabelais and Ronsard, and from there it was Englished by George Pettie (Books I–III, 1581) and Bartholomew Young (Book IV, 1586). In 1560, Thomas Wilson had written in *The Art of Rhetoric* that it was rhetoric (from the likes of Aristotle and Cicero) that had humanized and educated men, but for Guazzo and his followers, it was the informed practice of conversation.

[C]onversation is the full perfection of learning, and that it more avayleth a student to discourse one hours [*sic*] with his like, then to studie a whole day by himselfe in his studie. Yea and in conferring with his companions, if he have understood any thing amisse, he therby most commonly commeth to the right meaning of the matter, and cleereth his mind of many errours, and beginneth to perceive that the judgement of one alone may bee easily darkened with the veile of ignorance, or of some passion, and that amongst a multitude, it seldome falleth out that all are blinded: and finally, upon proofe he knoweth that vertue and knowledge set foorth in bookes, is naught else then a painted vertue: and that true vertue and learning, is gotten rather by practice then by reading.[7]

It was not solitary reading but communal conversation—*humanitas*—that Guazzo and his translators advocated. The alternative was unthinkable:

For to say that every man should have an eye only to his owne affaires, is nothing els, but to make man like to beasts. And besides, it is most certaine, that solitarinesse putteth many evil thinges into our heades, and maketh us beleeve that which is not. Neither hath it any thing in it but horror and terrour, enemies to nature. According whereto, it is daily seene that a man being by him selfe is fearefull, and being in company, is couragious …. For he that useth not company hath no experience, he that hath no experience, hath no judgment, and hee that hath no judgment, is no better then a beast. (vol. 1, pp. 46–7)

Such trust in the humanist community and the larger world was not, however, to suggest naiveté; Master Anniball Magnocavalli, the philosopher and physician who is providing this counsel to Guazzo in their dialogue (their conversation), acknowledges

that as some diseases of the body are infectious, so the vices of the minde take from one to another, so that a drunkard draweth his companions to love wine, a Carpet knight corrupteth and effeminateth a valiant man: and so much force hath continual conversation, that oft times against our wils, we imitate the vices of others. Thereupon it

---

[7] Stephano Guazzo, *The Civile Conversation of M. Steeven Guazzo*, trans. George Pettie and Bartholomew Young (2 vols, London, 1925), vol. 1, pp. 43–4. All further references are to this edition.

is saide, that the friends and familiers of Aristotle had learned to stammer: the friends of Alexander in discoursing, had got his roughnesse of speech: and dout not, but in haunting the companie of the evil, a man shal find by experience that a man is a woolfe to a man, not a God as I said before, and that according to the proverbe, A friend of fooles wil become like unto them, and hee which toucheth pitch shalbe defiled therwith. But in like case also, and by the same reason on the contrary side, vertue bringeth forth the like effect. And as a dead coale, laide to a lively, kindleth: so a naughty person meeting in companie with the good, partaketh with their conditions. Neither is a good aire and a mans owne native soile more helpeful to the health of the body, then the conversation and companie of the good is to diseased minds. (vol. 1, p. 44)

Conversation, it would seem, as it educates man, teaches him discernment. In the State of Guazzo, ugly alternatives are quickly dismissed—by a kind of fiat—and the largely unquestioned *value* of conversation is pursued at length. Anniball's dialectic with Guazzo never really allows a divided mind.

We do. Like Prescott and like many handbooks of rhetoric in Tudor England, we recognize linguistic practice as rhetorical exercise: the art of persuasion, the act of feigning, simulation and dissimulation. Conversations are constructed out of language, and language is itself a construction, formed by various forces in which various meanings (perhaps even contradictory meanings) reside. As the deployment of language, speech and conversation are never innocent. One of our best authorities on conversation—which she terms "social dialogue"—is Lynne Magnusson, who has this to say:

The sustained production of ordinary conversation is a remarkable social accomplishment. There are so many things that could go badly wrong, and yet they rarely do. The potential for trouble is always there and at virtually every level—the textual, the ideational, the experiential, and the interpersonal. At the textual level, speakers in conversation regularly produce well-coordinated speech exchanges, with speaker change recurring and one member talking at a time, despite the fact that turn order, turn type, and turn size are not prespecified or governed by any obvious set of rules. At the ideational level, speakers generally manage to make sense of one another's contributions, despite the fact that the interpretation of speakers' meanings draws upon complex processes of inference-making. The meanings communicated are not by any means transparent, even in what we think of as rudimentary exchanges: to make sense, hearers must draw not only upon what is communicated "in" words (words which are at best ambiguous and imprecise) but also upon what text and context co-construct as shared or tacit knowledge. At the experiential level, speakers are constantly managing to do things with their words—both in the sense that J.L. Austin expounded when he demonstrated that utterances themselves act upon the world and others and also in the sense that utterances can persuade or compel people to take actions that go beyond words. And finally, at the interpersonal level, talk enacts relationships—and the continuance of talk, in spite of the potential for eruptions of aggression and in spite of people's opposing impulses to assert themselves at the expense of others and to avoid the interference of others, works to cement and maintain relationships.[8]

It is true, of course, that, in order to continue, any conversation needs some kind of give-and-take, some kind of willed blindness or ignorance, some tacit compromise of subject and position. But that recognition has to be maneuvered alongside the fact that "the most commonplace speech acts negotiated in everyday conversation," as Magnusson says elsewhere, such as "advising, promising, inviting, requesting, ordering, criticizing, even complimenting"—that is, speech interchanges that abbreviate or are extracted from longer, fuller conversations—do so at considerable risk.[9] Language is, after all, not only self-promotion but self-projection (an idea as old as Aristotle, from whom the Renaissance inherited it), and the self, always fragile, can be more so when it is put forth in—*exposed by*—words. Magnusson could herself be accused of having a divided mind on the matter, since she can simultaneously affirm the miracle of social conversation—extended dialogue—and see the disparate, even disjunctive, forces at play within it. Such forces always dynamically threaten the little compromising acts that allow dialogue to proceed, the acts that allow us to pull disparate examples into some kind of larger, comprehensible order, such as agreeing that reason is what makes us human or that the Tudor recognition of Rabelais fell into three broad categories. Since conversation always takes so many inescapable rhetorical risks, we can understand the Renaissance interest in the form and its practice; what we need also, to understand it, is to engage in another Renaissance practice, that of partitioning the proposition into its constituent issues: anatomizing it.

Constructing Linguistic Habitus

Our proposition, once again, is that despite the complex significations inherent in words (not to mention conflicting intentions and receptions), there is still the possibility of holding conversations (or of understanding what happens when a Ronsard or a Rabelais is taken over by Tudor England). It is commonplace these days to begin the examination of language by turning to the binaries of Saussure—the distinction between the singular word, *parole*, and its transformation when embedded in an utterance, *langue*. But since we have already acknowledged that there are potentially multiple and conflicting forces within and behind any given word, that binarism tends to evaporate. V.N. Vološinov seems more representative when he notes that "[t]here are as many meanings of a word as there are contexts

---

[8] Lynne Magnusson, *Shakespeare and Social Dialogue: Dramatic Language and Elizabethan Letters* (Cambridge, 1999), p. 141.

[9] Magnusson, p. 17, drawing on Penelope Brown and Stephen Levinson, *Politeness: Some Universals in Language Usage* (Cambridge, 1987).

of its usage."[10] To help us understand what Vološinov may have in mind, we can turn to J.L. Austin's theory of words as lexical presentations of non-linguistic actions. He cites illocutions ("the performance of an act *in* saying something" such as questions, commands, affirmations, denials, promises) and perlocutions ("what we bring about or achieve by saying something, such as convincing, persuading, deterring, and even, say, surprising or misleading").[11]

Keir Elam finds even more helpful the earlier work of Ludwig Wittgenstein in his sense of *Sprachspiel*, or "language-game," as presented in the *Brown Book* of 1933–35 or, "more decisively," in the *Philosophical Investigations* of 1953. Here, Wittgenstein "employs the term 'game' in a very special sense, namely to indicate any distinct form of language-use subject to its own rules and defined within a given behavioural context" which, like Austin's speech-acts, brings something into being, yet "Wittgenstein's 'games' prove far more heterogeneous or many-leveled than Austin's illocutions or perlocutions." The emphasis is on fluidity in language usage. There are 73 language-games discussed in the *Brown Book*, fewer in *Philosophical Investigations*. Among them are giving orders and obeying them, describing the appearance of an object or giving its measurements, constructing an object from a description or drawing, reporting an event, speculating on an event, forming and testing a hypothesis, presenting in tables or diagrams the results of an experiment, making up a story and reading it, play-acting, singing catches, guessing, riddling, making and telling jokes, solving a problem in practical arithmetic, translating from one language to another, asking, thanking, cursing, greeting, praying.[12] Paraphrasing Wittgenstein, Anthony Kenny explains such examples as words that "cannot be understood outside the context of the non-linguistic human activities into which the use of the language is interwoven: the words plus their behavioural surroundings make up the language-game."[13] Elam notices other common features, "flexibility and multiformity" within the words and their deployment.[14] Such dynamic usage of words is what Magnusson can see resulting in

> a plenitude of colliding and overlapping discourses—discourses associated with the huge range of human enterprises specific to any time and place, discourses of groups, discourses of classes, of professions, of generations, and the like. Language is stratified,

---

[10] Vološinov, p. 79.

[11] J.L. Austin, *How to Do Things with Words* (2nd edn, London, 1978), pp. 99, 109. Austin is cited in Keir Elam, *Shakespeare's Universe of Discourse: Language-Games in the Comedies* (Cambridge, 1984), pp. 6–7.

[12] Elam, pp. 10–11.

[13] Anthony Kenny, *Wittgenstein* (Harmondsworth, 1973), p. 14.

[14] Elam, p. 12.

plural, heteroglossic. Discourses are specific to their historical, institutional, relational—and other—contexts, but they are also migratory, hybridizing, shape-shifting, continuously changing.[15]

It is the remarkable Rabelaisian world of sheer *copia*. What Magnusson is citing here in the ways words take on different significations and various shapes is Bakhtin's sense of multilayered words (heteroglossia) that is the basis for his *Dialogic Imagination* (translated by Michael Holquist in 1981) and *Rabelais and His World* (translated by Helene Iswolsky in 1965), and Vološinov's *Marxism and the Philosophy of Language* (translated by Ladislav Matejka and I.R. Titunik in 1986). It also bears close resemblance to Pierre Bourdieu's *habitus*, the circumstances that condition any individual's personal expression. But Bourdieu makes explicit a subtle shift of thought that may have been more implicit in the thinking of Wittgenstein and Vološinov, if not Austin. He defines *habitus* somewhat complexly in his *Outline of a Theory of Practice* (1977) in the translation of Richard Nice as "an acquired system of generative schemes objectively adjusted to the particular conditions in which it is constituted. [T]he habitus engenders all the thoughts, all the perceptions, and all the actions consistent with those conditions, and no others."[16] The shift is in the word "adjusted." The forces—at least the conscious forces inherent in a particular speaker's use of a particular word—allow the speaker to fine-tune the words he uses so that they can be embedded into the context of the sentence being spoken, and the context being addressed. They allow, that is, flexibility of expression so that disparities among speakers can be elided. They start from individual uses of language. In the event, in their execution, they permit—and construct—conversation.

Testing *Il Cortegiano*

We know how Tudor England viewed conversation, and we know what for them was the exemplary conversation: *Il Libro del Cortegiano, The Book of the Courtier* of Baldesar Castiglione made English in 1561 by Sir Thomas Hoby. Like Prescott's "Divided State," *The Courtier* is rooted in dialectic, an ongoing intricate interplay in fashioning the ideal courtier from Ottaviano's understanding of public needs to Bembo's revelation of private visions that energize and shape such counsel. Prolonged but differing attitudes help to dramatize the *conversazioni*, such as the continuing misogyny of Gaspare and Niccolò Frisio, which sharply modifies the Magnifico's extravagant praise of women in Book III. In the thin, high

---

[15] Magnusson, p. 8.

[16] Pierre Bourdieu, *Outline of a Theory of Practice*, trans. Richard Nice (Cambridge, 1977), p. 95.

mountain air of the remote city of Urbino where the impotent Duke Guidobaldo
Montefeltro employs thirty or forty copyists at transcribing Greek and Latin
manuscripts foundational to the humanists of the Quattrocento and Cinquecento,
there is an endless *paragore*, clashes of rhetoric and competitions of briefs
debating the superiority of sculpture or painting, ancient or vernacular languages,
politeness or rudeness, nature or art, love or hate, passion or spirit, duty or
freedom—continuing battles of linguistic wit that mingle the philosophic, the
essential, the pragmatic, and the trivial. Through the fine-tuning of four days of
conversation, Castiglione weaves a harmony of dialectic in which Lodovico
Canossa's extended definition of the courtier in Book I is realized in Ottaviano
Fregoso's prescriptive program in Book IV, clear coordinates for the particular
skills of the courtier listed in Book II balanced by the more generalized encomia of
admirable women as female counterparts in Book III. Meantime, the carpings of
Gaspare and Frisio serve as an obligatto, continually reminding the reader that
healthy courtiers may display weakness of character, understanding, or will, even
in the midst of the highest of speculations.

Together the varied discussants illustrate speech-acts, heteroglossia, and
habitus in decidedly Renaissance ways, managing dialectic in ways that preserve
the art of conversation:

> [T]he Count replied, "I should like us to discuss ... the question of drawing and of the
> art of painting .... [I]n the ancient world both painting and painters were held in the
> greatest respect, and the art itself was brought to the highest pitch of excellence. Of this,
> a sure proof is to be found in the ancient marble and bronze statues which still survive;
> for although painting differs from sculpture, both the one and the other derive from the
> same source, namely from good design. So if the statues which have come down to us
> are inspired works of art we may readily believe that so, too, were the paintings of the
> ancient world; indeed, they must have been still more so, because they required greater
> artistry."
>
> Then Signora Emilia, turning to Giovan Cristoforo Romano, who was seated with
> the others, asked him:
>
> "What do you think of this opinion? Would you agree that painting allows for
> greater artistry than sculpture?"
>
> "Madam," replied Giovan Cristoforo, "I maintain that sculpture requires more effort
> and more skill than painting, and possesses greater dignity."
>
> The Count then remarked:
>
> "Certainly statues are more durable, so perhaps they may be said to prove more
> dignified; for since they are intended for monuments, they serve the purpose for which
> they are made better than paintings. But, leaving aside the question of commemoration,
> both painting and sculpture also serve a decorative purpose, and in this regard painting
> is far superior. And if it is not, so to say, as enduring as sculpture, all the same it
> survives a long time, and for as long as it does so it is far more beautiful."
>
> Then Giovan Cristoforo replied:
>
> "I truly believe that you are not saying what you really think, and this solely for the
> sake of your Raphael; and perhaps, as well, you feel that the excellence you perceive in

his work as a painter is so supreme that it cannot be rivaled by any sculpture in marble. But remember that this is praise for the artist and not for his art."

Then he continued:

"Indeed, I willingly accept that both painting and sculpture are skilful imitations of Nature; yet I still do not understand how you can maintain that what is real and is Nature's own creation cannot be more faithfully copied in a bronze or marble figure, in which all the members are rounded, fashioned and proportioned just as Nature makes them, than in a picture, consisting of a flat surface and colours that deceive the eye. And don't tell me that being is not nearer the truth than merely seeming to be. Moreover, I maintain that working in stone is far more difficult, because if a mistake is made it cannot be remedied, seeing that repairs are impossible with marble, and the figure must be started again; whereas this is not the case with painting, which can be gone over a thousand times, being improved all the time as parts of the picture are added to or removed."

Then, with a smile, the Count replied:

"I am not arguing for the sake of Raphael, nor should you think me so ignorant as not to recognize the excellence shown by Michelangelo and yourself and other sculptors. But I am speaking of the art and not the artists. You say truly enough that both painting and sculpture are imitations of Nature; but it is not the case that the one seems to be what it portrays and the other really is so. For although statues are made in the round, like objects in real life, and painting is seen only on the surface, sculpture lacks many things to be found in painting, and especially light and shade: for example, the natural colouring of the flesh, which appears altogether changed in marble, the painter copies faithfully, using more or less light and shade according to need, which the sculptor cannot do. And even though the painter does not fashion his figures in the round, he does depict the muscles and members of the body rounded and merging into the unseen parts of his figures in such a way as to demonstrate his knowledge and understanding of these as well. The painter requires still greater skill in depicting members that are foreshortened and taper gradually away from the point of vision, on the principles of perspective."[17]

The officious Count Ludovico Canossa—the Bishop of Bayeux and diplomat to the Pope and subsequently to Francis I—is looking for a debate, and Emilia Pia, a close companion to the Duchess of Urbino, would seem to be provoking one by calling on Giovan Cristoforo Romano, by trade a sculptor and medalist. The Count is a close friend of Raphael and initiates the discussion in order to declare the superiority of painting. Giovan Cristoforo must defend his own livelihood and reputation. Clearly both men are called upon to defend their publicly known personal and professional commitments. And each, as Castiglione shapes the argument, calls upon strong reasons that would seem to lead to an impasse, their ideologically loaded assumptions leading, as Magnusson has noted, to "eruptions

---

[17] Baldesar Castiglione, *The Book of the Courtier*, trans. George Bull (Harmondsworth, 1967), pp. 96–9.

of aggression and ... opposing impulses to assert themselves at the expense of others." Their dialogue fissures the conversation rather than extends it. But that is not how conversation works; and it is not how Castiglione records the exemplary evenings at Urbino.

One answer may rest in what Bakhtin calls an "answer-word" that avoids a stalemate when sharply disjunctive positions are about to be foregrounded. Bakhtin defines this conscious technique in the fourth essay of the *Dialogic Imagination*:

> The word [such as *painting*] is born in a dialogue as a living rejoinder [to *sculpture* that is declared to be] within it; the word is shaped in dialogic interaction with an alien word that is already in the object. A word forms a concept of its own object in a dialogic way.
>
> But this does not exhaust the internal dialogism of the word. It encounters an alien word not only in the object itself: every word is directed toward an *answer* and cannot escape the profound influence of the answering word that it anticipates.
>
> The word in living conversation is directly, blatantly, oriented toward a future answer-word: it provokes an answer, anticipates it and structures itself in the answer's direction. Forming itself in an atmosphere of the already spoken, the word is at the same time determined by that which has not yet been said but which is needed and in fact anticipated by the answering word. Such is the situation in any living dialogue.[18]

The Count's key word is the one on which he ends—"artistry"—and it is, not coincidentally, the one Emilia picks up in her question to Giovan Cristoforo. And it is precisely artistry that Cristoforo responds to, but he redefines *artistry* in terms of *effort, skill,* and *dignity*. He anticipates the development of his own position: it is difficult to carve in marble where one mistake will ruin an entire work, and so a sculptor needs more skill than a painter, who can repaint over error; and the massive three-dimensional sculpture assigns more dignity to its subject than a flattened, two-dimensional painting can. In picking up on the Count's answer-word, Cristoforo not only challenges the Count to adjust the issues and defend painting on a sculptor's best grounds but also lays the foundation for his own extended statement of the case. The Count plays the same kind of Bakhtinian (or Wittgensteinian) game: he adopts the issue of *dignity* and seems to accommodate it while actually suspending judgment (*perhaps*), and turns the argument again to his favor by introducing new answer-words, *decorative* and *beautiful*. The massiveness of the sculpture would seem to prevent Cristoforo from doing much with *decorative*, so he turns the answer-word (or answer-issue) of beauty into a contemporary synonym, the painter Raphael. Clearly what he wishes to do is to point out the Count's ulterior purpose and the singularity of interest that may fundamentally weaken his argument. The Count makes use of this answer-word in developing a strong case for Raphael by praising the kind of art for

---

[18] M.M. Bakhtin, *The Dialogic Imagination: Four Essays*, trans. Michael Holquist (Austin, 1981), pp. 279–80.

which Raphael is widely known. The technique of the answer-word, that is, generates conversation by generating debate; but it generates debate by laying down keywords to guide its development. It is at once dialectical and progressive.

In *The Bonds of Love*, Jessica Benjamin describes the interaction somewhat differently. According to Benjamin, "the self is constituted to a large extent by what is mirrored back in the responses of the other; and so the self must negotiate a difficult tension between its own acts of assertion and its need for the recognition of the other."[19] For Magnusson, this results in what she calls "self-repair" or even "reciprocal self-maintenance."[20] It is the inversion of the answer-word, by which the speakers keep redefining the words laid down by their disputants in order to colonize them for themselves. This is true in the passage we are examining for *artistry, effort, skill* and *dignity* (although the Count redefines them by recontextualizing them), just as Cristoforo reconceives *beautiful* and introduces *proportioned* and *colours* which in turn become answer-words. The ideational dialectic is painting versus sculpture; the rhetorical dialectic is answer-word versus self-repair and self-maintenance. This latter, Magnusson continues, is further developed by Penelope Brown and Stephen Levinson when "they [adapt] Erving Goffman's concept of 'face-work'":

> The two aspects of "face" emphasized in their model, positive face relating to the "want to be approved by others" and negative face to the "want … that [one's] actions be unimpeded by others," roughly correspond to the two basic "needs" posited in Jessica Benjamin's general model of intersubjectivity: the need for recognition and the need for self-assertion.

"From discourse pragmatics," Magnusson sums, "comes the germ of a model for reciprocal self-maintenance."[21]

Thus the very divisive features of any speaker's individual *habitus*, and its potential disjunction from that of a second speaker in dialogue, can be profitably styled to permit conversation to continue while at the same time carving out a particular place for one's own staunch and unrelenting position. "[O]ne of the most important factors bearing on linguistic production," Bourdieu tells us, is "the anticipation of profit which is durably inscribed in the language habitus, in the form of an anticipatory adjustment … to the objective value of one's discourse." For Bourdieu, this adjustment is "without conscious anticipation," although as we have seen, this is not necessarily the case.[22] Either way, though, what it does is highlight the intermingled speeches in the dialectic, and foreground them.

---

[19] Jessica Benjamin, *The Bonds of Love: Psychoanalysis, Feminism, and the Problem of Domination* (New York, 1988), as summarized by Magnusson, p. 143.

[20] Magnusson, pp. 143–4.

[21] Magnusson, p. 144, citing Brown and Levinson, p. 58.

[22] Pierre Bourdieu, "The Economics of Linguistic Exchanges," *Social Science Information* 16 (1977): 653.

"Meaning," writes Vološinov, "does not reside in the word or in the soul of the speaker or in the soul of the listener" (we could read *disputant*). Rather, he continues,

> [m]eaning is the *effect of interaction between* [them] *produced via the material of a particular sound complex*. It is like an electric spark that occurs only when two different terminals are hooked together. Those who ignore them (which is accessible only to active, responsive understanding) and who, in attempting to define the meaning of a word, approach its lower, stable, self-identical limit, want, in effect, to turn on a light bulb after having switched off the current. Only the current of verbal intercourse endows a word with the light of meaning.[23]

The current of verbal intercourse is what we have been calling conversation.

Enter—and Exit—*Sprezzatura*

"The role of discourse in society is active," Jay Lemke contends; "it not only reconfirms and re-enacts existing social relationships and patterns of behavior, it also renegotiates social relationships and introduces new meanings and behaviors."[24] What binds the disputants together and suspends their fundamental divisions of attitude or perspective in the *Cortegiano* is what Castiglione terms *sprezzatura*: elegant style alone resolves fundamental antagonisms and basically irreconcilable beliefs, as well as the deep fractures caused by ambiguity and paradox in the conversations at Urbino. "I am sure that grace springs especially from this," the Count says; "we can truthfully say that true art is what does not seem to be art; and the most important thing is to conceal it, because if it is revealed this discredits a man completely and ruins his reputation."[25] This central doctrine of the *necessity of eloquence*, an art that seems not to be art, and nature that is not nature, goes unquestioned both theoretically and practically in the *Cortegiano*. But Lodevico introduces his fundamental principle by two different contextual corollaries that warn us not to accept this sort of eloquence without caution.

For one thing, we are told that *sprezzatura* disguises the practitioner and may delude him; for another, it is (at least initially) deceptive and false. *Sprezzatura*, that is, always entails subterfuge. A courtier's disposition and conduct always conceal his intentions to a greater or lesser degree; the elaboration of the self is mirrored in the elaboration of speech, but it is an eloquence that hides rather than reveals purpose. For Castiglione, there is no thought of binding answer-words and efforts of self-repair to prolong the art of conversation; rather, the art of

---

[23] Vološinov, pp. 102–3.

[24] Jay Lemke, *Textual Politics: Discourse and Social Dynamics* (London, 1995), p. 20.

[25] Castiglione, p. 67.

sprezzatura is the art of *dissimulation*—or an art opposed to Castiglione's *simulation* of Urbino and the humanist dialogues there. At its most extreme, *sprezzatura* echoes Pico's remarks in his correspondence with Ermalo Barbaro in the humanist *controversia* (not *conversazioni*) in the latter years of the Quattrocento: "the task of the rhetor is nothing else than to lie, to entrap, to circumvent, to practice sleight-of-hand."[26] Little wonder, then, that in its own time *Il Cortegiano* prompted a variety of responses, from Roger Ascham's straightforward recommendation that Castiglione "aduisedlie read, and diligentlie folowed, but one yeare at home in England, would do a yong ientleman more good, I wisse, then three years trauell abrode in *Italie*"[27] to George Whetstone's admiring and derivative *Heptameron of Ciuil Discourses* (1582), which recounts "the ciuill disputations and speeches of sundry well Courted Gentlemen, and Gentlewomen his Guestes during the time of my intertainment, with Segnior Phyloxenus" (sig. A2[v]), and to the more knowing cynicism of Aretino, whose *La Cortigiana*, the story of the grooming of Messer Maco to become a courtier, is a scurrilous satire on Castiglione's putative idealism.[28]

Yet *controversia* and *conversazioni*, even with answer-words and self-maintenance, function only when preserving dialectic, dialogue that knows no end. For Bakhtin, this is because one person's utterance keeps being recast through the utterance of another. As Gary Saul Morson and Caryl Emerson paraphrase Bakhtin:

> When this happens, the value systems and worldviews in these languages come to interact; they "interanimate" each other as they enter into dialogue. To the extent that this happens, it becomes more difficult to take for granted the value system of a given language. Those values may still be felt to be right and the language may still seem

---

[26] Quoted in James Richard McNally, "*Rector et Dux Populi*: Italian Humanists and the Relationship between Rhetoric and Logic," *Modern Philology* 67 (1969): 172.

[27] Roger Ascham, *The Scholemaster* (1570), sig. G4[v].

[28] Aretino's work is summarized in some detail in Hiram Haydn, *The Counter-Renaissance* (New York, 1950), pp. 567ff. In verses printed in *The Booke of the Courtier* (1561), Thomas Sackville commends Thomas Hoby's translation, remarking that "*No proude ne golden Court doth he set furth, / But what in Court a Courtier ought to be*" (sig. A2[v]), and Gabriel Harvey in a letter around 1578 and John Florio in his *Second Fruites* of 1591 speak of *Il Cortegiano* as a means of quickly picking up some Italian. Daniel Javitch chronicles contemporary references in "Rival Arts of Conduct in Elizabethan England: Guazzo's *Civile Conversation* and Castiglione's *Courtier*," *Yearbook of Italian Studies* 1 (1971): 180–81. Ben Jonson praises Castiglione in *Timber* (1640) and uses him in *Every Man in His Humour* (1601), as do John Marston in his *Satires* (1598) and *The Malcontent* (1604), John Webster and Thomas Dekker in *Westward Ho* (1607), and Henry Peacham, Thomas Nashe, John Taylor the Water Poet, Joseph Hall, and Shakespeare. Some of these borrowings are discussed by Mary Augusta Scott, "The Book of the Courtyer: A Possible Source of Benedick and Beatrice," *PMLA* 16 (1901): 475–502.

adequate to its topic, but not indisputably so, because they have been, however cautiously, disputed.

In fact, this dialogizing of languages is always going on, and so when these words attract tones and meanings from the languages of heteroglossia, they are often attracting already dialogized meanings. Having participated in more than one value system, these words become dialogized, disputed, and reaccented in yet another way as they encounter yet another. This potentially endless process pertains not only to particular words but also to other elements of language—to given styles, syntactic forms, even grammatical norms. Complex interactions of this sort serve as a driving force in the history of any language.[29]

But then, Louis A. Montrose has summed, "language use is understood to be always and necessarily dialogical, to be socially and materially determined and constrained"; more fundamentally yet, there always remains "the dialectic between the text and the world."[30]

Necessarily, then, Prescott's divided state remains divided. Indeed, if Prescott went looking for resolution, she may have found it in only one place, in her beloved Rabelais. There, near the end of Livre Quatre, Panurge and Pantagruel discover frozen words. For a split second, they say nothing at all.

---

[29] Gary Saul Morson and Caryl Emerson, *Mikhail Bakhtin: Creation of a Prosaics* (Stanford, 1990), p. 143.

[30] Louis A. Montrose, "Professing the Renaissance: The Poetics and Politics of Culture," in H. Aram Veeser (ed.), *The New Historicism* (New York, 1989), pp. 15, 24.

Chapter 2

"Defend his freedom 'gainst a monarchy"
Marlowe's Republican Authorship

Patrick Cheney

In this essay, I would like to open up the neglected topic of Marlowe's "republican authorship." The title phrase indicates my interest in sorting out the relationship in the Marlowe canon between two important topics of current scholarship: republicanism as an early modern political ideology; and authorship as an early modern literary practice. My general argument will be that during the late sixteenth century *Marlowe is the pioneer author in the writing of English republicanism.*[1]

Typically, Marlowe gets erased from our main critical narrative about the advent of English authorship. In a summarizing essay from *The Cambridge Companion to English Literature 1500–1600*, Wendy Wall locates the advent in Spenser and then in Jonson: "When Spenser and Jonson used the book format to generate the author's laureate status, ... they produced ... modern and familiar images of literary authority—classically authorized writers who serve as the origin and arbiter of a literary monument that exceeds its place in everyday cultural

This essay derives from two related papers: the first delivered at the Fourth International Marlowe Conference, Cambridge, England, 4 July 2003; the second at the international Lucan conference, Princeton, NJ, 4 October 2003. I am grateful to the conference organizers: Robert Logan, President of the Marlowe Society of America; and Nigel Smith and Denis Feeney. I am also grateful to Colin Burrow, Robert R. Edwards, and David Riggs for helpful readings, and to Letitia Montgomery for checking quotations and citations. Finally, I wish to thank the editors of this volume, Zachary Lesser and Benedict Robinson, for their scrupulous editorial eyes. The essay forms the foundation of a book under contract with Palgrave Macmillan, in the Early Modern Literature in History series edited by Cedric Brown and Andrew Hadfield, *Marlowe's Republican Authorship: Early Modern Political Representation*.

[1] In the introduction to *The Cambridge Companion to Christopher Marlowe* (Cambridge, 2004), I focus on Marlowe's emergence as a *pioneer author* in Elizabethan England, and later I adapt a few paragraphs from this discussion.

transactions."[2] As Wall intimates, the concept of the "laureate" poet now defines early modern authorship; in Richard Helgerson's original formulation, Spenser is Renaissance England's "first laureate poet" because he uses the nascent medium of print to present himself as national author, while Jonson and later Milton succeed Spenser in the laureate enterprise.[3] By contrast, in this essay I shall present Marlowe as Elizabethan England's *first counter-laureate author*: in particular, he uses poems and plays to contest the national authority of Spenser.[4]

Similarly, scholarship about the rise of English republicanism neglects Marlowe's pioneering role. Most notably, David Norbrook's *Writing the English Republic* recalls only that Marlowe was the translator of Book I of Lucan's *Pharsalia*.[5] When Norbrook discusses the pre-Stuart era, he cites Shakespeare and

---

[2] Wendy Wall, "Authorship and the Material Conditions of Writing," in Arthur F. Kinney (ed.), *The Cambridge Companion to English Literature 1500–1600* (Cambridge, 2000), p. 86. Wall mentions Marlowe only once in passing, seeing "The Passionate Shepherd to His Love" as an instance of the "social dimension of Renaissance writing," where "texts" could "travel" and were "open to inscription by readers," spawning "verse replies" such as Ralegh's "The Nymph's Reply" (p. 71). See also Wendy Wall, *The Imprint of Gender: Authorship and Publication in the English Renaissance* (Ithaca, 1993); and Jeffrey Masten, *Textual Intercourse: Collaboration, Authorship, and Sexualities in Renaissance Drama* (Cambridge, 1997). In "Playwrighting: Authorship and Collaboration" (in John D Cox and David Scott Kastan [eds], *A New History of Early English Drama* [New York, 1997], pp. 357–82), Masten aims to "resist categories of singular authorship" by mentioning a famous incident, when an atheist tract said to be owned by Marlowe got "shuffled" in with Kyd's papers (pp. 360–61). See also Richard Dutton, "Marlowe: Censorship and Construction," *Licensing, Censorship and Authorship in Early Modern English: Buggeswords* (Basingstoke, 2000), on the way Marlovian identity and authorship have been falsely "constructed" by others, not by the author himself (pp. 62–89). Today, critics privilege a "Marlowe effect" over Marlovian authorship; see Leah S. Marcus, "Textual Indeterminacy and Ideological Difference: The Case of *Dr. Faustus*," *Renaissance Drama* 20 (1989): 1–29; Thomas Healy, *Christopher Marlowe* (Plymouth, 1994), pp. 1–9; and J.A. Downie and J.T. Parnell (eds), *Constructing Christopher Marlowe* (Cambridge, 2000), esp. pp. 1–12.

[3] Richard Helgerson, *Self-Crowned Laureates: Spenser, Jonson, Milton and the Literary System* (Berkeley, 1983), p. 100. For Helgerson, Marlowe is a "professional" poet who "made play writing a part of an amateur career" (p. 36; see pp. 112, 147, 167n62, 217). In *Forms of Nationhood: The Elizabethan Writing of England* (Chicago, 1992), Helgerson includes Marlowe in a group of playwrights who wrote a nationhood of the common people (pp. 1, 197, 199–200, 204, 225, 242, 243). I go on to counter both of these classificiations.

[4] See Patrick Cheney, *Marlowe's Counterfeit Profession: Ovid, Spenser, Counter-Nationhood* (Toronto, 1997).

[5] David Norbrook, *Writing the English Republic: Poetry, Rhetoric, and Politics, 1627–1660* (Cambridge, 1999), p. 41. See also Nigel Smith, *Literature and Revolution in England 1640–1660* (New Haven, 1994), p. 204; and Colin Burrow, *Epic Romance: Homer to Milton* (Oxford, 1993), p. 186.

Jonson, Marlowe's two immediate heirs, but not Marlowe himself: "Elizabethan ... writers encouraged a degree of openness to alternative forms of political order. Shakespeare and Jonson vividly realized past republican cultures for a popular audience."[6] A critic who has moved the conversation back to the Elizabethan era, Andrew Hadfield, locates republican leanings in both Shakespeare and Spenser during the 1590s, without saying much about Marlowe.[7]

This scholarly situation is peculiar, given that Marlowe critics spent the past century emphasizing his commitment to the arch-republican value, liberty, without acknowledging its republican origins. Stephen Greenblatt can historicize "radical freedom" as the Marlovian gold standard, yet never mention the word "republicanism," while Jonathan Dollimore formally sets the pace that holds today: *Tamburlaine* is a "transgressive text: it liberates from its Christian and ethical framework the humanist conception of man as essentially free, dynamic, and aspiring; more consciously, this conception of man is not only liberated from a Christian framework but re-established in open defiance of it."[8]

Marlowe deserves to be placed at the forefront of any conversation about the writing of English republicanism.

In the sections following, I would first like to say a word about terms and methodology; next, provide preliminary evidence for the argument italicized above; then, look at one example from the Marlowe canon, *1 Tamburlaine*; and finally, address the question of significance.

Imagining Republican Language

At the top of the term list, the word *republican*. I am not arguing that Marlowe is a "republican author" the way Milton is; we do not have enough evidence to say so. I

---

[6] Norbrook, p. 12.

[7] Like Norbrook, Hadfield mentions Marlowe only in passing as the translator of Lucan ("Was Spenser a Republican?", *English* 47 [1998]: 170; and *Shakespeare and Republicanism* [Cambridge, 2005], pp. 63–5. See also Hadfield's *Shakespeare and Renaissance Politics* [New York, 2003]). On Spenser as well, see David Scott Wilson-Okamura, "Republicanism, Nostalgia, and the Crowd," and Andrew Hadfield, "Was Spenser Really a Republican After All? A Reply to David Scott Wilson-Okamura," both in *Spenser Studies* 17 (2003): 253–73 and 275–90; and Graham Hammill, "'The thing / Which never was': Republicanism and *The Ruines of Time*," *Spenser Studies* 18 (2003): 165–83. The scholar who paves the way for this work is Markku Peltonen, *Classical Humanism and Republicanism in English Political Thought, 1570–1640* (Cambridge, 1995), who surveys the presence of republican thought during Elizabeth's reign, but who does not mention Marlowe.

[8] Stephen Greenblatt, *Renaissance Self-Fashioning: More to Shakespeare* (Chicago, 1980), p. 212; and Jonathan Dollimore, *Radical Tragedy: Religion, Ideology and Power in the Drama of Shakespeare and His Contemporaries* (Chicago, 1984), p. 112.

suggest rather that Marlowe's works unmistakably participate in a cultural conversation, at once political and literary, that recent scholars describe as republican; and further, that Marlowe performs an inaugural Elizabethan role in this conversation.

Scholars make clear that republicanism is intricate as a topic in its own right. As Norbrook puts it, "'Republicanism' ... was not a fixed entity. Nor, for that matter, was 'royalism'," and he demonstrates how the two concepts intertwine during the period, sometimes amicably. In particular, he distinguishes between republicanism as a "language" and as a "programme." He sees as misleading the argument of J.G.A. Pocock that, before 1649, "English republicanism was 'a language, not a programme,'" alternatively suggesting that "republican language was a more powerful presence than has been recognized." Importantly here, the presence Norbrook describes emerges well after Marlowe's death, as the dates in his title indicate (1627–60). Relatedly, Norbrook distinguishes between republicanism as an imaginative idea and as a "political practice," and he suggests that for Tudor "humanists" like Sir Thomas More and Sir Philip Sidney, "who lived under a well-established monarchy, republicanism was indeed a matter of imagination," not the political practice it became for mid-seventeenth-century republicans like Henry Marten. According to Norbrook, "Historians of political thought have remarked on the absence of explicit republican theory in England before the 1650s; they have paid less attention to the many situations in which republican political practice was actively imagined."[9]

Norbrook's formulations allow us to discern a historical evolution to republicanism and to place Marlowe within it. Marlowe belongs to a phase of English republicanism that we might call *imaginative* and *linguistic*; this phase is *pre-programmatic*, *pre-practical*. In such a phase, which is influenced by humanism and its recollection of classical thought, writers from More and Sidney to Shakespeare and Jonson conduct political debate "obliquely through the dramatization and publication of the classics." Primarily, Norbrook refers to Arthur Gorges and Thomas May, who in 1614 and 1627 respectively printed complete

---

[9] Norbrook, pp. 18, 5–6, 12. For a critique of Norbrook—and Peltonen—see Blair Worden, "Republicanism, Regicide, and Republic: The English Experience," in Martin van Gelderen and Quentin Skinner (eds), *Republicanism: A Shared European Heritage* (2 vols, Cambridge, 2002), vol. 1, pp. 308–14. Worden criticizes both Norbrook and Peltonen for bridging the gap between "two approaches" to republicanism that he believes need to be separated: Skinner's model of "constitutional republicanism," which depends on "kingless government" and emerges historically during the Interregnum (p. 307); and Pocock's model of "civic republicanism," which depends on "political action and civic virtue" and emerges before the Interregnum (p. 308). See Quentin Skinner, *Liberty before Liberalism* (Cambridge, 1998), pp. 11, 22, 54–5; and J.G.A. Pocock, *The Machiavellian Moment: Florentine Political Thought and the Atlantic Republican Tradition* (Princeton, 1975).

translations of Lucan's *Pharsalia*, both including prefatory material outlining their political agendas.[10]

Finally, we can follow Norbrook and others in defining governmental republicanism as "'a state which was not headed by a king and in which the hereditary principle did not prevail in whole or in part in determining the headship.'"[11] To put it more affirmatively, republicanism is "the spirit of free and open speech amongst equals" as instituted by political or constitutional program— what Norbrook calls a "politics of open speech and dialogue." When it comes to defining republicanism succinctly, however, perhaps no one can compete with Lucan himself: "libera regum"—free of kings (6.301).[12]

Let us see where we are: *obliquely imagined republican language*. This is hardly solid ground for conventional scholarship. The ground begins to tremble once we place Marlowe on it. His meteoric life and career were truncated at the age of twenty-nine; insoluble problems plague the two sets of evidence to which we have access: the archive of Marlowe's life and his thirteen extant works.[13] Yet it is precisely on such ground that we may hear a challenge for our critical methodology about the authorship of English republicanism in the early modern period.

Republican Representation

Without question, we will find it difficult to discern a republican form of government in Marlowe's works. What we can discern is what I term "republican representation": the author's representational foregrounding of his own republican frame of art. In *Lucans First Booke*, the author conducts political debate about

---

[10] Norbrook, p. 13. On Gorges and May as Marlowe's successors in translating Lucan, see J.B. Steane, *Marlowe: A Critical Study* (Cambridge, 1964), pp. 266–71.

[11] Norbrook, p. 17, quoting Zera S. Fink, *The Classical Republicans: An Essay in the Recovery of a Pattern of Thought in Seventeenth Century England* (Evanston, 1945), p. x.

[12] Norbrook, pp. 12, 20, 29. Quotations from Lucan come from *Lucan: The Civil War, Books I–X*, Loeb Classical Library, trans. J.D. Duff (London, 1928), except for Book I, where English translations come from Christopher Marlowe, *Lucans First Booke* (1600). Quotations from Marlowe's poems come from Stephen Orgel (ed.), *Christopher Marlowe: The Complete Poems and Translations* (Harmondsworth, 1971).

[13] Marlowe wrote seven plays (*Dido, Queen of Carthage, Tamburlaine, Parts One* and *Two, The Jew of Malta, Edward II, The Massacre at Paris, Doctor Faustus*); five poems (*Ovid's Elegies* [a translation of the *Amores*], "The Passionate Shepherd to His Love," *Lucans First Booke, Hero and Leander*, a Latin epitaph on Sir Roger Manwood); and a Latin prose dedication to Mary Sidney Herbert, prefacing Thomas Watson's 1592 *Amintae gaudia*. For an authoritative collection of the biographical archive, see Constance Brown Kuriyama, *Christopher Marlowe: A Renaissance Life* (Ithaca, 2002), pp. 173–240: "Appendix: Transcriptions and Translations of Selected Documents."

republicanism obliquely. He actively imagines republican political practice; and he creates a formal English republican language, without putting it into program. In his corpus of works as a whole, both poems and plays, Marlowe represents republicanism for his own late-Elizabethan era and for the first half of the seventeenth century, as the English nation moves toward the nightmare of a Lucanian Civil War.

Yet here we might observe the near blackout on Marlowe's pioneering authorship of English republicanism. It is not simply Norbrook and Hadfield who have little to say; it is Gorges and May as well.[14] Why did Marlowe get erased from this important historical conversation? One answer is that from Lucan to Milton, Marlowe alone writes republicanism *without being a patriotic author*. The English writers discussed by Norbrook and others take up republican thought because they are *loyal* to England. With Marlowe, we have a rather different case; who would call him a patriot?[15] To examine this question, we can do no better than turn to Blair Worden's gauge for measuring "republicanism" within written documents: whether an author "aim[s]" to "undermine" rather than "fortify" the "English monarchy." Worden's gauge, which criticizes "literary representations" and is based on patriotic activism, cannot measure Marlowe's republican authorship, but in fact helps explain why it has been erased: "What we seek in vain is evidence that imaginative literature reflected or fostered a desire for republican rule."[16] *Desire for republican rule*: this methodological standard aims to exclude not simply the "imaginative" discourse emphasized by Norbrook but *the unpatriotic imaginative discourse* that first appears in the works of Marlowe.

Here, then, we have a genuine contradiction: Marlowe is the first author to *trouble* the writing of English republicanism. Perhaps like everything associated with Marlowe, his is an afflicted republicanism, not of the pure color. For his complex psyche, we might say, liberty was not the grand solution but a deep structural problem.[17]

To historicize Marlowe's authorship of English republicanism more accurately, we need to return to his own political moment. Specifically, we may complement Norbrook's story about the seventeenth-century writing of English republicanism with Patrick Collinson's formulation about "the monarchical republic of Queen

---

[14] This topic needs to be studied; to my knowledge, no one has looked into the Marlovian underpinnings of either Gorges's or May's translations. As Steane's printing of the prologue by all three translators allows us to see (pp. 266–7), Gorges does not appear to need Marlowe for the famed opening line, yet May appears to *imitate* Marlowe's version, changing only one important word (italicized here), perhaps borrowed from Gorges:

> Marlowe: "Wars *worse* then civill on Thessalian playns"
> Gorges: "A *more* then civill warre I sing"
> May: "Warres *more* then civill on Aemathian plaines"

[15] For details, see Cheney, *Marlowe's Counterfeit Profession*, pp. 23–4.

[16] Worden, pp. 312, 311, 309.

[17] On Marlowe and freedom, see Cheney, *Marlowe's Counterfeit Profession*, pp. 21–5.

Elizabeth I."[18] Collinson argues that "Elizabethan England was a republic which happened to be a monarchy: or vice versa." Remembering the town of Swallowfield in 1596, and analyzing the debates in the 1572 Parliament on Mary Queen of Scots and the 1584 Bond of Association requiring allegiance to Elizabeth, Collinson discovers a paradoxical environment in which a monarchy operates through republican principles. Swallowfield was "in effect, a self-governing republic"; the Mary Stuart debate revealed that "the monarchy is taken to be not an indelible and sacred anointing but a public and localized office"; and the Bond of Association, which ostensibly "defended the life of the Queen," constituted "a quasi-republican statement" that relied on the "body politic" to enforce punishment against Elizabeth's enemies.[19]

The available evidence suggests that Marlowe was alert to the fault line within Queen Elizabeth's monarchical republic. The single most important piece of evidence is that Marlowe is the first Englishman to translate the classical author whom Norbrook calls the "central poet of the republican imagination," and the poem that became the central literary text of republicanism, Lucan's counter-imperial epic, the *Pharsalia*. We do not know what Marlowe's plans were for his translation, which the classicist Charles Martindale calls "arguably one of the most underrated masterpieces of Elizabethan literature," and which C.S. Lewis judges of "very great merit"—so much so that he was convinced Marlowe couldn't have written it.[20] Marlowe's authorship is no longer in dispute; indeed, his masterpiece is significant to the development of English literature. In the words of O.B. Hardison, Jr., *Lucans First Booke* is "the only sustained sixteenth-century heroic poem in blank verse after Surrey [in his translation of the *Aeneid*]."[21]

---

[18] Patrick Collinson, "The Monarchical Republic of Queen Elizabeth I," in John Guy (ed.), *The Tudor Monarchy* (London, 1997), pp. 110–34. For Norbrook's brief discussion of Elizabethan republicanism, including reliance on Collinson's paradigm, see pp. 11–14; see also Hadfield, *Shakespeare and Renaissance Politics,* ch. 3.

[19] Collinson, pp. 119, 111, 122, 125. Not everyone is persuaded by Collinson's brief argument (Nigel Smith, personal communication, October 4, 2003). Yet enough subsequent work on the Elizabethan interest in "republicanism," especially by Peltonen but also by Norbrook, Hadfield, Hammill, and others, argues for the merit of Collinson's formulation.

[20] Norbrook, p. 24; Charles Martindale, *Redeeming the Text: Latin Poetry and the Hermeneutics of Reception* (Cambridge, 1993), p. 71; C.S. Lewis, *English Literature of the Sixteenth Century, Excluding Drama* (1954; London, 1973), p. 486. On the excellence of Marlowe's translation, see also W.R. Johnson, *Momentary Monsters: Lucan and His Heroes* (Ithaca, 1987), pp. xii, 3, 14–16, 57n23, 75; and Jane Wilson Joyce (trans.), *Lucan: "Pharsalia"* (Ithaca, 1993), p. xvi. For publication details, see Millar MacLure (ed.), *The Poems: Christopher Marlowe* (London, 1968), pp. xxxiv–vi.

[21] O.B. Hardison, "Blank Verse before Milton," *Studies in Philology* 81 (1984): 265. MacLure goes further: Marlowe's *"Lucan* remains the chief monument in undramatic unrhymed English pentameters between Surrey and Milton" (p. xxxvi). Steane adds: "In this

Despite the historic achievement of Marlowe's "heroic poem," Renaissance critics have ignored it. We possess only a few article-length studies and notes.[22] While critics tend to focus on the quality of Marlowe's line-by-line translation, they also emphasize both the temperamental and the biographical kinship between two authors who did not survive their twenties: these free-spirited young men became enmeshed in the violence of an imperial engine, and both authors appear to have died, quite amazingly, at work on the same poem.[23] However true Marlowe remained to Lucan in his translation, critics agree that he made the *Pharsalia* his own; in the words of J.B. Steane, "Marlowe's Lucan is in fact an English poem."[24]

Yet it is Norbrook who most helps us understand what Marlowe scholars neglect: "The first book of the *Pharsalia* was in fact much cited by two of the leading seventeenth-century theorists of republicanism, James Harrington and Algernon Sidney."[25] Whatever Marlowe's intentions might have been, we can classify his translation of Lucan's first book as a republican document: it is the first great literary representation of republicanism in the English Renaissance. In other words, Book I of the *Pharsalia* was not just any book; it may not even be the best book, but during the English Renaissance it was the arch-republican book, a Lucanian republican epic in brief.[26]

Typologically, Book I stands on its own two feet because it ends with the Bacchic Roman matron's frenzied prophecy of Pompey's severed head, which rolls climactically in Book VIII: "This headless trunk that lies on Nilus' sand / I

---

poem blank verse has already, virtually before Shakespeare, become the Shakespearean instrument" (pp. 276–7).

[22] Steane, pp. 249–79; Roma Gill, "Marlowe, Lucan, and Sulpitius," *Review of English Studies* 24 (1973): 401–13; James Shapiro, "'Metre meete to furnish Lucans style': Reconsidering Marlowe's *Lucan*," in Kenneth Friedenreich, Roma Gill, and Constance B. Kuriyama (eds), *"A Poet and a filthy Play-maker": New Essays on Christopher Marlowe* (New York, 1988), pp. 315–25; Clifford J. Ronan, "*Pharsalia* 1.373–8: Roman Parricide and Marlowe's Editors," *Classical and Modern Literature* 6 (1986): 305–9; Cheney, *Marlowe's Counterfeit Profession*, pp. 227–37; and Georgia Brown, "Marlowe's Poems and Classicism," in the *Cambridge Companion to Marlowe*, ed. Cheney, pp. 120–24.

[23] On the "temperamental kinship" between Marlowe and Lucan, see Harry Levin, *The Overreacher: A Study of Christopher Marlowe* (Cambridge, 1952), p. 10; and Steane, who emphasizes their "violent and early deaths" (p. 254), their reputations as "bold, independent mind[s], given to strong antipathies and enthusiasms, with an irreverent and ironical streak which courted danger" (p. 255), their "partisan" works hopelessly backing the defeated (p. 256), their commitment to "hyperbole" (p. 257), their "unorthodoxies in artistic and religious matters" (p. 257), and "the most striking affinity," their "sadis[m]" (p. 258). On the late dating of *Lucans First Booke*, see Lewis, p. 486; and Shapiro, pp. 323–4.

[24] Steane, p. 270; see also Clifford Leech, *Christopher Marlowe: Poet for the Stage*, ed. Anne Lancashire (New York, 1986), pp. 34–5; and Gill, pp. 403–4.

[25] Norbrook, pp. 36–7.

[26] For classicist commentary on Book 1, see Elaine Fantham (ed.), *Lucan: "De Bello Civili": Book II* (Cambridge, 1992), pp. 23–34.

know."[27] In a 1598 continuation of *Hero and Leander*, Henry Petowe appropriates this Lucanian image to portray the truncated authorship of Marlowe himself: "This history, of *Hero and Leander*, penned by that admired poet Marlowe, but not finished (being prevented by sudden death), and the same … resting like a head separated from the body." Among other things, Petowe's image helps us to see the congruence between *Hero* and *Lucan*, narrative poems that otherwise seem radically different.[28]

The first extant edition of *Lucans First Booke* does not appear until 1600—seven years after many biographers believe Marlowe was assassinated by one faction of the government or the other, including by order of the Queen—but the poem shows up in the Stationers' Register on 28 September 1593, back-to-back with *Hero and Leander*.[29] What has escaped attention is that *Lucans First Booke*, whether in manuscript or a lost edition, almost certainly fired the Lucan revival of the 1590s, which included Daniel's *Civil Wars* (1595), Drayton's *Mortimeriados* (1596), and Shakespeare's *Titus Andronicus* (published 1594), *The Rape of Lucrece* (1594), and *Julius Caesar* (performed 1599).[30]

---

[27] *Lucan: The Civil War, Books I–X*, Book I, lines 684–5: "Hunc ego, fluminea deformis truncus harena / qui iacet, agnosco."

[28] Petowe quoted from Orgel (ed.), p. 91. Lucan inscribes the Ovidian myth of Hero and Leander *twice* in his counter-Virgilian epic (6.55–6, 9.954–60). Burrow notes how in Lucan's second inscription of the Hero and Leander myth Caesar "hunts Pompey down" by "pass[ing] … the Hellespont, scene of Hero and Leander's fatal love" (p. 181), without recalling Marlowe's poem. In her translation of Lucan's first inscription of the landscape underlying the myth, Joyce appears to have detected Marlovian relevance:

All those hands together, by mounding earth in the Hellespont,
Could, instead, have connected Sestos to Abydos;

…

could have changed any part of the world for the better,
even if Nature said 'No'. (Lucan, *Pharsalia* 6.55–60)

Where having spied her tower, long star'd he on't,
And pray'd the narrow toiling Hellespont
To part in twin, that he might come and go,
But still the rising billows answered 'No'. (Marlowe, *Hero and Leander*, II, 149–52)

Moreover, Marlowe's famed architectural description of Venus' Church (I, 135–57) may find its blueprint in Lucan's description of Cleopatra's palace (10.111–46); and both *Hero* and *Lucan* conclude with the same graphic image: of a female oppressed by masculine power.

[29] In his biography, *The World of Christopher Marlowe* (London, 2004), David Riggs argues that Marlowe was assassinated by order of Queen Elizabeth herself. See also David Riggs, "The Killing of Christopher Marlowe," *Stanford Humanities Review* 8 (2000): 239–51.

[30] On Lucan in the Middle Ages and the Renaissance, see William Blissett, "Lucan's Caesar and the Elizabethan Villain," *Studies in Philology* 53 (1956): 553–75; O.A.W. Dilke,

Further evidence lies in a second pioneering translation: Marlowe is the first European author to translate the one taboo work in the Ovid canon, the *Amores*, into the vernacular.[31] Ovid is not formally a republican author the way Lucan is, but he is the anti-monarchical author *par excellence*, including in the *Amores*, as Marlowe translates it in Elegy 1.15.32–3: "Verse is immortal, and shall ne'er decay. / To verse let kings give place, and kingly shows." As the arbiter of power and truth, the poet with his "verse" is superior to the sovereign with his "show."

In *Marlowe's Counterfeit Profession,* I argued that Marlowe's Ovidian poetry inscribes a "counter-nationhood," a nonpatriotic form of nationalism that subverts Elizabethan royal power with what Ovid calls *libertas* (*Amores* 3.15.9)—and Marlowe translates as "liberty" (*Ovid's Elegies* 3.14.9)—in order to present "the poet" as "the true nation," to quote Leo Braudy's succinct formulation.[32] Marlowe's Lucanian poetry, however, needs to be rerouted as a second classical road into the Elizabethan political sphere—specifically, as a republican form of nationalism in opposition to monarchical power. Marlowe's twin translations of Rome's two greatest counter-imperial epicists, at the beginning and the end of his career, construct for his work a bifold representational framework that includes both Ovidian counter-nationalism and Lucanian republicanism.[33] Any full study of Marlowe's representational politics needs to distinguish between the two and then discuss their interwoven texture.

A third and fourth piece of evidence follows from Marlowe's two translations. The third is well known: Marlowe infuses Ovidianism throughout both his poems and his plays. What I would like to emphasize is a neglected point recently made by Heather James: that Tudor and Stuart writers appropriated sweet and mellifluous Ovid for political purposes, including anti-monarchical and even

---

"Lucan and English Literature," in D.R. Dudley (ed.), *Neronians and Flavians: Silver Latin I* (London, 1972), pp. 83–112; Charles Martindale, "The Epic of Ideas: Lucan's *De Bello Civili* and *Paradise Lost,*" *Comparative Criticism* 3 (1981): 133–56; Clark Hulse, *Metamorphic Verse: The Elizabethan Minor Epic* (Princeton, 1981), pp. 210–14; A. Donald Sellstrom, "*La Mort de Pompée*: Roman History and Tasso's Theory of Christian Epic," *PMLA* 97 (1982): 830–43; Winthrop Wetherbee, "Dante, Lucan, and Virgil," in Robert von Hallberg (ed.), *Canons* (Chicago, 1984), pp. 131–48; Richard C. McCoy, *The Rites of Knighthood: The Literature and Politics of Elizabethan Chivalry* (Berkeley, 1989), pp. 103–26; Gerald M. MacLean, "The Debate over Lucan's *Pharsalia,*" *Time's Witness: Historical Representation in English Poetry, 1603–1660* (Madison, 1990), pp. 26–44; David Quint, *Epic and Empire: Politics and Generic Form from Virgil to Milton* (Princeton, 1983), pp. 5–10, 131–60; Burrow, pp. 180–99; Smith, pp. 204–9, 224–30; Andrew Shifflett, "'By *Lucan* Driv'n About': A Jonsonian Marvell's Lucanic Milton," *Renaissance Quarterly* 59 (1996): 803–23; and Norbrook, pp. 23–62.

[31] For details, see Cheney, *Marlowe's Counterfeit Profession*, pp. 49–67.

[32] Leo Braudy, *The Frenzy of Renown: Fame and Its History* (New York, 1986), p. 135.

[33] On Ovid and Lucan as counter-imperial epicists, see Philip Hardie, *The Epic Successors of Virgil: A Study in the Dynamics of a Tradition* (Cambridge, 1993).

republican ones.[34] The fourth piece of evidence requires more pause because it has been more neglected: Marlowe also infuses Lucanism throughout his poems and plays. Back in 1956, William Blissett suggested that the "heroic figures of Marlowe's plays are ... blood brothers to [Lucan's] Caesar," citing Tamburlaine, Machiavel, Gaveston, and the Guise, all of whom themselves cite Lucan's Caesar as their model for conduct.[35] To this list we can add Mephistophiles, who detects Faustus' innate Caesarism (A-text, III, i, 43). Blissett also sees Marlowe's Lucanian characterology as "supplemented by allusions to details in Lucan," the "most important" being "the general pervasion of the Lucanic point of view," and including Marlowe's "wealth of geographical and ethnological detail," his "rationalism" or contempt for orthodox supernaturalism, and finally Marlowe's mighty line.[36]

Blissett's short discussion deserves to be augmented. While Renaissance critics have become obsessed with Ovid in Marlowe (and Shakespeare), we might wish to become obsessed with Lucan in Marlowe (and therefore Shakespeare).[37] Once we do, we discover how Lucan's model of Caesar as an anti-hero illuminates Marlowe's famed invention of dramatic character, the overreacher. For instance, Norbrook identifes the "sublime" as a key signature of Lucan's anti-monarchical poetics, seeing it in opposition to Virgil's "monarchical monumentalism," and he notes that in the seventeenth century Thomas Hobbes objected to "Lucan's aiming at sublimity," which Hobbes "identified with soaring fancifully above due limits."[38] Students of Marlowe will quickly grasp the relevance of the Lucanian sublime for Marlowe; what we might have forgotten is how precisely the Marlovian sublime is at once Lucanian and republican.

A fifth and final piece of evidence brings us to the heart of the matter. Marlowe's poems and plays habitually narrate a story about the loss of liberty. Marlowe's experiments in tragedy in his plays can be identified as in some sense republican documents. Greenblatt and his heirs emphasize Marlowe's theatrical originality for putting at center stage a series of aliens, outsiders, and exiles—an African queen, a Scythian shepherd, a German scholar, a Maltese Jew, even an English homoerotic king who lacks clear political organization—without recognizing that such figuration forms a strong republican ethos. Dido might speak

---

[34] Heather James, "Ovid and the Question of Politics in Early Modern English," *ELH* 70 (2003): 343–73. Robert R. Edwards adds that Ovid was "unwillingly political in the direct imperial reception of his work" (personal communication, September 12, 2003).

[35] Blissett, pp. 563–5; see *1 Tamburlaine*, III, iii, 152; *Jew of Malta*, Prologue, 19; *Edward II*, I, i, 173; *Massacre at Paris*, ii, 95; xix, 66; xix, 85. Quotations of Marlowe's plays come from *Christopher Marlowe: The Complete Plays*, ed. Mark Thornton Burnett, Everyman Library (Rutland and London, 1999).

[36] Blissett, pp. 565–6.

[37] On the influence of Marlowe's *Lucan* on Shakespeare, see Emrys Jones, *The Origins of Shakespeare* (Oxford, 1977), p. 273; on Jonson, see Steane, p. 268n1.

[38] Norbrook, p. 137.

for all of Marlowe's figures when she says, "I am not free. O would I were!" (III, iv, 5). Thus, Marlowe's much-debated interest in Machiavelli needs to be reconsidered, since it is well known that in *The Jew of Malta* he is the first to put the arch-republican author of *The Prince* and *The Discourses* on the English stage.[39] To this *dramatis personae*, we can add, from Marlowe's poems, an Ovidian lover, a passionate shepherd, a pair of star-crossed lovers, and of course those egregious Gemini of anti-republicanism at the core of Lucan's Roman civil war, Caesar and Pompey. Accordingly, the famed Marlovian narrative, in both poems and plays, tells how a freedom-seeking individual is oppressed, always to annihilation, by those in power, whether represented by a corrupt government or by the angry gods, or by both: "Adders, and serpents, let me breathe a while!" (*Doctor Faustus*, A-text, V, ii, 120).[40]

Republican Authorship in *1 Tamburlaine*

Once we acknowledge the presence of republican discourse in Marlowe's poems and plays, we are ready to approach its strangeness. I propose to do so through *1 Tamburlaine*. The passage quoted in my essay title shows Ceneus, a lord working for the King of Persia, criticizing Tamburlaine as a republican:

> He that with shepherds and a little spoil
> Durst, in disdain of wrong and tyranny,
> Defend his [freedom] 'gainst a monarchy. (II, i, 54–6)[41]

---

[39] On Marlowe and Machiavelli, see Irving Ribner, "Marlowe and Machiavelli," *Comparative Literature* 6 (1954): 348–56; Mario Praz, "Machiavelli and the Elizabethans," *Proceedings of the British Academy* 14 (1928): 49–97; Howard S. Babb, "Policy in Marlowe's *The Jew of Malta*," *ELH* 24 (1957): 85–94; N.W. Bawcutt, "Machiavelli and Marlowe's *The Jew of Malta*," *Renaissance Drama* 3 (1970): 3–49; Catherine Minshull, "Marlowe's 'Sound Machevill,'" *Renaissance Drama* 13 (1982): 35–53; Margaret Scott, "Machiavelli and the Machiavel," *Renaissance Drama* 15 (1984): 147–74; and Cheney, *Marlowe's Counterfeit Profession*, pp. 136–156. Yet this work focuses exclusively on Machiavelli as the monarchical author of *The Prince*, not the republican author of *The Discourses*. (NB: I consider *The Prince* as much a republican work as *The Discourses*.) Graham Hammill is now researching the topic of Marlowe and Machiavelli (personal communication, October 16, 2002).

[40] On this Lucanian idea, cf. D.C. Feeney, *The Gods in Epic: Poets and Critics of the Classical Tradition* (Oxford, 1991), p. 285: "He has not abandoned the gods, they have abandoned him"; see also Martindale, *Redeeming the Text*, pp. 70–71.

[41] Curiously, Burnett's text contains a typo right at the key word, mistakenly printing "kingdom" instead of "freedom" (personal communication, June 15, 2003).

The phrasing here is precise: Tamburlaine emerges as a republican freedom-fighter. As a shepherd, he disdains political tyranny and sets out to defend his own freedom, and that of his friends, against the wrong of monarchical power. As Tamburlaine himself tells his future wife Zenocrate, "I love to live at liberty" (I, ii, 26).

Recurrently, Tamburlaine voices his commitment to the republican idea of liberty, even in matters of appetite: "Then let us freely banquet and carouse" (IV, iv, 5). Not surprisingly, what the shepherd finds intolerable is slavery: "[I] must maintain my life exempt of servitude" (I, ii, 31). Indeed, the word "free" and its cognates occur 13 times in this play. Marlowe's archly masculine hero takes freedom so seriously that he opens a door we might not expect: at the end of the play, Tamburlaine identifies the female as the political agent of freedom, telling the Soldan, "Thy princely daughter here shall set thee free; / She that hath calmed the fury of my sword" (V, i, 437–8).

Another recurrent word in *1 Tamburlaine* is the plural "friends," which occurs 11 times.[42] Marlowe's use of "friends" speaks to the communal ethos of Tamburlaine's identity and regime; he begins with two close friends, Techelles and Usumcasane, and he soon acquires a third, Theridamus; and together these four men overrule a number of single monarchs around the East: Mycetes (Act I), Cosroe (Act II), Bajazeth (Acts III–V), and the Soldan and his prospective son-in-law, the King of Arabia (Act V). As this inventory suggests, Marlowe structures the play precisely around the opposition between a sturdy republican coalition and a sliding set of monarchs. As Tamburlaine voices his ethos of friendship: "These are my friends, in whom I more rejoice / Than doth the King of Persia in his crown" (I, ii, 240–41). Friendship opposes kingship, and in doing so helps define Tamburlaine's republican rule.[43]

At times, Tamburlaine's republican discourse of friendship is startlingly precise. As he tells Theridamus, Techelles, and Usumcasane, "We will reign as consuls of the earth, / And mighty kings shall be our senators" (I, ii, 196–7). The word "consuls" identifies the leading office of the Roman republican government, as, for instance, Shakespeare records in the prose Argument to *The Rape of Lucrece*, the narrative about the end of the Roman Empire and the birth of the Roman Republic: Lucrece's suicide is so charged that it "changed" the "state government ... from kings to consuls" (Argument, 45).[44] In Marlowe's first line,

---

[42] Compared with 33 times in *Edward II*; six in *Dido*; ten in *2 Tamburlaine*; five in *The Jew*; eight in *The Massacre*; and seven in *Faustus*. The total of 21 uses of "friends" in the two *Tamburlaine* plays reveals how important this concept is to Marlowe at the outset of his London theatrical career.

[43] On friendship and republicanism, see Laurie Shannon, *Sovereign Amity: Figures of Friendship in Shakespearean Contexts* (Chicago, 2002).

[44] In the *Riverside Shakespeare*, ed. G. Blakemore Evans, et al. (Boston, 1997). See Patrick Cheney, *Shakespeare, National Poet-Playwright* (Cambridge, 2004), ch. 4.

Tamburlaine tells his friends that they shall reign as consuls of a republican government; in the second, he measures how his new republican regime will radically change Eastern government: by deposing "kings" and reducing them to "senators."

As this representation intimates, however, Marlowe's play does not allow pure republican government to reign unalloyed. For, as the title page to the 1590 edition advertises, Marlowe's republican "shepherd" becomes a "mighty monarch." We have here a rather complex political representation. Initially, Marlowe presents his hero as a republican freedom-fighter who opposes slavery and monarchy and who locates his government in a group of "friends" operating as "consuls." But then Marlowe lets Tamburlaine's imperialist desire and discourse dominate the play; this freedom-fighter is obsessed with becoming a king. As Tamburlaine asks his friends, "Is it not passing brave to be a king, / And ride in triumph through Persepolis" (II, v, 53–4). In fact, it is Tamburlaine's obsession with kingship that readers and viewers likely remember most. Thus, he makes his monarchical goal no secret, proclaiming, "I shall be the Monarch of the East" (I, ii, 184; see I, i, 43). Later, after defeating Mycetes and his brother Cosroe, he places the crown on his head: "I [will] wear it in despite of them / As great commander of this eastern world, / If you but say that Tamburlaine shall reign" (II, vii, 61–3). As the condition in the last line indicates, and as the line following insists, Tamburlaine's imperial rule exists through republican vote: "*All.* Long live Tamburlaine, and reign in Asia!" (II, vii, 64).

It is the Persian King Cosroe who first expresses confusion about Marlowe's complex political representation: "The strangest men that ever nature made! / I know not how to take their tyrannies" (II, vii, 40–41)—the plural here being precisely to the republican point. The complexity only intensifies as the play progresses, for Tamburlaine insists that his republican kingship is paradoxically ordained: "fates and oracles of heaven have sworn / To royalise the deeds of Tamburlaine / And make them blest that share in his attempts" (II, iii, 7–9)—an idea the play voices repeatedly (for example, IV, iv, 135–6). In other words, Marlowe's new Elizabethan icon shows a contradiction of terms: *the divine right of a republican king.* In all its grim violence, this seems to register not so much Queen Elizabeth's monarchical republic as its photographic negative.

We can gain further access to Tamburlaine's political weirdness by recalling his origins in the master of weirdness himself: Lucan.[45] On the one hand, the

---

[45] No one better expresses Lucan's weirdness than John Henderson, "Lucan / The Word at War," in A.J. Boyle (ed.), *The Imperial Muse: Ramus Essays in Roman Literature of the Empire to Juvenal through Ovid* (Berwick, 1988): "Read Lucan. You must read Lucan. His poem breaks rules, inflicts pain and suffering. Don't bother to reclaim *this* classic in the name of a 'literature': this text screams a curse on its readers and upon itself—not at every moment in its duration, or you may begin to lose the edge of its imprecation, but in a press of destabilising counter-creation" (p. 123).

republican Tamburlaine explicitly identifies Lucan's arch monarch, Caesar, as his military model:

> My camp is like to Julius Caesar's host,
> That never fought but had the victory;
> Nor in Pharsalia was there such hot war
> As these my followers willingly would have. (III, iii, 152–5)

Here Marlowe presents his hero self-consciously voicing his Lucanian origin, as Tamburlaine compares his own "camp" to the "host" of Caesar, and his battle against Bajazeth to Caesar's battle against Pompey at Pharsalus. If Jamie Masters is correct about "the conflict at the heart of Lucan's relation to the epic genre"— the poet's identification with both Caesar's "ambition" and Pompey's "remorse"— we might be struck by Blissett's argument that Tamburlaine, like Marlowe's overreacher in general, identifies only with Caesarian ambition.[46]

On the other hand, the last line of the speech just presented shows Tamburlaine identifying a republican authority—the will of his followers—as the key to his military triumph. Thus, we need to distinguish between Tamburlaine and Caesar: if Lucan's despot is an absolutist tyrant, Marlowe's hero is what we might term a republican tyrant. As the Messenger informs the Soldan:

> Did your greatness see
> The frowning looks of fiery Tamburlaine,
> That with his terror and imperious eyes
> Commands the hearts of his associates,
> It might amaze your royal majesty. (IV, i, 12–16)

In these terms, Tamburlaine's paradox is that he uses his eyes of imperialism to form a republican army organized around the "hearts of his associates." No wonder the "royal majesty" of the Soldan should be amazed. Consequently, Tamburlaine also shows a resemblance to Lucan's Pompey, whose republican drive is always controlled internally from an absolutist command center. As Marlowe brilliantly puts it in his translation, "Pompey could abide no equal, / Nor Caesar no superior."[47] Collinson speaks of "an anti-monarchical virus of early sixteenth-century humanism," yet Marlowe, we might say, with his weird Lucanian humanism, is a *virus with attitude.*[48]

While emphasizing the viral infection distempering Marlowe's republican representation, we still might be interested to know how alertly it taps into a vital

---

[46] Jamie Masters, *Poetry and Civil War in Lucan's "Bellum Civile"* (Cambridge, 1992), pp. 9–10.

[47] *Lucan: The Civil War, Books I–X*, Book I, lines 125–6: "Nec quemquam iam ferre potest Caesarve priorem / Pompeiusve parem."

[48] Collinson, pp. 119–20.

historical phenomenon. In a valuable essay, David Armitage reconstructs a Machiavellian paradox that bears uncannily on Marlowe's play: a republican government needs to balance its primary value, liberty, with the glory and greatness of imperial dominion. According to Armitage, the Machiavellian paradox derives from the Roman historian Sallust and is inherited by "British republicans" between the sixteenth and nineteenth centuries, from Richard Beacon in 1594, to James Harrington in 1656, to Algernon Sidney in 1663–64, to David Hume in 1752:[49]

> ... his Sallustian and Machiavellian tradition encouraged the belief that the greatness of the republic derived originally from its liberty. However, Sallust's continuation of his narrative showed that the consequences of pursuing such *grandezza* would lead inevitably to the loss of that liberty both for the republic and for its citizens. The virtuous and the courageous became greedy, ambitious and impious, the character of the republic was changed, and the government itself became cruel and intolerable.[50]

As Machiavelli saw, "*Imperio* and *libertà* would, at last, be incompatible." Yet the drive to solve "Machiavelli's dilemma" is precisely what organizes republican theory thereafter. For our purposes, the most important solution comes from Henry Bolingbroke in *The Idea of a Patriot King* (1738), which features "a monarch committed above all to the public good, who would hence be that republican oxymoron, a patriot king." In *1 Tamburlaine*, 150 years in advance of this republican document, it is as if Marlowe parodies the Machiavellian idea of the patriot king, cynically turning the republican ideal into a republican tyrant. Remarkably, Marlowe's response to Machiavelli turns out to resemble William Gladstone's biting nineteenth-century critique of "Bolingbroke's admirer, Disraeli": "Liberty for ourselves, Empire over the rest of mankind."[51]

Can we imagine a better slogan for Marlowe's strange republican tyrant? Is this not a fit epitaph for his own republican authorship?

Conclusion

Marlowe's republican authorship might prove significant initially because it helps us to historicize Marlowe as an early modern author. During the past four hundred years, commentators have turned up an impressive list of original Marlovian achievements: the first to translate Lucan and Ovid, the first to make blank verse the standard on the stage, the first to put Machiavelli in the theater, and so forth. As we have seen, Marlowe is also the first important Elizabethan author to write

---

[49] David Armitage, "Empire and Liberty: A Republican Dilemma," in *Republicanism: A Shared European Heritage*, vol. 2, pp. 30, 35–46.

[50] Armitage, pp. 30–31.

[51] Armitage, pp. 33, 36, 42, Gladstone quoted at p. 42.

English republicanism. Marlowe's republican authorship, however, is strange and perhaps unique; it does not show a patriotic political program but an afflicted imaginative expression at once obsessed with and tormented by the republican fantasy of freedom and always bound by empire. By recalling Marlowe's pioneering role in writing imperial republicanism, we may begin to reconstruct his place in English literary history.

Additionally, Marlowe's republican authorship might prove significant because it helps us to fill in an important phase in a much larger historical narrative, linking republican thought in classical Rome with that in mid-seventeenth-century England. In his essay, "Classical Liberty and the Coming of the English Civil War," Quentin Skinner observes in passing that the Elizabethan age was "exactly ... the first time" when the major authors of classical civil liberty "became available in English." Skinner singles out the main documents: Nicholas Grimalde's 1556 translation of Cicero's *De officiis* (with a dual language version in 1558), Henry Savile's 1591 translation of Tacitus' *Histories* and *Agricola*, Richard Grenewey's 1598 translation of Tacitus' *Annals* and *Germania*, and Philemon Holland's 1600 translation of Livy's *History of Rome*. He adds to this list Thomas Heywood's 1608 translations of Sallust's *Bellum Catiliniae* and *Bellum Iugurthinum*, and Cicero's key text, Aristotle's *Politics,* translated in 1598 from Louis Le Roy's French translation.[52] For Skinner, this Elizabethan print practice is part of the origin of seventeenth-century republicanism.

Nonetheless, Skinner's essay title reveals his real topic, the attempt to show the origins of the English Civil War in classical views of civil liberty: "By the time Charles I confronted his Parliament in 1640, ... these observations by the Roman historians about 'free states' and the attendant dangers of enslavement had all been turned into works of English political thought."[53] We can extend this conclusion, and sketch out the Elizabethan crucible of mid-seventeenth-century republicanism, especially the late sixteenth-century fascination with alternate forms of government and a willingness to criticize the Queen's government, represented in the circles surrounding the earl of Essex and Sir Walter Ralegh, within which authors such as Spenser, Marlowe, and Shakespeare moved. Marlowe's writing of *1 Tamburlaine*, like his translation of Lucan and indeed all of his poems and plays, emerged from this environment.

The Elizabethan phase of the 1590s, I believe, catches classical liberty and English republicanism precisely in its *representational phase*, rather than in a constitutional one. The Elizabethan representational phase plays a transitional role between "classical liberty" and "the English Civil War." By translating "the central poet of the republican imagination," and by troubling that imagination through a new theatrical icon, the republican tyrant, Marlowe comes to play a counter-laureate role in the advent of English authorship.

---

[52] Quentin Skinner, "Classical Liberty and the Coming of the English Civil War," in *Republicanism: A Shared European Heritage*, vol. 2, pp. 9–10.

[53] Skinner, "Classical Liberty and the Coming of the English Civil War," p. 13.

Chapter 3

"Much More the Better for Being a Little Bad," or, Gaining by Relaxing
Equity and Paradox in *Measure for Measure*

Peter G. Platt

Late in Act V of Shakespeare's *The Comedy of Errors*, Duke Solinus asks, upon seeing the twin Antipholi, "And so of these, which is the natural man, / And which the spirit? Who deciphers them?"[1] In this moment of confusion and inquiry, the Duke recognizes doubleness and interpretive complexity. A man who had read the world and the law in a single-minded and inflexible fashion—"I am not partial to infringe our laws ...; by law thou art condemned to die" (I, i, 4, 25)—encounters "twin-ness"—"Stay, stand apart. I know not which is which" (V, i, 365)—and mitigates his earlier harsh ruling: "Thy father hath his life" (V, i, 392).

Solinus's words are a classic case of Shakespearean paradox: that is, an astonished expression of the encounter with double or multiple perspectives that usually accompanies epistemological change in Shakespeare's plays. This doubleness fascinated John Keats; he called it "negative capability": "that is when a man is capable of being in uncertainties, Mysteries, doubts, without any irritable reaching after fact & reason." This is a quality, said Keats, that "Shakespeare posessed [*sic*] so enormously."[2]

This recognition of the paradoxical nature of the world, I would argue, is a prerequisite for cognitive growth in Shakespeare—for his characters and for his audience. Those trapped in a single-minded, monomaniacal view of human

Special thanks go to Angela Balla, Bradin Cormack, and Benedict Robinson for suggestions and encouragement at just the right time.

[1] William Shakespeare, *The Comedy of Errors*, in Stephen Greenblatt et al. (eds), *The Norton Shakespeare* (New York, 1997), V, I, 334–5. All further references to the texts of Shakespeare will be taken from this edition, unless otherwise noted.

[2] John Keats, "To George and Tom Keats," in *The Letters of John Keats: 1814–1821*, ed. Hyder Edward Rollins (2 vols, Cambridge, 1958), vol. 1, p. 193.

experience tend to be the ones doomed in the Shakespearean universe. To return to my opening example, Duke Solinus of Ephesus both overrides his earlier univocal reading of the letter of the law that automatically sentences Syracusans to death and allows Egeon to live *only after* hearing Egeon's story and encountering the double perspective that his twin sons represent.

First, we need to examine ever so briefly what paradoxes were supposed to mean and do in the early modern period. "Paradox" in Greek (*para-doxon*) means contrary to received teaching or opinion. This is the denotation in Cicero's *Paradoxa stoicorum* and the one that gets repeated throughout the Renaissance. Another definition available to the sixteenth century was what Thomas Playfere, an Elizabethan preacher, called in 1595 "the intermingling of extremities."[3] These senses of paradox necessarily suggest a challenge both to conventional thought and to single, stable truths. Rosalie Colie's magisterial book on Renaissance paradox has highlighted the role of paradox in undoing certainty and conventional wisdom. The figure inevitably involves an "exploitation of the fact of relative, or competing, value systems. The paradox is always somehow involved in dialectic: challenging some orthodoxy, the paradox is an oblique criticism of absolute judgment or absolute convention."[4] Colie rightly sees paradox's intimate relationship with epistemology and the negotiation of the boundaries of the known.

My sense of the Renaissance paradox is threefold: it challenges conventions and commonly held opinions; it startles its "audience" into marvel and amazement; and it contains opposites without necessarily resolving them. But paradox could be more than a rhetorical figure. As I have argued elsewhere, a geographical site— Venice—could do the work of the verbal paradox. Indeed, the Renaissance Venice of contemporary accounts and of Shakespeare's *The Merchant of Venice* and *Othello* was a location that could force a reconfiguring of thought, knowledge, and evidence.[5]

The concept of equity, too, performed paradoxical functions in early modern legal discourse, negotiating between universal law and strict justice on the one hand and "the randomness of particular circumstance" on the other; Duke Solinus's changed ruling is a helpful Shakespearean example.[6] Indeed, at the heart of early modern equity discussions lay a paradoxical proverb usually attributed to Cicero

---

[3] Thomas Playfere, *A Sermon preached at Saint Maryes Spittle in London on Tuesday in Easter weeke, 1595* (1596), p. 21, cited in Bryan Crockett, *The Play of Paradox: Stage and Sermon in Renaisssance England* (Philadelphia, 1995), p. 19.

[4] Rosalie Colie, *Paradoxia Epidemica: The Renaissance Tradition of Paradox* (Princeton, 1966), p. 10.

[5] See Peter G. Platt, "'The Meruailouse Site': Shakespeare, Venice, and Paradoxical Stages," *Renaissance Quarterly* 54.1 (Spring 2001): 121–54.

[6] Kathy Eden, *Poetic and Legal Fiction in the Aristotelian Tradition* (Princeton, 1985), p. 44.

and found in his *De officiis*: *summum Ius, summa iniuria* [Extreme justice is extreme injustice].[7]

Shakespeare's *Measure for Measure* participates in this paradoxical discourse, even in its title.[8] For critics and editors have long recognized that—in the area of justice, mercy, and equity—the phrase "measure for measure" could cut in opposite directions. In his Arden edition of the play, J.W. Lever notes that the roots of the saying seem to be double: one, from Matthew 7: 2—"with what measure ye judge, ye shalbe judged, and with what measure ye mete, it shalbe measured to you again"[9]—stressed "just retribution and reward, or the just exaction of revenge."[10] The counter-sense is proverbial and suggests "moderation or temperance as a virtue. 'He that forsakes measure, measure forsakes him' ...."[11] Even on the level of title, then, there seems to be a paradox involving strict justice and mitigation.

Situated in their context, however, the lines from Matthew complicate matters further. Part of the Sermon on the Mount, Matthew 7 begins with Jesus saying in the Geneva version, "Ivdge not, that ye be not iudged." After the previously cited lines on measure, Jesus continues warning *against* judgment:

> And why seest thou the mote that is in thy brothers eye, and perceiuest not the beame that is in thine owne eye? Or how sayest to they brother, Suffer me to cast out the mote out of thine eye, and behold, a beame is in thine owne eye? Hypocrite, first cast out that beame out of thine owne eye, and then shalt thou see clearly to cast out the mote out of your brothers eye.

When returned to its context, then, "with what measure ye judge, ye shalbe judged,

---

[7] See Cicero, *On Duties* (*De officiis*), 1.10.33, eds M.T. Griffin and E.M. Atkins (Cambridge, 1991), p. 14. Cicero notes that this is "a proverb well worn in conversation" (p. 14). See also Erasmus's adage "*Summum jus, summa injuria*," in *Collected Works of Erasmus*, vol. 32, trans. and ed. R.A.B. Mynors (Toronto, 1989): "Extreme right is extreme wrong means that men never stray so far from the path of justice as when they adhere most religiously to the letter of the law. They call it 'extreme right' when they wrangle over the words of a statute and pay no heed to the intention of the man who drafted it" (p. 244).

[8] For a very compelling discussion of paradox and *Measure for Measure*, see Jonathan Bate, *The Genius of Shakespeare* (London, 1997), pp. 301–16.

[9] Matthew 7: 1, 3–5, in *The Geneva Bible: The Annotated New Testament, 1602 Edition*, ed. Gerald T. Sheppard (Cleveland, 1989). Unless otherwise noted, references are to this edition.

[10] J.W. Lever, Introduction to William Shakespeare's *Measure for Measure*, The Arden Shakespeare (1965; London, 1987), p. 3. All further references to *Measure for Measure* will be taken from this edition unless otherwise noted. See M.P. Tilley, *A Dictionary of the Proverbs in England in the Sixteenth and Seventeenth Centuries: A Collection of the Proverbs Found in English Literature and the Dictionaries of the Period* (Ann Arbor, 1950), M801.

[11] Lever, p. 3; see Tilley, M803.

and with what measure ye mete, it shalbe measured to you again" seems less a text of retribution and revenge and more one of moderation and mitigation. Yet, if editors sometimes forget the context of the lines, so does Shakespeare's Duke Vincentio, who proclaims in Act V, scene 1, as he calls for Angelo's punishment, "An Angelo for Claudio, death for death; / Haste still pays haste, and leisure answers leisure; / Like doth quit like, and Measure still for Measure" (V, i, 407–9). Whether he is posing as severe in order to get Isabel to be merciful and pardon Angelo or is demonstrating a newfound severity, the Duke reveals the potential for the lines from Matthew to be invoked with a sense of retribution and revenge behind them.

Just to underscore the paradoxicality of this scriptural citation—and thus Shakespeare's title—we need to emphasize the tension that exists between sixteenth- and early seventeenth-century commentaries on this passage. The gloss on Matthew 7: 2–5 in the 1560 edition of the English Geneva Bible stresses the need for hesitation and moderation in judgment: "He commandeth not to be curious or malicious to trye out, and condemne our neighbors fautes: for hypocrites hide their owne fautes, and seke not to ame[n]de them, but are curious to reproue other men's." But the marginal commentary from the 1602 edition stresses the much harsher interpretation of the lines: "We ought to finde fault one with another, but we must beware we doe it not without cause, or to seem holier than they, or in hatred of them."[12] If it has always been difficult to decipher what *Measure for Measure* means, that is at least partly because—in Shakespeare's England as now—it is difficult to know what "measure for measure" means.

To attempt an account of the paradoxes surrounding legal judgment in *Measure for Measure*, this essay will begin by examining some classical sources for the concept of equity before looking at the forms it could take in Tudor and Stuart England. I will argue that equity—which, through its paradoxical status, was meant to solve and reconfigure legal problems—could create new paradoxes and contradictions instead. I will then return to Act V of *Measure for Measure*, where equity is held out as a potential solution to the legal quandaries of the play. Part of equity's power—as theorists from Aristotle to Edmund Plowden noted—is its relationship to fiction and imaginative possibility, a relationship on which Duke Vincentio draws as he attempts to repair Vienna by staging mercy. Lowell Gallagher has called this paradoxical power equity's "inherent deregulatory aspect" and its "destabilizing action." Because equity is "a discursive space that always exceeded the boundaries of the written text of the law," it allows for

---

[12] It is as if, in the margins of the *Geneva Bible*, Escalus (1560 edn) and Angelo (1602 edn) were debating justice and equity. For a similar reading of Luke 6: 36–42, see Elizabeth Marie Pope, "The Renaissance Background of *Measure for Measure*," *Shakespeare Survey* 2 (1949): 66–9.

interrogation of the legal problems at hand as well as ways of imagining diverse solutions.[13] Ultimately, however, equity cannot solve the problem of justice in *Measure for Measure*, for this play suggests that law—or measure—is unable to contain the incommensurability of human experience. Unlike the paradox with which I started—one that allowed Solinus a way of reconfiguring his vision of the world—paradoxes of equity in *Measure for Measure* provide a justification for, rather than a mitigation of, strict justice and close down rather than open up interpretive possibility and legal flexibility.[14]

Indeed, as we will see in the versions of equity that follow, equity's very flexibility—its commitment to mitigating the severity of the written law—could create rather than solve legal difficulties. For a concept that at times advocates going "above the law" leaves open the possibility of subjective or even tyrannical interpretation and action. As Ian Maclean has helpfully framed the issue, "equity as interpretation becomes also equity as application; the jurist or judge performs the law by deciding its relationship to an individual case …. Interpretation thereby passes from a subservient to a dominant rôle vis à vis the text."[15] One of the many paradoxes of equity is that—in *performing* a law—a judge, chancellor, or king could in fact take away from the mitigation that equity ideally brings to a legal case; the law, and even justice itself, could become subordinate to the individual interpreter.

From Plato on, equity has been a concept used to redress difficulties arising from inflexible laws being brought to bear on flexible and multiple human behavior. In short, equity acknowledges the tension between the measure of law and the incommensurability of human experience. As Plato says in the *Statesman*:

> … law could never, by determining exactly what is noblest and most just for one and all, enjoin upon them that which is best; for the differences of men and actions and the fact that nothing, I may say, in human affairs is ever at rest, forbid any science whatsoever to promulgate any simple rule for everything and for all time.[16]

---

[13] Lowell Gallagher, *Medusa's Gaze: Casuistry and Conscience in the Renaissance* (Stanford, 1991), pp. 145, 161, 252.

[14] This is obviously an issue raised by *The Merchant of Venice* as well. In a longer version of this essay, I will argue that equity meets a similar fate in the earlier play. Portia's seemingly equitable position—in which she claims to believe in seasoning justice with mercy—ends up being a reinscription and a reassertion of the letter of the law.

[15] Ian Maclean, *Interpretation and Meaning in the Renaissance: The Case of Law* (Cambridge, 1992), p. 177. Maclean adds that "equity as application … raises the spectre of extensive interpretation as correction of the law or addition to it which … is a matter of dispute among Renaissance lawyers" (p. 177).

[16] Plato, *Statesman*, 294B, trans. Harold N. Fowler, Loeb Classical Library (London, 1925). Another *locus classicus* is Cicero's *De inventione*: "There are then certain matters

At equity's root, then, is the recognition of the uncertain, shifting, restless, and paradoxical nature of the world.[17]

Aristotle's definition of equity was often cited in the Renaissance and thus provides an important touchstone for any discussion of early modern equity. Book V of his *Nichomachean Ethics* leaves little doubt that simply defining equity requires entrance into the realm of paradox. Aristotle goes to great lengths to sift through the paradox that is "the problem about the equitable": it is just, and it is not; equity is both similar to and different from the just. And "what creates the problem" is that the equitable achieves justice by *correcting* justice.[18]

Justice needs correction, according to Aristotle, because "all law is universal but about some things it is not possible to make a universal statement which will be correct." When such a case arises—"when the legislator fails us and has erred by over-simplicity"—it becomes essential "to correct the omission—to say what the legislator himself would have said had he been present, and would have put into his law if he had known" (p. 1796). But in a paradox that would characterize discussions of equity throughout the early modern period, Aristotle reasserts that equity is "better than one kind of justice—not better than absolute justice but better than the error that arises from the absoluteness of the statement" (p. 1796). Error comes not from absolute justice but from an absolute *statement* of justice; Aristotle seems uneasy with criticizing law even as he necessarily must do so.

He closes with a call for flexibility in law—not an abandonment of the rule but a recognition that "when the thing is indefinite the rule also is indefinite, like the lead rule used in making the Lesbian mouldings; the rule adapts itself to the shape of the stone and is not rigid, and so too the decree is adapted to the facts" (p. 1796). Or, as Wesley Trimpi has noted, "Paradoxically, the generality of a legal code is deficient because it can never be general enough—since, could it have

---

that must be considered with reference to time and intention and not merely by their absolute qualities. In all these matters one must think what the occasion demands and what is worthy of the persons concerned, and one must consider not what is being done but with what spirit anything is done, with what associates, at what time, and how long it has been going on" (2.59.176, trans. H.M. Hubbell, Loeb Classical Library [London, 1949]).

[17] See Hans-Georg Gadamer, *Truth and Method*, translation revised by Joel Weinsheimer and Donald G. Marshall (2nd edn, New York, 1989): "Aristotle shows that every law is in a necessary tension with concrete action, in that it is general and hence cannot contain practical reality in its full concreteness .... The law is always deficient, not because it is imperfect in itself but because human reality is necessarily imperfect in comparison to the ordered world of law, and hence allows of no simple application of the law" (p. 318).

[18] Aristotle, *Nicomachean Ethics*, 5.10, in *The Complete Works of Aristotle*, ed. Jonathan Barnes (2 vols, 1984; Princeton, 1985), vol. 2, p. 1795. All future references to Aristotle will be to this edition and will follow the quotation in parentheses.

been so, it would have included the exception."[19] What I hope is clear is not only that equity is paradoxical but also that Aristotle needs the figure of paradox to describe equity: he must *use* paradox to analyze the paradox of striving for universality in a world of dizzyingly multiple possibilities.

Another part of the complexity of equity was what Stuart Prall has called "a confusion of definitions .... [T]here is the timeless question of whether equity is a principle of justice transcendent and distinct from the law (legal justice) or whether it is of the same substance as the positive law but expresses the spirit rather than the letter of that particular law." Prall sees this contrast as fundamentally one between the Greek (and Aristotelian) *epieikeia* and the Roman *aequitas*.[20]

Someone who attempted to bridge the gap between these two conceptions of equity was Christopher St. German.[21] Historian John Guy has suggested that this reconciliation—indeed, St. German's entire theory of equity—is influenced by the writings of the Parisian Jean Gerson (1363–1429) and his *Regulae morales*. Still, although equity was introduced to Tudor England through a variety of sources, none was more important than St. German's *A Dialogue betwixt a doctor of divinity and a student in the laws of England* (1530, 1532), commonly called *Doctor and Student*.[22] St. German seems to have written to defend English law in general and the Chancery court in particular.[23] As a commentator on St. German

---

[19] Wesley Trimpi, *Muses of One Mind* (Princeton, 1983), p. 270. For other important discussions of the classical tradition of equity and its implications for early modern fiction-making and interpretation, see Joel B. Altman, *The Tudor Play of Mind: Rhetorical Inquiry and the Development of Elizabethan Drama* (Berkeley, 1978); Colin Burrow, *Epic Romance: Homer to Milton* (Oxford, 1993), pp. 134–9; Eden, *Poetic and Legal Fiction*, esp. pp. 25–61; Maclean, pp. 171–8; Lorna Hutson, *The Usurer's Daughter: Male Friendship and Fictions of Women in Sixteenth Century England* (London, 1994), esp. pp. 144–51; and Kathy Eden, *Hermeneutics and the Rhetorical Tradition: Chapters in the Ancient Legacy and Its Humanist Reception* (New Haven, 1997), esp. pp. 11–19.

[20] Stuart E. Prall, "The Development of Equity in Tudor England," *The American Journal of Legal History* 8 (1964): 1, 2.

[21] Alistair Fox and John Guy, *Reassessing the Henrician Age* (Oxford, 1986), pp. 183-4. See Prall, p. 3.

[22] See *St. German's Doctor and Student*, eds T.F.T. Plucknett and J.L. Barton (London, 1974). All future references will be to this edition and will follow the quotation in parentheses.

[23] See Plucknett and Barton, Introduction to *St. German's Doctor and Student*, pp. xliv–li. Important studies of equity in English law include H.D. Hazeltine, "The Early History of English Equity," in Paul Vinogradoff (ed.), *Essays in Legal History* (London, 1913), pp. 261–85; R.W. Turner, *The Equity of Redemption* (Cambridge, 1931); F.W. Maitland, *Equity: A Course of Lectures* (1936; 2nd edn, Cambridge, 1969), esp. pp. 1–42; Prall; Edward Hake, *Epieikeia: A Dialogue on Equity in Three Parts*, ed. D.E.C. Yale (New

has noted, in carving out a theory for equity and Chancery, St. German, like Aristotle, saw that "[l]aws must of necessity be framed in general terms, but the circumstances in which they may fail to be applied are infinitely variable. It therefore follows that a case may arise in which the literal application of the law would frustrate rather than promote the object which the legislator had in view."[24]

The situation was, again, paradoxical: the written law—the function of which was to facilitate the object of the legislator—could actually "frustrate" this object. What's more, as the Doctor tells the Student in Chapter 16 of the First Dialogue, there are times when to be right is to be wrong:

> ... be not ouer moch ryghtwyse for the extreme ryghtwysenes is extreme wrong/ [as who sayeth yf thou take all that the wordes of the law gyueth thē thou shalte somtyme do agaynst the lawe.] And for the playner declaracyon what equytie is thou shalt vnderstande that syth the dedes and actes of men/for whiche lawes ben ordayned happen in dyuers maners infynytlye. It is not possyble to make any general rewle of the lawe/but that it shall fayle in some case .... And therfore to folowe the wordes of the lawe/were in some case both agaynst Iustyce & the common welth: wherfore in some cases it is *good and even* necessary to leue the wordis of the lawe/& to folowe that reason and Justyce requyreth/& to that intent equytie is ordeyned/that is to say to tempre and myttygate the rygoure of the lawe. (97)

By following the "wordes of the law," one can "somtyme do agaynst the lawe," can go "both agaynst Iustyce & the common welth." As a result, "in some cases it is *good and even* necessary to leue the wordis of the lawe" in order to "folowe that [which] reason and Justyce requyreth" and "to tempre and myttygate the rygoure of the lawe." There is a recognition here that law can work against itself—or at least against its seeming intention.

Arriving at the intention behind a law is a central quality of equity, as the Doctor claims: "equytie rather foloweth the intent of the lawe/then the wordes of the lawe" (99). To prove this point, he gives several helpful examples:

> As yf a man make auowe that he wyll neuer eate whyte meate/& after it happenyth hym to come there where he can gette none other meate. In this case it behouyth hym to breke his auowe for that partyculer case is excpeted secretly from his general auowe by this equytie or epykay as it is sayd byfore. Also yf a law were made in a cytie that no man vnder the payn of deth shuld open the gates of the cytie byfore the sonne rysynge/yet yf the Cytyzens byfore that houre fleynge from theyr enemyes come to the gates of the cytie & one for sauynge of the cytyzens openyth the gates [byfore the houre

---

Haven, 1953); J.H. Baker, *An Introduction to English Legal History* (3rd edn, London, 1990), esp. pp. 112–28.

[24] Plucknett and Barton, p. xliv.

appoynted by the lawe:] yet he offendyth not the law/for that case is exceptyd from the sayd general law by equytie. (97–9)

Whether having to make dietary adjustments in order to survive or opening the city gates in an emergency, living life equitably means occasionally breaking vows, promises, and laws in order to achieve a greater good; it means living with a certain amount of contingency and flexibility.[25] Or, as Gerson would have it, "The diversity of human temperament is incomprehensible—not just in several men, but in one and the same man—and not, as I say, in different years or months or weeks, but in days, hours, and moments."[26]

Discussion of equity was not restricted to legal writings. The discourses of law and religion overlapped in the links between equity and the Christian concept of the letter and the spirit. Based in 2 *Corinthians* 3: 5–6 ("God, Who also hath made vs able ministers of the new Testament, not of the letter, but of the Spirit: for the letter killeth, but the Spirit giueth life"[27]), the distinction between the letter and the spirit was often connected to the distinction between law and the general on the one hand and equity and the particular on the other.[28] William West's *Symboleography* (1594) puts the matter very clearly: "For it is to bee understood that the law hath two parts, *Carnem* & *Animam*: the letter resembleth the flesh ..., and the intent and reason the soule."[29] John Selden was even more frank, though also disapproving: "Equity in law, is the same that the Spirit is in Religion, what every one pleases to make it."[30]

William Perkins is a crucial figure who connects these strains of law and theology. His *Epieikeia: or, A treatise of Christian Equitie and moderation* (1604) links equity to a moral Christian life:

---

[25] For the opening of the gates *topos*, see also Cicero, *De inventione*, 2.52.123.

[26] Jean Gerson, quoted in Gallagher, p. 6. Treatises on equity by writers like Gerson and St. German, according to Gallagher, were shaped by the religious discourse of casuistry, "the science of resolving problems of moral choice, known as 'cases of conscience'" (p. 1; see also p. 9). Other helpful discussions of casuistry include Wylie Sypher, "Shakespeare as Casuist: *Measure for Measure*," *Sewanee Review* 58 (1950): 275–6; A.E. Malloch, "John Donne and the Casuists," *Studies in English Literature* 2 (1962): 57–76; and Camille Wells Slights, *The Casuistical Tradition in Shakespeare, Donne, Herbert, and Milton* (Princeton, 1981).

[27] *Geneva Bible, 1602*, ed. Sheppard.

[28] For an important meditation on this connection, see Erasmus's adage "*Summum jus, summa injuria*." See also Eden, *Poetic and Legal Fiction*, pp. 136–8.

[29] William West, *Symboleography* (1594), cited in W. Nicholas Knight, "Equity, *The Merchant of Venice*, and William Lambarde," *Shakespeare Survey* 27 (1974): 97.

[30] John Selden, *Table Talk* (1689), ed. S.W. Singer (1855; Freeport, 1972), p. 49. For Selden's sense of equity as legal relativism, see below.

Equitie and Christian moderation whether publike or priuate, is the true badge of Christianitie. Without publike Equitie, what is the court of Iustice, but turned into the seate of Iniquitie? and without priuate equity, what is mans life humane societie, neighbourhood, nay friendship, nay kindred, nay marriage itself but euen a potion of poyson in a golden cuppe?[31]

But Perkins's most elegant formulation for our purposes comes in his statement about what equity is *not*: it is not justice, and it is not mercy. Though many link equity and mercy in the early modern period, Perkins keeps them distinct and reveals once again the paradoxical quality of equity:

> … two sortes of men are here reproueable. First such men, as by a certain foolish kind of pittie, are so carried away, that would haue nothing but *mercy, mercy,* and would haue all punnishments, forfaitures, penalties, either quite taken away, and remitted, or at least lessoned, and moderated, they would also haue extremitie of the lawe executed on no man. This is the high way to abolish lawes, and consequently to pull downe authoritie, and so in the end to open a dore to all confusion, disorder, and all licentiousness of life …. [I]n the second place, this doctrine and the very scope of this text, condemnes another sort of men, which are more combersome; that is to say, such men as haue nothing in their mouthes, but *the lawe, the lawe*: and *Iustice, Iustice*: in the meane time forgetting, that Iustice alwaies shakes hands with her sister mercie, and that all lawes allowe a mittigation. (sig. A8[r-v])

Equity, then, is tougher than mercy but softer than justice and law: Perkins sees equity as that which reminds us that these binaries collapse into kinship; Justice needs to shake hands with her sister and mitigate the law. Otherwise, "you make the name of iustice, a couer for crueltie" (sig. A5[r]).

Richard Hooker, another early modern figure who wrote on the connection between law and theology, warns in Book V of his *Of the Laws of Ecclesiastical Polity* of the dangers of rigid, "generall lawes," which he claimed

> … are like generall rules of physick, accordinge whereunto as no wise man will desire himselfe to be cured, if there be joygned with his disease some special accident, in regard whereof that whereby others in the same infirmitie, but without the like accident, recover health, would be to him either hurtefull, or at the least unprofitable: So we must not, under a colourable commendation of holie ordinances in the Church, and of reasonable causes whereupon they have been grounded for the common good, imagen that all mens cases ought to have one measure.[32]

---

[31] William Perkins, *Epieikeia: or, A treatise of Christian Equitie and moderation* … (1604), sig. ¶6[r-v]. Further citations are to this edition.

[32] Richard Hooker, *Of the Laws of Ecclesiastical Polity*, Book V, ed. W. Speed Hill (Cambridge, 1977), 9.2, pp. 43–4.

Just as a similar disease requires different treatment because of its particular nature, its "special accident," Hooker claims—in a phrase with Shakespearean resonance—that no "one measure" can successfully be applied to "all mens cases." Finally, stressing equity's power to correct the law, Hooker importantly concludes his definition by claiming that the problem is "not that the lawe is unjust, but unperfect; nor equitie against, but above the lawe; bindinge mens conciences in thinges which law cannot reach unto."[33]

But Hooker also raises a different issue that came to be crucial in discussions of equity: whether equity resides within the law or outside and above the law. It was just this uncertainty about where equity lay that led some who wrote about the concept to worry about its ability to correct and mitigate law. Because human laws were shadows of divine laws, John Calvin found the flexibility intrinsic to equity anathema:

> Others—which is a fault more common than criminality—think that unjust which legislators have sanctioned as just, and on the contrary, pronounce that to be laudable which they have forbidden .... The controversy of these is by no means repugnant to that original idea of equity ... for when men dispute with each other on the comparative merits of different laws, it implies their consent to some general rule of equity. This clearly argues the debility of the human mind, which halts and staggers even when it appears to follow the right way.[34]

For Calvin, the paradoxical suppleness of equity—capable of making the unjust just and the forbidden laudable—called all law, divine as well as human, into question.

But even some defenders of equity felt that it was important to stress that the written law had equity built into it—that equity was not, as Hooker had it, "above the law," but lurked within, awaiting the wise interpreter who could find it. An important example of this argument appears in one of Edmund Plowden's *Reports*, "Eyston v Studd" (Eliz. 16), in which Plowden discusses the double, paradoxical power of equity to extend or limit the law:

> ... it is not the Words of the Law, but the internal Sense of it that makes the Law, and our Law (like all others) consists of two parts, *viz.* of Body and Soul, the Letter of the Law is the Body of the Law, and the Sense and Reason of the Law is the Soule of the Law, *quia ratio legis est anima legis* .... And equity, which in Latin is called Equitas, enlarges or diminishes the Letter according to its Discretion .... Equity or *Epichaia* makes an Exception ... from the general Words of the Text, which Exception is as

---

[33] Hooker, 9.3, p. 44.

[34] John Calvin, *Institutes of the Christian Religion*, trans. John Allen, (2 vols, Philadelphia, 1936), vol. 1, p. 295.

strong as if it had been expressly put in the Act ....[35]

Equity can enlarge or diminish the law "according to its discretion," but Plowden's version of equity—unlike the view put forth in Hooker—is part of the law, its "internal Sense." Equity is law's soul, while the letter is law's body. The paradox of equity has been made part of a Christian binary system that does not threaten law's predominance.[36]

The clearest articulation of equity as law's "internal sense" comes in Edward Hake's *Epieikeia: A Dialogue on Equity in Three Parts*, which was written in about 1600 but stayed in manuscript until 1953. In putting forth his theory of internal equity, Hake cites St. German's Chapter 16, on the limits of the letter of the law: "*in some cases it is necessarye to leave the wordes of the lawe and to followe that* [which] *Reason and Justice requireth, and to that intent is Equity ordeyned.*" Instead of emphasizing correction and mitigation—and the concomitant ambiguity and paradox—Hake attempts to resolve the problem of equity, which, he says, "is of some tearmed *tacita exceptio*, yea, even in that chapter yt is said to be a secreat exception, that is, an exception secreatlie understoode in every generall rule of every positive lawe ...." But attempting to resolve paradoxes, Hake creates new ones: "Equity which seemeth to be owte of the lawe or besides the lawe, bicause it is not to be seene in the wordes of the lawe (but yet within the lawe as being within the meaninge of the lawe), is by the judge or expositor of the lawe to be applyed to the same lawe."[37] Unlike Hooker, Hake does not see equity as "owte of the lawe or besides the lawe."

But just what Hake does see is difficult to pin down. Equity "is not to be seene in the wordes of the lawe," but it is there, "within the lawe as being within the meaning of the lawe." The burden, it seems, is on the judge or expositor to find the meaning, the "secreat exception," beneath the letter of the law. While this approach may seem only to reformulate the notion that equity uncovers intention, it is different, for Hake will not let go of the law, will not look beyond it. Law *does* "fayle in the deciding of a particularity," but when this failure occurs, "the judge or expositor of the lawe is thereuppon by and by to investigate the hidden sense or *Equity* thereof ...."[38]

---

[35] Edmund Plowden, "Eyston v. Studd," in *The Commentaries, or Reports of Edmund Plowden* (London, 1779), pp. 465–6. He also notes a gap between the two types of equity, which he calls "a great Diversity ..., for the one abridges the Letter, the other enlarges it, the one diminishes it, the other amplifies it, the one takes from the Letter, the other adds to it" (p. 467). For his solution, see my final paragraphs.

[36] For an extremely useful explication of Plowden's being "virtually identified with the range of learning associated with the equity of statutes" by later Tudor and Stuart writers on equity, see Lorna Hutson, "'Our Old Storehowse': Plowden's Commentaries and Political Consciousness in Shakespeare," *Shakespeare Yearbook* 7 (1996): 258.

[37] Edward Hake, *Epieikeia*, pp. 13, 15.

[38] Hake, p. 23.

If the danger in interpreting equity as beyond the law is that either legal or extra-legal relativism could ensue, the danger in Hake's view of equity residing secretly in the law is that the judge or chancellor could have too much interpretive power, could become a tyrannical beast unrestrained by the law. In the mid-seventeenth century, John Selden worried in a similar fashion about the power of the chancellor, going so far as to suggest that equity allowed a kind of legal relativism:

> Equity is a roguish thing: for Law we have a measure, know what to trust to; Equity is according to the Conscience of him that is Chancellor, and as that is larger or narrower, so is Equity. 'Tis all one as if they should make the Standard for the measure we call a Foot, a Chancellor's Foot; what an uncertain Measure would this be? One Chancellor has a long Foot, another a short Foot, a Third an indifferent Foot: 'Tis the same thing in the Chancellor's Conscience.[39]

For Selden, equity—that which is supposed to combat the problem of measuring the incommensurable—makes measurement impossible because it shifts with every new interpreter.

The implications are even more serious when we factor in the monarch's role in the system of equity. King James, perhaps unsurprisingly, defended equity in several of his writings. But the way in which he developed the concept raises serious questions—questions that make their way into Shakespeare's *Measure for Measure*. In *The True Lawe of Free Monarchies* (1598), written before he ascended the English throne, James used equity as a method by which a king could moderate his absolutism:[40]

> For albeit it be trew that I haue at length prooued, that the King is aboue the law, as both author and giuer of strength thereto; yet a good king will not onely delight to rule his subiects by the lawe, but euen will conforme himselfe in his owne actions thervunto,

---

[39] Selden, p. 49.

[40] This discussion takes me—with some trepidation—into debates that continue to rage among historians of early modern England. For the purpose of this essay, I am taking my definition of "absolutism" from Johann P. Sommerville: "The theory of absolutism vested sovereign power in the ruler alone and forbade disobedience to the sovereign's commands unless they contradicted the injunctions of God Himself" ("English and European Political Ideas in the Early Seventeenth Century: Revisionism and the Case of Absolutism," *Journal of British Studies* 35 [April 1996]: 168). Historians such as Glenn Burgess and Paul Christianson have seen James—as his reign progressed—moving from absolutism to constitutionalism. His views on equity, though, are remarkably consistent. As far as James and equity are concerned, then, once an absolutist, always an absolutist. For the consistency and coherence of James's comments on equity, see Mark Fortier, "Equity and Ideas: Coke, Ellesmere, and James I," *Renaissance Quarterly* 51.4 (Winter 1998): 1255–81.

alwaies keeping that ground, that the health of the common-wealth be his chiefe law: And where he sees the lawe doubtsome or rigorous, he may interpret or mitigate the same, lest otherwise *Summum ius* bee *summa iniuria*: And therefore

generall lawes, made publickely in Parliament, may vpon knowen respects to the King by his authoritie bee mitigated, and suspended vpon causes onely knowen to him.[41]

We have reentered the paradoxes of equity: because *"Summum ius* [can] bee *summa iniuria"*—Extreme justice can be extreme injustice—the true comprehension of the law is achieved only by going "aboue the law." But here the stakes are higher, for by allying himself with equity—like the king, equity is "aboue the law"—James is able to justify mitigating or suspending those "generall lawes, made publickely in Parliament ... vpon cause onely knowen to him." What seems to be mitigation of the letter of the law can in fact become a kinder, gentler absolutism.

James also stresses the mitigating quality of equity in his handbook on kingship, *Basilikon Doron*, written for his son Prince Henry and first published in Edinburgh in 1598. Invoking once again the Ciceronian paradox of equity, James tells Henry to "Vse Iustice, but with such moderation, as it turne not in Tyrannie: otherwaies *summum Ius*, is *summa iniuria* ... for lawes are ordained as rules of virtuous and sociall liuing, and not to bee snares to trap your good subiects: and therefore the lawe must be interpreted according to the meaning, and not to the literall sense thereof: *Nam ratio est anima legis* [For reason is the soul of law]." Interpreting law literally can lead to tyranny, but so can being too loose with the law: "what difference is betwixt extreame tyrannie, delighting to destroy all mankinde; and extreame slacknesse of punishment, permitting euery man to tyrannize ouer his companion." For James, the solution comes both in recognizing that extremities can collapse into sameness—*"Nam in medio stat virtus* [For virtue lies in the middle] ... and the two extremities themselues, although they seeme contrarie, yet growing to the height, runne euer both in one"—and in achieving moderation and equity: "For Iustice, by the law, giueth euery man his owne; and equitie in things arbitrall, giueth euery one that which is meetest for him."[42] But in this last quotation we are back to the problem explored in the *True Lawe*: who is to decide "that which is meetest" for "euery man"?

The answer, of course, is the King—and the Court that represented the "King's conscience": the court of Chancery. A major controversy erupted in 1616 when Sir Edmund Coke challenged the reversal of a common law decision by the Chancery. Eventually, Coke, who vehemently defended common law, was taken off the

---

[41] King James VI and I, *Political Writings*, ed. Johann P. Sommerville (Cambridge, 1994), p. 75.

[42] James VI and I, pp. 43–5.

King's Bench, as James defended Chancery's decision.[43] For Coke, the

common law of England was "the golden metwand, whereby all men's causes are justly and evenly measured."[44]

Taking an approach that envisioned an elasticity to the law that Coke refused to accept, Thomas Egerton, Lord Ellesmere, issued a famous defense of equity and Chancery in the *Earl of Oxford's Case* of 1616: "Equity speaks as the Law of God speaks," Ellesmere asserted, and went on to claim that "[t]he Cause why there is a *Chancery* is, for that Mens Actions are so divers and infinite, That it is impossible to make any general Law which may aptly meet with every particular Act, and not fail in some Circumstances."[45] Claiming what Coke could never accept, Ellesmere recognized what Aristotle had: the incommensurability of human experience required a flexible legal measurement; the golden metwand was insufficient.

In June of the same year, James addressed the Star Chamber and defended both Chancery and equity:

> ... this is a Court of Equitie, and hath power to deale likewise in Ciuill causes: It is called the dispenser of the Kings Conscience, following alwayes the intention of Law and Iustice; not altering the Law, not making that blacke which other Courts made white, nor *e conuerso*; But in this it exceeds other courts, mixing Mercie with Iustice, where other Courts proceed onely to the strict rules of Law: And where the rigour of the Law in many cases will vndoe a Subiect, there the Chancerie tempers the Law with equitie, and so mixeth Mercy with Iustice, as it preserues men from destruction.[46]

James addresses and critiques the idea that Chancery and equity distort, reinvent, transform law: they do *not* make "that blacke which other Courts made white." But James also makes it clear that what undergirds equity is the King: "The Chancerie is vndependant of any other Court, and is onely vnder the King." Chancery and equity exist to correct "the rigour of the Law," but the King is the final judge: "the King onely is to correct it."[47] The problem is that, in Ian Maclean's words, "No clear demarcation can be drawn between legitimate extension of the law to *casus omissi* and illegitimate correction or emendation of the law by the judge or interpreter."[48] The court of Chancery and its use of equity become an extension of

---

[43] For a very lucid summary of the interrelated *Magdalen College Case*, *Earl of Oxford's Case*, and *Doctor Gouge's Case*, see Fortier, esp. pp. 1259–67.

[44] Sir Edward Coke, *The Fourth Part of the Institutes of the Laws of England* (4th edn, London, 1669), p. 290.

[45] *Earl of Oxford's Case*, p. 6, quoted in Fortier, p. 1262.

[46] James VI and I, p. 214.

[47] James VI and I, pp. 214–15.

[48] Maclean, p. 178.

the King's power: the Chancellor mitigates any violation of the spirit of the law, but the King—and certainly not Edward Coke—is the only one who can correct the court. He claims to be a "King of reasonable vnderstanding," but equity and his ultimate control over it potentially give him power that flies above the law.[49]

As my earlier discussion suggests, *Measure for Measure* is a play that, even in its title, engages with the paradoxes surrounding equity and justice. And there is little question that the Shakespearean plays that explore these issues evince a sympathy toward mitigating the harshness of the letter of the law. Further, in 1603—close to the date of Shakespeare's composition of *Measure*—Samuel Daniel held out equity and its personification in Lord Ellesmere as a hope for solving the problem of strict justice and rule by the letter of the law.[50] One of his *Certain Epistles* (1603), "To Sir Tho[mas] Egerton, Knight, Lord Keeper of the Great Seal of England," announces that Lord Ellesmere is the embodiment of true justice, one who can navigate the paradoxical space between "rigor and confused uncertainty."[51] Daniel goes on to celebrate Ellesmere by celebrating equity:

> Which equity, being the soul of law
> The life of justice, and the spirit of right,
> Dwells not in written laws, or lives in awe
> Of books—deaf powers that have nor ears nor sight—
> But out of well-weighed circumstance doth draw
> The essence of a judgment requisite,
> And is that Lesbian square, that building fit,
> Plies to the work, not forc'th the work to it;
>
> Maintaining still an equal parallel
> Just with the th'occasions of humanity,
> Making her judgments ever liable
> To the respect of peace and amity;
> When surly law, stern and unaffable,
> Cares only but itself to satisfy,

---

[49] James VI and I, p. 215.

[50] Elizabeth Marie Pope notes significantly that there was an "outburst of concern with the theory of government" around the time of James's accession. In addition to *Measure for Measure* and Daniel's poem, 1603 and 1604 brought—among many other texts—Perkins's *Treatise of Christian Equity and Moderation* discussed earlier, Ben Jonson's *Panegyre* on the King's initial entrance into Parliament, as well as two reprintings of James's *True Lawe of Free Monarchies* and seven reprintings of his *Basilikon Doron* (nine, Pope notes, "if we count the Welsh translation and William Willymat's digest in Latin and English verse"). Pope, p. 70.

[51] Samuel Daniel, "To Sir Tho[mas] Egerton, Knight, Lord Keeper of the Great Seal of England," line 5, in *Selected Poetry and A Defense of Rhyme,* eds Geoffrey G. Hiller and Peter L. Groves (Asheville, 1998), pp. 157–65. All further references are to this edition.

And often innocency scarce defends,
As that which on no circumstance depends.

But equity, that bears an even rein
Upon the present courses, holds in awe
By giving hand a little, and doth gain
By'a gentle relaxation of the law;
And yet inviolable doth maintain
The end whereto all constitutions draw,
Which is the welfare of society,
Consisting of an upright policy. (lines 121–44)

Neither dwelling "in written laws" nor living "in awe of books," equity is adaptable, plying "to the work, not forc[ing] the work to it." Significantly, too, equity works paradoxically, achieving wondrous power or "awe" by loosening power, "by giving hand a little"; it "doth gain / By'a gentle relaxation of the law."

In spite of Shakespeare's plays' general sympathy toward equitable principles, however, *Measure for Measure* seems less certain than Daniel's poem that equity can provide "the welfare of society, / Consisting of an upright policy." The whole process of judging in the play becomes deeply vexed, as my examination of the paradoxes of the title has already suggested. G. Wilson Knight, with whose interpretation of the Duke I vehemently disagree, is nevertheless certainly right to claim that this play reveals that "'justice' is a mockery: man, himself a sinner, cannot presume to judge."[52] But Knight is too confident that, Christ-like, the Duke resolves the problems of justice that plague this play. By emphasizing the inability of human beings to judge each other, Knight claims, the Duke and the play remind us that only God can judge. In a more convincing argument that stresses the distinction between the jurisdictions of the secular common law courts and the ecclesiastical courts, David Lindley claims that the Duke recognizes in the Barnardine scene (V, iii) "the vulnerability of the governor before a greater law than his own."[53] And Huston Diehl has recently included the Duke among those characters who reveal the play's interrogation of the problems of judgment: these difficulties lie not only in Angelo and Isabella but in the Duke's performances as "an imperfect, even a bungling, playwright." With this interrogation, she argues, Shakespeare "creates in his audience a profound sense of the infinite space that separates them from the divine."[54]

---

[52] G. Wilson Knight, *The Wheel of Fire: Interpretation of Shakespeare's Tragedy* (1930; New York, 1964), p. 76.

[53] David Lindley, "The Stubbornness of Barnardine: Justice and Mercy in *Measure for Measure*," *Shakespeare Yearbook* 7 (1996): 347.

[54] Huston Diehl, "'Infinite Space': Representation and Reformation in *Measure for Measure*," *Shakespeare Quarterly* 49 (1998): 410.

Building on Diehl's point, I would argue that—as we saw with James's reading of his role in relation to equity—the Duke's seemingly equitable gestures serve ultimately to consolidate his power. As Diehl has noted, "like the law as Calvin conceives it, the play can only reveal, not correct, imperfection, and it thus arouses a longing for what it acknowledges it cannot deliver: divine forgiveness."[55] I would add that the play also cannot deliver equity—that which is supposed to correct imperfection in the law—even though it arouses a yearning for both equity and equitable leaders.

Many critics have noted that equity plays a role in *Measure*, but there is disagreement about what this role is and who plays it.[56] Ernest Schanzer sees Escalus as equity personified because he is able to provide "the *via media* between the two excesses in the administration of justice. He possesses the proper mixture of severity [Angelo] and mercy [Duke] which marks the ideal judge."[57] Initially compelling, this idea is less convincing when we remember that Escalus shows both the problem of being too lax and the problem of being too severe. He reveals the former in Act II, scene 1, when he lets Pompey go and worries that "[p]ardon is still the nurse of second woe" (281). Although Escalus is discussing Claudio's case, the comment has clear implications for the comic subplot. Yet Escalus turns away from equity and mercy when he encounters Pompey again in Act III: "Double and treble admonition, and still forfeit in the same kind! This would make mercy swear and play the tyrant" (III, ii, 187–9). And he becomes just this sort of tyrant in Act V, scene 1, when he calls for Friar Lodowick (the Duke's alias) to be sent to prison and tortured for slandering the Duke: "To th'rack with him!—We'll touse you / Joint by joint, but we will know his purpose" (309–10). On closer inspection, Escalus seems capable of calling for both of Perkins's extremes ("Mercy, Mercy" and "the Law, the Law") but not of negotiating the paradox of equity.

---

[55] Diehl, p. 410.

[56] See G. Wilson Knight, pp. 73–96; Wilbur Dunkel, "Law and Equity in *Measure for Measure*" and J.W. Dickinson, "Renaissance Equity and *Measure for Measure*," both in *Shakespeare Quarterly* XIII (1962): 275–85 and 287–97; Ernest Schanzer, *The Problem Plays of Shakespeare: A Study of* Julius Caesar, Measure for Measure, Antony and Cleopatra (New York, 1963), esp. pp. 114–20; Harold Skulsky, "Pain, Law, and Conscience in *Measure for Measure*," *Journal of the History of Ideas* 25 (1964): 147–168; Lever, pp. lxiii–lxxii; Harriet Hawkins, *Measure for Measure: Harvester New Critical Introductions to Shakespeare* (Brighton, 1987), ch. 2; Graham Bradshaw, *Shakespeare's Scepticism* (Ithaca, 1987), pp. 164–218, especially his discussion of the conflict between legal and moral obligation in the play; Richard Wilson, *Will Power: Essays on Shakespearean Authority* (London, 1993), pp. 118–57; Crockett, pp. 104–8; Barnaby and Wry; Diehl; and Debora Kuller Shuger, *Political Theologies in Shakespeare's England: The Sacred and the State in* Measure for Measure (New York, 2002), esp. pp. 72–101.

[57] Schanzer, p. 116. See also Dickinson, who calls Escalus "the type of the just judge …. Escalus illustrates equity" (p. 294).

Other critics have seen the returned Duke as a force of equity, undoing the letter of the law and replacing it with the kind of divine forgiveness that Diehl sees lacking in the play; in this version, both Angelo and Isabella need to learn from the Duke how to mitigate their severity.[58] But the Duke's return and his subsequent actions raise as many questions about equity as they answer.[59]

The Duke wants miraculous and histrionic *effects* in Act V, and establishing himself as an equitable leader is thus bound up with theatricality. Unsurprisingly, paradoxes abound. First, Isabella must be Mariana's substitute again: claiming to have slept with Angelo, she once more plays the role of seemingly sexualized nun. After this part of the Duke's play has produced the proper confusion and anxiety, Mariana is brought on stage. She, too, plays a paradox. Asserting to the Duke that she is neither a married woman, nor a maid, nor a widow, she asserts that she is nevertheless not "nothing" (V, i, 178):

My lord, I do confess I ne'er was married
And I confess besides, I am no maid.
I have known my husband; yet my husband
Knows not that ever he knew me. (185–8)

Not long after, Mariana unveils herself to Angelo, who continues to deny sleeping with her, though he admits to having broken off "some speech of marriage" when "her reputation was disvalued / In levity" (216, 220–21). It takes Lucio's unveiling of the Duke to bring Angelo to confession:

O my dread lord,
I should be guiltier than my guiltiness
To think that I can be undiscernible,
When I perceive your Grace, like power divine,
Hath looked upon my passes. (365–8)

Angelo recognizes the Duke as God's substitute and significantly makes no appeal to the law. Asking merely that his "confession" be his "trial" (370), Angelo

---

[58] See especially G. Wilson Knight; Roy Battenhouse, "*Measure for Measure* and the Christian Doctrine of Atonement," *PMLA* 61 (1946): 1029–59; R.W. Chambers, "The Jacobean Shakespeare and *Measure for Measure*," *Man's Unconquerable Mind* (London, 1939), pp. 277–310; M.D.H. Parker, *The Slave of Life* (London, 1955); and Neville Coghill, "Comic Form in *Measure for Measure*," *Shakespeare Survey* 8 (1955): 14–27. For a compelling complication of this view, see Pope and, more recently, Peter Lake (with Michael Questier), *The Antichrist's Lewd Hat: Protestants, Papists, & Players in Post-Reformation England* (New Haven, 2001).

[59] Still others see Isabella as equity's spokesperson. See, most recently, Cohen, esp. pp. 443–6.

requests immediate death. But instead the Duke sends Mariana and Angelo away to be married.

One unveiling that does not take place at this time is the revelation to Isabella that Claudio is alive; in fact, Vincentio reiterates the fiction that her brother is dead, telling her "That life is better life, past fearing death, / Than that which lives to fear" (395–6). Stephen Greenblatt has called the Duke's practices in this play, especially at moments like this, "the techniques of salutary anxiety ..., inflicting anxiety for ideological purposes."[60] And the ideological purpose here, first and foremost, is to assert himself as an equitable ruler. In order to do that, though, he must summon the specter of revenge and strict justice so that he can be seen to correct them, to be Equity itself.

The Duke first raises the issue of strict justice to the people gathered at the city gate while he is still disguised as Friar Lodowick. He tells the crowd that he has been "a looker-on here in Vienna," where he has seen "laws for all faults, / But faults so countenanc'd that the strong statutes / Stand like forfeits in a barber's shop, / As much in mock as mark." There are "laws for all faults" and "strong statutes" that need enforcing. Once fully himself again, he builds on this foundation by invoking the "measure for measure" passage from Matthew: "An Angelo for Claudio, death for death; / Haste still pays haste, and leisure answers leisure; / Like doth quit like, and Measure still for Measure" (V, i, 407–9). While I agree with Andrew Barnaby and Joan Wry that the Duke "misapplies its central lesson in recalling not its new ethical ideal but rather the Old Testament ethic of an eye for an eye," I would argue that this misreading is an intentional part of his "equity effect": he raises the possibility of a retributive punishment in order ultimately to correct it with his staged mercy.[61] In doing so, he brings this paradoxical scriptural text into the site of paradox that his stage has become.

For Mariana is now asked to take on the paradoxical role of wife-widow, a part that she does not wish to play: "I hope you will not mock me with a husband" (V, i, 415). It is left to Isabella to beg for mercy for Angelo, and Mariana invokes the paradoxical language of equity to try to convince Justice Isabella: "They say best men are moulded out of faults, / And, for the most, become much more the better / For being a little bad" (437–9).[62] The Duke has clearly manipulated his play towards this moment. While some critics have seen him trying to lead Isabella away

---

[60] Stephen Greenblatt, *Shakespearean Negotiations: The Circulation of Social Energy in Renaissance England* (Berkeley, 1988), p. 138.

[61] Barnaby and Wry, p. 1244.

[62] Compare Bassanio's urgent command to Portia-as-Balthazar in the trial scene of *Merchant*: "Wrest once the law to your authority. / To do a great right, do a little wrong" (IV, I, 210–11).

from her own form of strict justice and towards mercy and (Christian) love,[63] I would argue that the main point for the Duke here is not Isabella but the equitable persona that he is fashioning for himself. A merciful plea from Isabella would add another important piece to his play—would add to the effect—but he will stage the *coup d'equitie*.[64]

Yet Isabella helps him out more than he could have imagined, for her words—unlike Portia's in *Merchant*—focus not on mercy seasoning justice but on legal and logical loopholes:

> Let him not die. My brother had but justice,
> In that he did the thing for which he died:
> For Angelo,
> His act did not o'ertake his bad intent,
> And must be buried but as an intent
> That perish'd by the way. Thoughts are no subjects;
> Intents, but merely thoughts. (5.1.440–46)

First, Isabella maintains that Claudio was correctly sentenced, while Angelo would be killed for an act he did not actually commit; she upholds the letter of the law in her brother's case. Even more helpful for the Duke—who wants to establish himself as the most equitable—she goes on to argue *against* equity, which typically made a claim in favor of intention over action; here, "Intents [are] but merely thoughts." It is a speech that poses as merciful but is not.[65] The Duke looks even more equitable at the end, then, because Isabella raises rather than dissipates the specter of strict justice. And, although Mariana takes Isabella's speech as a plea for mercy, none is granted until the Duke unveils Claudio and thus Angelo's crime disappears. What follows is a series of pardons and proposed marriages, an "orgy

---

[63] This position is eloquently laid out—but not adopted—by Craig Bernthal, "Staging Justice: James I and the Trial Scenes in *Measure for Measure*," *Studies in English Literature* 32 (1992): "Christian humanist exploration of mercy's relationship to justice ... [justifies] Vincentio's deceptive behavior on the grounds that he is acting for the benefit of Isabella's spiritual growth, forcing her to recognize the value of mercy by forcing her to act on her own stated beliefs" (p. 254). For a skeptical view towards any Christian reading that would celebrate the Duke's mercifulness, see Cole, esp. pp. 440–45.

[64] For a reading that finds paradox and undecidability everywhere in the play, see Lars Engle, "*Measure for Measure* and Modernity: The Problem of the Sceptic's Authority," in Hugh Grady (ed.), *Shakespeare and Modernity: Early Modern to Millenium* (London, 2000), pp. 85–104.

[65] For our purposes, it is also worth noting that Isabella uses paradox—so often an ally of equity—against equity. Like Diana describing Bertram in *All's Well That Ends Well*, Isabella is claiming "He's guilty, and he's not guilty" (*All's Well*, V, iii, 289).

of clemency," as A.D. Nuttall would have it.[66] Although the ending of the Duke's play is not without its problems—he first proposes to Isabella while she and Claudio are embracing, and she famously does not respond to his second proposal—the Duke's equitable position (within the play, at least) has been established.[67]

In closing, I would now like to turn to fictions and speculate on why they seem to be a mode for conveying the paradoxes of equity, whether the context is a law court, the Duke's Vienna, or King James's palace. If, as St. German said, equity recognizes that the greatest justice can be the greatest injustice, that "yf thou take all that the wordes of the law gyueth the thou shalte somtyme do agaynst the lawe," equity is also essentially an act of imagination, an act of fiction. According to Edmund Plowden:

> in order to form a right Judgement when the Letter of a Statute is restrained, and when enlarged, by equity, it is a good way ... to *suppose* that the Law-Maker is present, and that you have asked him the Question you want to know .... [Y]ou must give yourself such an Answer as you *imagine* he would have done .... [I]t is a good way to put Questions and give Answers to yourself thereupon, in the same manner *as if* you were actually conversing with the Maker of such Laws.[68]

Plowden suggests turning to fiction, imagination, dramatic dialogue—"conversing with the Maker of such Laws"—to negotiate the paradoxical waters of equity, which contain "great Diversity."[69]

Equity attempts to deal with the paradoxes of true justice, then, by turning to the "suppose," the "imagine." Or to use Constance Jordan's helpful paradox, "the law ventures into art to be more true to itself."[70] Thomas Ridley, writing in 1607, makes a related point:

---

[66] Nuttall, p. 239.

[67] The notion that there is an icy silence between Claudio and Isabella—simply because there is silence—strikes me as misguided, though many have maintained this position. Why else would the Duke break off his first proposal so abruptly if he does not see that he has botched his discovery scene? "Give me your hand and say you will be mine. / He is my brother too: but fitter time for that" (V, I, 490–91).

[68] Plowden, p. 467, emphasis added. See also Trimpi's formulation of the fictions of equity: "It is only as a fiction ... that one might summon the original lawmaker from the dead to interpret his general statute *as if* he could have foreseen or could now see all individual cases and its application to them" (p. 272).

[69] Plowden, p. 467.

[70] Constance Jordan, *Shakespeare's Monarchies: Ruler and Subject in the Romances* (Ithaca, 1997), p. 140.

> A fiction ... [is] an assumption of the Law upon an untruth, for a truth, in a certaine thing possible to be done, and yet not done: vpon which fiction the Doctors hold there wait two things, the one is Equitie, the other Possibilitie .... [I]f that which is in controuersie may be obtained by any other meanes than by a fiction, a fiction is not to be afforded: but if ordinairie meanes cannot be had, then fictions may be entertained to supply the defect of the ordinairie meanes, that thereby, although the truth bee otherwise, yet the effect of the Law may be all one .... [T]he law cannot proceed to a fiction without equitie ....[71]

Fictions of equity operate, then, on "certaine thing[s] possible to be done and yet not done."

And this is the quality—what Kathy Eden has called "equity's accommodative power"[72]—that Shakespeare's plays often explore and that gives his fictions of equity a sometimes exhilarating sense of "possibilitie": in *The Comedy of Errors*, as we saw earlier, Duke Solinus of Ephesus, after encountering paradox, practices equity by overriding the letter of the law and allowing Egeon to live; in *A Midsummer Night's Dream*, Hermia and Lysander flee "the sharp Athenian law" (I, i, 162), and in the forest find ways to "see these things with parted eye, / When everything seems double" (IV, i, 186–7), to gain by relaxing; and in *Othello*, Othello's tales of love and travel—of wonders and paradoxes—convince the Duke not to allow Brabantio "to read in the bitter letter / After [his] own sense" "the bloody book of law" (I, iii, 68–9, 67).[73] Although arguably all of these examples contain problems that equity cannot fully solve, the "as if" of equity nevertheless affords these plays some new, more expansive way of imagining the world.

What makes *Measure for Measure* (and *The Merchant of Venice*, for that matter) different is that in these plays equity ultimately fails to provide this new perspective, fails to offer a way out of the letter's prison, even if the equitable figures attempt to convince their audiences—in the play and in the theater—otherwise. Like Selden, Shakespeare seems aware that equity can lead merely to legalistic relativism or absolutism. Perhaps worse, it can be used by an interpreter who closes down rather than opens up possibilities. Or as Harold Skulsky so aptly puts it, "Viennese justice is restraint and not scope."[74] Is Vienna a more equitable place by the end of *Measure for Measure*? Almost certainly not, though the Duke has emerged a more equitable-seeming leader. We may be tempted to say, like

---

[71] Thomas Ridley, *A View of the Civile and Ecclesiastical Law* (London, 1607), sigs. Q2^{r-v}, Q3^r.

[72] Eden, *Hermeneutics and the Rhetorical Tradition*, p. 14.

[73] There is a hint of Ridleian "possibilitie" in Isabella's remark to the Duke early in Act 5: "Make not impossible / That which but seems unlike" (V, I, 54–5).

[74] Skulsky, p. 168. Cohen makes the same point, stressing the forced marriages at the play's close: "unions that represent not the removal but the imposition of restraint, and that celebrate not freedom but authority" (pp. 454–5).

Escalus meditating on Claudio's fate, "But there's no remedy" (II, i, 278). In the spirit of equity, however, Shakespeare leaves his play famously open-ended and gives Isabella and us some room to move, to think, to imagine an ending. Her response is, perhaps unsurprisingly, paradoxical: eloquent silence that testifies to equity's limitations and possibilities.

PART 2
Authors in Conversation

Chapter 4

Allegory, Irony, Despair
Chaucer's *Pardoner's* and *Franklin's Tales* and Spenser's *Faerie Queene*, Books I and III

Judith H. Anderson

In the following essay about allegory, irony, and despair in the *Pardoner's Tale* and Book I of *The Faerie Queene* and in the *Franklin's Tale* and Book III, I start with verbal echoes as a way of suggesting the plausibility of an interpretive context, but I concentrate instead on intertextual relations between Chaucerian and Spenserian texts that are broader—more imaginative and conceptual—than local and explicitly verbal. Whether in art or life, readers and writers register, remember, and imitate much else in literary models besides the odd word or phrase.[1] Subtler relations among texts manifestly exist and convey meaning: tonal allusions, motifs and images, rhythmic effects, tropes, structural paradigms, ideological formations, and the like. Such relations are significant in culture and relevant to its historical expressions, and their observation not only modifies and enhances previously recognized dimensions of meaning but also discovers new ones. The most historically interesting and engaged interpretations of earlier texts are often found in the writers who imitate and revise not only their content but also, and inseparably, their forms. In Gerald Bruns's words, such a later text can elicit from the earlier one "that which remains unspoken."[2] Particularly in the Renaissance, with its desire to recover the past, to return *ad fontes*, to the fountains and sources—to the deep "well" in Spenser's word for Chaucer—writers tried actually to converse with their predecessors, as Petrarch did literally in his letters to

---

[1] Lynn Enterline has suggested how a figure like Ovid's suffering Hecuba could become "a 'mirror' or 'example'"—to which I'd add, a rhetorical "place"—"for pupils to imitate," ostensibly to develop their own styles but inevitably with further "social, imaginary, and personal" impact. Both Shakespeare's Lucrece and his Hamlet, she notes, use Ovid's Hecuba as just such a mirror "in and through which to understand and to express what they claim to be their 'own' emotions" (*The Rhetoric of the Body from Ovid to Shakespeare* [Cambridge, 2000], pp. 19, 25–6).

[2] Gerald Bruns, *Inventions: Writing, Textuality, and Understanding in Literary History* (New Haven, 1982), pp. 55–6.

classical authors such as Cicero and Livy. Their conversations with their deepest sources were touched by the primary sense of the word *converse* in the Renaissance itself: "to live with," "to dwell among." What follows listens to the conversation between Spenser's texts and Chaucer's.

Theresa Krier has recently suggested an allusion to the *Pardoner's Tale* in *The Faerie Queene*, Book IV, occurring in lines that A.C. Hamilton's second edition cross-references with the temptation of Despair in Book I (ix.46, vs.1–2; 47, vs. 7–8).[3] The allusive lines, spoken by the Spenserian narrator, are these:

> O Why doe wretched men so much desire,
>   To draw their dayes vnto the vtmost date,
>   And doe not rather wish them soone expire,
>   Knowing the miserie of their estate,
>   And thousand perills which them still awate,
>   Tossing them like a boate amid the mayne,
>   That euery houre they knocke at deaths gate? (IV.iii.1)[4]

Where Hamilton hears the despairing Spenserian questions "Why then doest thou, O man of sin, desire / To draw thy dayes forth to their last degree" and "Is it not better to doe [that is, to die] willinglie, / Then linger till the glasse be all out ronne," Krier hears within the Chaucer-laden context of Book IV an allusive memory of the old man's knocking on his "moodres gate"—Mother Earth—in the *Pardoner's Tale*.[5] In the early cantos of Book IV, Krier has in mind Spenser's explicit invocation of "Dan *Chaucer*, well of English vndefyled," numerous verbal echoes and narrative memories of Chaucer's poems, and the more generalized incorporation of chthonic mothers that invites the memory of Mother Earth here.[6] I would accept both Hamilton's and Krier's recollections—the one of Despair and the other of the Pardoner—and would further suggest that their coincidence is (even literally) predictable from the vantage point of the first book of Spenser's epic romance. Awareness of Chaucer's *Pardoner's Tale* and especially of its "olde

---

[3] Edmund Spenser, *The Faerie Queene*, ed. A.C. Hamilton (rev. edn, Harlow, 2001), p. 428, note on stanza 1. Throughout I have used the standard abbreviation vs. for verse(s).

[4] Citations of *The Faerie Queene*, unless otherwise specified, are from the Variorum edition: *The Works of Edmund Spenser*, eds Edwin Greenlaw et al. (11 vols, Baltimore, 1932–57), vols 1–6. Each citation has been checked for variants against the Yamashita-Suzuki text of 1590 in Hamilton's edition. With a single possible exception, noted below, the variants involve insignificant differences in spelling, most commonly the interchangeable letters *i* and *y*.

[5] *The Faerie Queene*, I.ix.46–7. *The Riverside Chaucer*, ed. Larry D. Benson (3rd edn, Boston, 1987), p. 199, vs. 729.

[6] Theresa Krier, *Birth Passages: Maternity & Nostalgia, Antiquity to Shakespeare* (Ithaca, 2001), pp. 210–12. Quotation from *The Faerie Queene*, IV.ii.32.

man" is brooding and pervasive through much of Book I. It begins with the old man Archimago and climaxes in the related character of Despair. Conspicuously and ironically, it involves the Redcrosse Knight's recurrent encounters with mirrors of himself that he fails to recognize and the progressive identification of sleep, or rest, with death.

An older Chaucer criticism, as Marshall Leicester has distilled it, identifies the Pardoner as "the *eunuchus non dei*, the embodiment of the *vetus homo*, the Old Man whose body is the body of this death and who is guilty of sinning against the Holy Ghost."[7] Specifically, this is the Bible's Old Man who fails to put on the New, as urged in Ephesians 4: 22–4. Criticism has also established that the "olde man," as well as the three rioters, is an aspect or a reflection of the Pardoner.[8] More than the Pardoner fully realizes, he meets himself in his tale about the search for Death. Like the Pardoner, the rioters gamble, overplay their hands, and through greed indeed find death, but the more secret, less openly motivated parallels between the "olde man" and the Pardoner are the unforgettable ones, at once more poignant and more terrible. This restless, haunting product of the Pardoner's imagination not only enables the rioters to achieve their desire for Death, but also expresses his own death wish:

> Thus walke I lik a restles caityfe
> And on the ground, which is my mothers gate
> I knocke with my staffe erlyche and late
> And say, leue mother let me in
> Lo howe I vanisshe, flesshe, bloode and skyn
> Allas, whan shal my bones ben at reste[?][9]

Chaucerians have referred the restless wish of the "olde man" to Augustinian despair, which is the inverse of pride, an abyss of guilt at once self-centered, self-

---

[7] H. Marshall Leicester, Jr., *The Disenchanted Self: Representing the Subject in the Canterbury Tales* (Berkeley, 1990), p. 39. Leicester cites Robert P. Miller, "Chaucer's Pardoner, the Scriptural Eunuch, and the *Pardoner's Tale*," *Speculum* 30 (1955): 180–99.

[8] Leicester, p. 46. Donald R. Howard, *The Idea of the Canterbury Tales* (Berkeley, 1976), pp. 357–8, 361; and Alfred Kellogg, "An Augustinian Interpretation of Chaucer's Pardoner," in his *Chaucer, Langland, Arthur: Essays in Middle-English Literature* (New Brunswick, 1972), p. 257. Carolyn Dinshaw credits the Pardoner with more awareness than do most, since she finds in the "olde man" not an ironic, sub- or semi-conscious reflection of the Pardoner's imagination but a self-knowing one. For her, the "olde man" is "an incarnation of the pardoner's anguished knowledge of his fragmentariness" (*Chaucer's Sexual Poetics* [Madison, 1989], p. 179).

[9] Unless otherwise specified, subsequent citations of Chaucer are to *Works 1532*, supplemented by material from the editions of 1542, 1561, 1598, and 1602 (1968; London, 1976). The present reference to the *Pardoner's Tale* is on f.lxxviii^r. Throughout, I have changed solidi to commas and have expanded contractions in Thynne's text of Chaucer.

tormenting, and self-destructive.[10] In relation to the Pardoner, Leicester cites a modern description of such despair from Kierkegaard's *Sickness unto Death* that is sufficiently suggestive in relation to Spenser's figure Despair to bear repeating:

> Literally speaking, there is not the slightest possibility that anyone will die from this sickness or that it will end in physical death. On the contrary, the torment of despair is precisely this inability to die .... If a person were to die of despair as one dies of a sickness, then the eternal in him ... must be able to die in the same sense as the body dies of sickness. But this is impossible; the dying of despair continually converts itself into a living. The person in despair cannot die; "no more than the dagger can slaughter thoughts" can despair consume the eternal, the self at the root of despair, whose worm does not die and whose fire is not quenched .... [This] is precisely the torment, is precisely what keeps the gnawing alive and keeps life in the gnawing ... [that he] cannot reduce himself to nothing.[11]

Similarly, Spenser's Despair, having failed at the last minute to secure the death of Redcrosse, tries to hang himself, "But death he could not worke himselfe thereby; / For thousand times he so himselfe had drest, / Yet nathelesse it could not doe him die" (I.ix.54).

Whereas critics of Chaucer have reproached the rioters for taking the boy's personification of death literally, it might more accurately be said that the rioters take this personification realistically in the substantive, Platonic sense.[12] Of course, with consummate irony, the rioters eventually do achieve death as a physical reality, though only with their own extinction. But before then, rushing off to slay the thief Death, they look less like a trio of literalists than like three drunks entering a fantasy world, or, as it turns out, an allegory. Once in this fictive world—part deictic and part nondeictic, part real and part Real[13]—they don't understand the

---

[10] On the relation of pride to despair, besides Kellogg, see Harry Rusche, "Pride, Humility, and Grace in Book I of *The Faerie Queene*," *Studies in English Literature* 7 (1967): "Despair, like all the sins that threaten the Christian's quest for salvation, is a result of the egocentrism created by pride" (38–9). For a more extensive and learned examination of "The Left Hand of God: Despair in Medieval and Renaissance Tradition," see Susan Snyder's essay in *Studies in the Renaissance* 12 (1965): 18–59; she writes, for example, that "Augustine points out the paradox of the travelers to Emmaus who walked with the risen Christ without recognizing him: the living walked with the dead but bereft of hope *they* were in fact dead, while he was Life itself" (p. 58). Throughout the essay, Snyder keys her discussion to Spenser's rendering of despair in Book I, canto ix.

[11] Leicester, p. 48.

[12] For example, Howard, p. 357: "taking the personification literally, they attempt to 'slay' Death"; Dinshaw, p. 178: "The three [rioters], of course, take this talk [the boy's] literally." On use of the Platonized real in allegory, see Stephen A. Barney, *Allegories of History, Allegories of Love* (Hamden, CT, 1979), pp. 22–3.

[13] See Carolynn Van Dyke's persuasive characterization of literary allegory as a "synthesis of deictic and nondeictic generic codes" (*The Fiction of Truth: Structures of*

significance of the "olde man" and his allegorically resonant directions, but they do recognize that he has some connection with the Death they seek. They remark his odd appearance, "al forwrapped saue thy face," and his "great age" and later, after he has spoken, they accuse him of being Death's "espye," one "of his assent," and even like Death himself, a "thefe" (f.lxxviii^r-v). That "espye" in its cognate verbal form can mean "to lie in ambush for" or "to set a snare for" and "to discover (a person or thing that is concealed)," "to discover or disclose (a person) as to identity or condition," is surely more relevant to the rioters' meeting with the "olde man" than they recognize, even as their words, responding to the old man's and highlighting their ironic resonance, cue readers further into the allegory.[14]

The "olde man" himself conveys a spooky excess of significance, even while his figure is insistently natural—real in this lowercase sense. This synthesis of deictic with nondeictic is very much part of his power and, paradoxically, of the resemblance to him of Spenser's more abstract figure Despair, a point to which I'll return later. Here, I would emphasize again that everything about the "olde man" works on a natural, or deictic, level. Even his most hauntingly resonant words evoke the image of a frail old man steadying his steps with a cane or staff as he walks—tap, tap, tap, or, "knocke, knocke, knocke." His words project the thoughts that match his deictic movement and appearance, much as might those of a personifier of animal-stories for children. The technique is dramatic, imaginative, and poignantly empathetic. Little wonder the rioters do not recognize the old man's full meaning: this is not the boy's earlier, stylized picture of an emblematic, nondeictic Death brandishing dart or spear, but death in a living form, the death wish arising from despair. We hear the affective power of this figure, as figure, resisting single-minded translation to the containment of an abstractive and bloodless system, be it psychoanalytical or theological, or both.

What I have called an excess of significance in or about the old man's figure, however, starts with the very suddenness of his appearance. Coming up over a stile, the "olde man" is initially, so to speak, right in the rioters' faces. Spookily wrapped up, aged but willing to walk all the way to India, and conceiving, if only in a manner of speaking, of a bargain of youth for age that sounds odd, if not unnatural, the "olde man" delivers directions to the rioters that are about as loaded with nondeictic meaning as anything Spenser ever wrote: his directions feature a "croked way," as distinct from a straight one, and the archetypal tree associated

---

Meaning in Narrative and Dramatic Allegory [Ithaca, 1985], p. 40). I follow Van Dyke in using *deictic* and *nondeictic* as convenient summary terms for all the binaries in her argument (or in mine), such as particular and universal, concrete and abstract, natural and emblematic, real and Real. *Deictic* itself signifies "directly pointing out" or "demonstrative." In a linguistic context, it indicates a word that particularizes and points, such as the demonstrative pronoun *this*. It derives from Greek δεικτικός, "able to show, showing directly." By "genre," Van Dyke means "a set of conventions based on an inferable semiotic code" *and* "the texts that realize the code—or realize it to a significant degree" (pp. 20–21).

[14] *MED*, s.v. *Aspien*, 2.(a), 4b, 4c; *OED*, s.v. *Espy sb.*, 1.b.

with the Fall and more generally—via Servius on Vergil's *silva* ("wood, forest")—
with matter itself, with the root beneath the tree, *radix malorum*, which takes form
in this *Tale* as gold florins and fleshly *cupiditas*, the greed that motivates the
Pardoner's entire sermon.[15] Oblivious to obvious moral and spiritual meaning, as
well as to the old man's pious warnings, the vice-ridden rioters achieve the death of
the body that is denied the "olde man." The Pardoner, their creator, enters the
allegory with them, as earlier he might have been said to have entered the tavern,
where his vivid dramatizations of life cross into direct discourse:

> By goddes preciouse herte, and his nayles
> And by the blode of Christ, that is in hayles
> Seuene is my chaunce, and thyn is fyue and thre
> By goddes armes, if thou falsly play me
> This daggar shal thorowe thyn herte go. (f.lxxviiiʳ)

But all the Pardoner achieves in his allegory—I think without fully realized
awareness—is an expression of his otherwise repressed death wish. His fragmented
personality, much remarked by modern psychoanalytic interpreters, achieves ironic
wholeness, a wholeness that is not wholeness, in the sharing of this wish by teller,
"olde man," and unruly rioters. This self-canceling wholeness realizes content
subversively latent in allegorical form itself, in its contradictory impulses to
inclusion and division. Such latency is not characteristically *expressed*, as it is both
here and in Spenser's first Book.

Allegory often projects elements of a complex whole, such as a person or
human consciousness, as separate personifications, as in the instance of both the
"olde man" and the rioters, who mirror the Pardoner in some respect. It also
combines temporal narrative with non-temporal abstraction to produce an analytical
process. The more allegorical the text, the more these characteristics will be
evident in it, or tautologically, vice versa. In Spenser's first Book, unmistakably an
allegory from its outset, the Pardoner's "presence" is a memory—refracted,
progressive, elusive, persistent.[16] It is recurrently evoked by the text through the

---

[15] On Servius' gloss, see William Nelson, *The Poetry of Edmund Spenser: A Study*
(New York, 1963), p. 159: Servius' commentary on *silva*, namely, "that in which beastliness
and passion dominate," was standard throughout the Middle Ages and in the Renaissance
entered the dictionaries. Now linked with *hyle*, the "Vergilian forest … becomes a figure
variously signifying the material stuff upon which the divine ideas are impressed, the
activities of this world, the passions of the body, the earthly or fleshly aspect of human life."

[16] "Refraction," a term I use here to describe the relation between two different poems,
occurs in Spenser criticism to describe the recurrence within and between different parts of
The Faerie Queene itself. Spenser's poem often uses a kind of refraction to relate largely
disparate figures to a single type, model, or, as I would argue here, to a nondeictic
abstraction; as Peter Hawkins has observed, in such phenomena we recognize less the
presence of the original than the "degrees" of its presence ("From Mythography to Myth-

sheer weight of repeated coincidence in meaning arising within a shared technique, the weight of a particular traditional content merging with a particular conventional form. For content, especially the Bible and Augustine are common cultural denominators in both texts, and for form, allegorical projection or mirroring. Spenser's avowed awareness of Chaucer's poetry, which is prominent in Book I, as in all but one of the other books of *The Faerie Queene*, is itself a relevant factor and *a condition of plausible interpretation*.

In Book I, while Archimago's temptation of Redcrosse is a consequence of the events it follows—his entrance into the Wandering Wood and his battle with the serpent-woman Error—it marks the first clear failing of the Knight's faith and the beginning of his descent to despair, the ironic nadir of his quest for holiness and wholeness in a self-contradictory allegorical medium. If, as some argue, this medium is a stand-in for meaning itself in this life, then Spenser's poem focuses more specifically on a potential that is present more latently and fleetingly in Chaucer's. Archimago, whose name suggests both imagination, the image-making faculty, and its product or "chief image," is a shape-shifter and impersonator, an artist who manipulates the imaginations of others to produce tempting but guilty illusions. Dressed as a hermit, "Bidding his beades," framing his stories of "Saintes and Popes" with "*Aue-mary*'s," he is a representative of the Catholic Church and one who, like the Pardoner, can "file his tongue as smooth as glas" (i.30, 35). He is pointedly called "the old man," the *vetus homo*, a reference reinforced by "aged sire," and he turns out to be on a continuum with the fallen nature of everyman, who is figured in this book by the Redcrosse Knight (ii.5). Archimago is the first of many figures who mirror Redcrosse in such a way that we understand them to be at once inside and outside him, an ironic realization that Archimago's actual impersonation of Redcrosse brings home. His figure suggests that Spenser may have read the Pardoner's story of the "olde man" and the rioters in much the same way, and two additional considerations enforce this possibility. The false dream Archimago gets from the Cave of Morpheus—that is, from sleep, or, Redcrosse's merely but thoroughly natural condition—conspicuously alludes to Chaucer's *Book of the Duchess* and likewise indicates that Spenser either read Chaucer's poem allegorically or found in it the potential thus to repackage it. Earlier, the description of the Wandering Wood noticeably includes Chaucer's wood in *The Parliament of Fowls* among its sources, and the subsequent motif spanning Book I that associates trees with the nature of flesh begins here. Fradubio, the tree man physically rooted in bad faith, is a particularly and ironically telling mirror of Redcrosse and a memorable embodiment of this archetypal arboreal motif, coincidentally present in the *Pardoner's Tale* as well.

As Redcrosse progresses in bad faith, the resemblance of his situation to the Pardoner's develops further. Redcrosse's inconclusive battle with Sans Joy, who figures his own joylessness and the emotional condition of his eventually conscious despair, leads under the aegis of Pride, the deceptively showy surface of restless, inner discontent, to the bottom of hell. Implicitly, this hell is within Redcrosse, whose joylessness takes him there in the night. It is a subterranean hell that explicitly evokes the descent into earthly matter in Vergil's sixth book, as glossed by Servius, and Redcrosse's descent occurs while he is in bed and presumably dreaming, as before at Archimago's hermitage. Within its infernal precincts, natural rest moves closer to the "deadly sleepe" first witnessed in that hermitage and then more openly in the poignant speeches of Despair (i.36, cf. 32):

> Is not short paine well borne, that brings long ease,
> And layes the soule to sleepe in quiet graue?
> Sleepe after toyle, port after stormie seas,
> Ease after warre, death after life does greatly please. (I.ix.40)[17]

At "the furthest part" of Hell, a "Deepe, dark, vneasie, dolefull, comfortlesse" cave much like Despair's, the tale of Aesculapius' reuniting the scattered members of Hippolytus signals the restoration to wholeness not of Redcrosse but ironically of Sans Joy, his joylessness, the sickness of spirit gnawing within him (v.36–9).[18] Since the story of Hippolytus also reads as an account of jealousy and betrayal from either Redcrosse's or Una's different points of view, it serves as a reflection of and on their division "into double parts" at Archimago's hermitage, even while holding both parts in unholy communion (ii.9).[19] Like the Pardoner's, this Aesculapian wholeness is not wholeness, but a perverse reunion of Redcrosse's parts, and it fulfills the psychic fragmentation Redcrosse embraced when, abandoning Una, he took up with Duessa, double being or duplicity (Latin *duo*, "two," and *esse*, "to be").

When Despair finally takes form as a character in Book I, his appearance mirrors that of the miserable Redcross Knight when he emerges from Orgoglio's dungeon: "A ruefull spectacle of death and ghastly drere," Redcrosse has "sad dull eyes deepe sunck in hollow pits," "bare thin cheekes," and "rawbone armes," all reflected in the face of Despair, whose "hollow eyne / Lookt deadly dull, and stared as astound; / His raw-bone cheekes through penurie and pine, / Were shronke into his iawes, as he did neuer dine" (viii.40–41; ix.35). In the dungeon, Redcrosse has explicitly wished for physical death in order to escape his living one, his "hollow, dreary, murmuring voyce" resounding, "O who is that, which brings me happy choyce / Of death, that here lye dying euery stound" (viii.38)?

The Knight's Despair combines elements of the Pardoner with those of the

---

[17] See Judith H. Anderson, "Redcrosse and the Descent into Hell," *ELH* 36 (1969): 481–5.

[18] Despair's cave is "Darke, dolefull, drearie, like a greedie graue" (I.ix.33).

[19] For additional discussion of this unholy communion, see Anderson, "Redcrosse and the Descent into Hell," 487–8.

"olde man." Despair is a preacher who, like the Pardoner, preys on guilt and manipulates the imagination with a finely tuned psychological finesse. He plants traps easy to see through, if only his victim were confident of salvation and deaf to the appeal of repose he offers. Repeatedly, he calls Redcrosse's failings to mind, rubbing salt in the wound of his diseased conscience, and he drives him to desperation by picturing vividly the torments of the damned. His counsel is deadly in every sense, and, as we have seen, like the Pardoner's "olde man," he explicitly embodies a death-wish, which is paradoxically a wish for the death that can never die, described so fittingly by Kierkegaard.

Above all, Despair is an artist with words. This is the deepest source of his affective power and of his reality (small *r*) as a temptation, despite the openness of his evil intent and even of his name. While clearly a nondeictic abstraction, Despair is heard and felt as a deictic experience. Described as "charmed," "inchaunted," and "bewitch[ing]," the cadences of Despair have an arresting, hypnotic attraction (ix.30, 48, 53). The resonance of his words, like those of the Pardoner's "olde man," is moving and hauntingly memorable, and may also be the deepest source of his likeness to this aged precursor in Chaucer:

Who trauels by the wearie wandring way,[20]
    To come vnto his wished home in haste,
    And meetes a flood, that doth his passage stay,
    Is not great grace to help him ouer past,
    Or free his feet, that in the myre sticke fast?
… … …

He there does now enioy eternall rest
    And happie ease, which thou doest want and craue,
    And further from it daily wanderest:
    What if some litle paine the passage haue,
    That makes fraile flesh to feare the bitter waue?
    Is not short paine well borne, that brings long ease,
    And layes the soule to sleepe in quiet graue?
    Sleepe after toyle, port after stormie seas,
Ease after warre, death after life does greatly please. (I.ix.39–40)

Striking testimony to the comforting appeal of the last four lines, which I cited earlier by themselves, is to be found in their having been a staple of British military funerals during the twentieth century.[21]

Coming face to face with Despair is a new experience for Redcrosse, even

---

[20] The Yamashita-Suzuki text in Hamilton (ed.) has "trauailes" rather than "trauels"; either spelling enables the pun, although the former may do so more insistently for a modern reader.
[21] My source for this eye-witness story is the late Charles Boxer, an officer in the British Army in World War II and subsequently an academic historian.

though he has earlier been depressed and has even wished for death. Building on the foundation of Redcrosse's earlier feelings, Despair newly tempts the Knight to a conscious, willful disbelief in his own salvation. Significantly, Despair's is the first cave that Redcrosse actually enters voluntarily, while awake, and with Una. The marked contrast of this situation with that at or in earlier caves or cave-like enclosures—Error's, Morpheus', Night's, Aesculapius', Orgoglio's—signals the difference in meaning. Likewise, the naming of Despair outright even before he appears and the simple fact that he has an English name advertising, rather than half masking, his full identity differentiate the kind and level of experience he embodies from those of Archimago, Lucifera, Sans Joy, and Orgoglio. In this striking respect, Despair resembles the Pardoner, who not merely discloses but even insists on his own vice, fraud, and malice, yet whose sermon, especially the words of its "olde man," touches and disturbs us.

It would be easy, if unimaginative, to see this resemblance, this defiance of our wariness, as Spenser's effort to overgo Chaucer: after all, what could be a greater accomplishment than to make us feel the appeal of a figure as physically ugly and unqualifiedly evil as Despair? It would be equally easy, and to my mind more inviting, more generous, and more plausible, to see it as homage to the Chaucerian "well of English" and deep tonal source from within the relatively more abstract and analytical form Spenser chooses to speak to his audience. Is this not the sort of homage artists often pay their precursors, sometimes acknowledging their influence or inspiration in the title of a painting or poem? Looked at this way, a central thread of the narrative fabric in Book I becomes an intensification and more extensive examination not alone of a Chaucerian theme, despair, but also of Chaucerian character, irony, and allegorical reflection. While very much a new creation and a different sort of poem, Book I becomes also a reading of Chaucer and a text in the history of interpretation, as well as in the history of form. The relation between the *Pardoner's Tale* and Book I likewise becomes an intertextuality that is truly inter-text, *text* being understood as a whole.

Gerald Bruns observes of a manuscript culture, which was still very much alive in Spenser's time, that the appropriation and "embellishment" of another text "is an art of disclosure, as well as an art of amplification. Or rather, amplification is not merely supplementation but also interpretation: the act of ... eliciting from it [the earlier text] that which remains unspoken" (55–6). To a considerable extent, his observation applies to the relation between the *Pardoner's Tale* and Book I: the "olde man" haunts the imagination of Book I and what is implicit in the form of the Pardoner's allegory becomes focal there. But this application is by no means an isolated instance of broader, imaginative and conceptual, relations aside from but not excluding specific verbal echoes between Chaucer's poems and Spenser's epic romance. Further to exemplify and to explore this fact, I will pursue the suggestive bearing of the *Franklin's Tale* on Book III, which, like that of the *Pardoner's Tale* on Book I, ought to be apparent but has not proved so. This relationship, too, involves allegory, irony, and despair.

Once again, a verbal echo offers an initial clue but affords only information of a general sort. In the first canto of Book III, when Britomart rebukes six knights trying to force Redcrosse to exchange the love of Una for that of Malecasta, her words closely recall the Franklin's: "Ne may loue be compeld by maisterie; / For soone as maisterie comes, sweet loue anone / Taketh his nimble wings, and soone away is gone" (25).[22] This allusion to Chaucer fits Spenser's immediate context, invites us to think of the *Franklin's Tale* as Britomart's quest begins, and appears to require no further explanation. In due course, a number of other memories in Book III add to its Chaucerian cast, recalling tales of desire and marriage similarly appropriate to its subject matter: notably, memories of the *Tale of Sir Thopas*, the *Wife's Prologue*, and old January and young May in the *Merchant's Tale*, the prototypes of Malbecco and Hellenore.[23]

Given these Chaucerian memories, I would look more closely at a motif, a technique and tonal allusion, and a sub-genre in the fourth canto of Book III. This is the canto of generic complaints, first Britomart's, then Cymoent's, and finally Arthur's, each complaint inviting comparison with the others. Britomart's comes when she reaches the seacoast in her restless quest for Artegall. It is the place to which "her grieuous smart," a love wound that makes her feel "nought but death her dolour mote depart," seems naturally to draw her. There, she sits upon "the rocky shore," and

> ... having vewd a while the surges hore,
> That gainst the craggy clifts did loudly rore,
> And in their raging surquedry disdaynd,
> That the fast earth affronted them so sore,
> And their deuouring couetize restraynd,
> Thereat she sighed deepe, and after thus complaynd. (III.iv.6–7)

In the Petrarchan complaint she then utters, the sea of passion within mirrors that without her. Like the Petrarchan religion of love itself, her woes as a near-hopeless lover reflect the images of religious despair, here those of storm and shipwreck associated by Augustine and others, *via* the Vulgate's Psalm 101 and the "profundum marum" of the Vulgate's Psalm 67: 23, with the abyss of despair.[24]

---

[22] Compare the *Franklin's Tale*, f.lx^v: "Loue wol not be constrayned by maistry / Whan maistrye cometh, the god of loue anon / Beateth his wynges, and farewel he is gon."

[23] For the *Tale of Sir Thopas* in Book III, see my essay "The 'couert vele': Spenser, Chaucer, and Venus," *English Literary Renaissance* 24 (1994): 646–7. Book III.x.10, vs. 1–3, also recalls both I.ix.11, vs. 1–4, and the *Wife's Prologue*, lines 263–4 (lineation of Benson [ed.], *The Riverside Chaucer*).

[24] See Snyder, pp. 18, 54, 58; Snyder specifies Augustine's commentary on Psalm 101 and Gregory's *Moralia* for the imagery of storm and shipwreck. Augustine, Chrysostom, Gregory, Bernard, and Bonaventura are among those referring to despair as a deep abyss

Britomart pleads first with the sea and later with the "God of winds" that the billows might abate, for otherwise her

> ... feeble vessell crazd, and crackt
> Through thy strong buffets and outrageous blowes,
> Cannot endure, but needs it must be wrackt
> On the rough rocks, or on the sandy shallowes. (III.iv.9–10)

Reminiscent of Petrarch's sonnet 189 as Britomart's complaint is, this Petrarchan subtext has no "craggy clifts" or "rough rocks" awaiting the storm-tossed ship. But her lament finds a parallel to them in the lovelorn Dorigen's fear of "the grysly rockes blake" in the *Franklin's Tale*, where Dorigen stands on a cliff overlooking the sea and casts "her eyen downwarde fro the brinke" (f.lxi[r]).[25] "Fro the brinke" is suggestively suicidal, hence despairing, and from it she pleads, "But thilke god, that made the wynde to blowe / As kepe my lorde,"

> And wolde god that all these rockes blake
> Were sonken in to hell for his sake.
> These rockes slee myn hert for feare. (f.lxi[v])[26]

Earlier, Dorigen's extensive complaint about the rocks questions the wisdom and motives of God as creator and provider:

> Eterne god, that through thy purueyaunce

(related is the image of despair as a prison). I have combined "profundum marum" and abyss, perhaps the most common image of despair. In connection with Britomart's sea imagery, Hamilton (ed.), *The Faerie Queene*, cites Psalm 69: 15 (the Vulgate's 68: 16), which is clearly related as well.

[25] I am not suggesting the absence of rocks from Petrarch's *Rime sparse* by noting their presence in the *Franklin's Tale*. My point is simply that the rocks are not in Spenser's immediate subtext, sonnet 189, and anything less immediate lacks its *prima facie* force. For the combination of rocks and boats in the *Rime sparse*, see, for example, poems 80 ("Chi è fermato di mensar sua vita / su per l'onde fallaci et per li scogli / scevro da morte con un picciol legno ... "; "He who has decided to lead his life on the deceiving waves and near the rocks, separated from death by a little ship ... "), 135, 235 ("Né mai saggio nocchier guardò da scoglio / nave did merci preziose carca"; "Nor did ever a wise helmsman keep from the rocks a ship laden with precious merchandise"), 264: *Petrarch's Lyric Poems: The "Rime sparse" and Other Lyrics*, trans. and ed. Robert M. Durling (1976; Cambridge, 1995). None of these parallels is psychologically or emotionally as close to Britomart's as are Petrarch's sonnet 189 and the complaint of Dorigen, Chaucer's notably female speaker. For a discussion of sonnet 189 as the immediate subtext, see note 29.

[26] On the well-established connection between suicide and despair, see Snyder, pp. 50–57.

Ledest this worlde, by certayne gouernaunce
In ydel, as men sayn, doste thou nothing make
But lorde, these grisly fendely rockes blake
That semen rather a foule confusyon
Of werke, than a fayre creacion
Of suche a parfyt god, wyse and ful stable
Why haue ye wrought this werke unresonable:[27]
For by this werke, north, south, west, ne este
There nys fostred, man, byrde, ne beste
It dothe no good, but anoyeth
Se ye nat lorde, howe mankinde it distroyeth[?] (f.lxi^{r-v})

When Dorigen's unwelcome wooer Aurelius later underwrites the illusion by which the rocks disappear, an appalled Dorigen herself declares "such a mister or meruayle ... ayenst the processe of nature" (f.lxiii^v). Thus trapped and punished through an artful illusion for her "unnatural" wish to get rid of the rocks, she is ironically "astonyed," turned to stone herself, in this favorite Spenserian pun.[28]

Dorigen's plight has been variously interpreted in the latter half of the twentieth century. For example, Elaine Tuttle Hansen first sees Dorigen's complaint about the rocks and God as meant by the *Tale* (implicitly by the Franklin and complicitly by Chaucer) to indicate "the inappropriateness and irrationality of such intense desire in a woman [for her husband's safe return]." Hansen later makes the metafictional suggestion that the rocks are "a multivalent symbol" among whose significations are "masculine fantasies about the monstrosity of female sexuality, another version of Scylla and Charybdis, and the dangers embodied in Dorigen as heroine that stand in the way of [her husband] Arveragus's return to a chaste wife." In an earlier criticism represented by E. Talbot Donaldson, Dorigen is a naive idealist who resents the rocks because they are not "for the best in the best of all possible worlds." In his view, she subsequently "makes an analogy between ... [Aurelius'] bad behavior and nature's in allowing the ugly rocks to remain where they are" and thus combines her disapproval of Aurelius' adulterous desire with the rocks symbolizing a natural threat to her love's safe return. In this older, new critical reading, Dorigen is culpable, if only of innocence and foolishness; in the more recent feminist one, she is the pawn in a patriarchal tale and the object over which a homosocial contest in culturally valent "fredom" and true "gentillesse" is waged. In an impressive ideological omnium-gatherum, Stephen Knight describes the overdetermined rocks as "a classic *fin amor* 'impossible task'; a reification of Dorigen's insecurity when she is alone; [and] the key to her challenge ... to providence [hence to hegemony]." He adds that they also reflect "the water relations of the ur-Dorigen [combined fairy mistress and propertied Breton queen], and in a more contemporary transformation they hinder trade as well as Arveragus'

---

[27] I have substituted "gh" for the "yogh" in "wrought."

[28] Elaine Tuttle Hansen, *Chaucer and the Fictions of Gender* (Berkeley, 1992) notes this pun (p. 279).

return …. Lastly they are a Breton [coastal] reality."[29] What Spenser might have made of Dorigen's "grysly rockes blake" is uncertain, but that he, too, would have seen allegory in the focal motif they constitute seems hardly in doubt.

In view of the "rocky" site of Britomart's Petrarchan complaint and the rocks in it upon which the "God of winds" (for Dorigen, the "god, that made the wynde to blowe") threatens to wreck her vessel, it seems a curious coincidence that instead of remaining in the endlessly self-enclosed circle of Petrarchan sonneteering, Britomart turns from it in a fit of vengeance actively to pursue her quest by venting her frustration on Marinell, both the "rocky-hart[ed]" son of the sea himself and "loue's enimy," as he is described, and thus associated with the source of her torment (III.iv.26, IV.xii.7, cf. 13).[30] Marinell, whose name signifies "sea" (Latin *mare*) is the son of Dumarin (French "of the sea-farer," or "sailor") and the sea nymph Cymoent (Greek *knma*, "wave") and hence by denomination one-sided and self-centered. Violently unhorsed by Britomart, he lies in "deadly stonishment," as deadly still as a stone, and when his mother comes to lament over his fallen body even "the hard rocks could scarse from teares refraine," as happens again much later, when Florimell, in love with "stony heart[ed]" Marinell from the opening of Book III, complains so piteously that "ruth it moued in the rocky stone" of her prison (III.iv.19, 35; IV.xii.5, 13). In contrast to Dorigen, Britomart is empowered to act against the threatening sea-rocks embodied in Marinell—at this point in her career, in any case.

Dorigen's complaint to God about the rocks is not as directly about passionate love, however, as Britomart's is. Nor is the complaint to and about Night that Spenser's Prince Arthur, lovelorn like Dorigen, utters at the end of the same canto that begins with Britomart's complaint. But Arthur, like Dorigen, complains about the natural order.[31] At the same time, the resemblance of Arthur's condition in this canto to Britomart's is enforced not only by the generic forms of their plaintive utterances but also by a barrage of specific verbal echoes, which insist on our also noting this relationship. Losing sight of Florimell in the "griesly shadowes" of night, for example, Arthur wanders "Like as a ship, whose Lodestarre suddenly / Couered with cloudes, her Pilot hath dismayd," a recollection of Britomart's similar image in her complaint of Love, her "lewd Pilot," who "saile[s] withouten

---

[29] Hansen, pp. 272, 277; E. Talbot Donaldson (ed.), *Chaucer's Poetry: An Anthology for the Modern Reader* (2nd edn, New York, 1975), p. 1088; Stephen Knight, "Ideology in 'The Franklin's Tale'," *Parergon* 28 (1980): 23.

[30] On the Petrarchan circle and Britomart's lament, see Susanne Lindgren Wofford, "Britomart's Petrarchan Lament: Allegory and Narrative in *The Faerie Queene* III.iv," *Comparative Literature* 39 (1987): 28–57, esp. 34–43. Behind Wofford's view of this circle is John Freccero's classic discussion, "The Fig Tree and the Laurel: Petrarch's Poetics," in Patricia Parker and David Quint (eds), *Literary Theory/Renaissance Texts* (1975; Baltimore, 1986), pp. 20–32.

[31] Mark Rasmussen has also remarked this similarity between Arthur's and Dorigen's complaints in a paper read at The New Chaucer Society conference in July, 2002.

starres, gainst tide and wind"; this connection is reinforced by the "thousand fancies" and "sad sorrow, and disdaine" that Arthur here inherits from Britomart's earlier behavior in this canto (III.iv.5, 8–9, 15, 52–4). Via Arthur, Britomart is thus further related to Dorigen and indirectly to Dorigen's complaint about nature. In a summary word, canto iv thereby *triangulates* the relation of these three figures.

Arthur's complaint apostrophizes Night as the "foule Mother of annoyance sad, / Sister of heauie death, and nourse of woe," whose ugliness has been thrust down to hell to dwell in "*Herebus* blacke house, / (Blacke *Herebus* thy husband ...)" (iv.55). Like Dorigen in the *Franklin's Tale*, who asks, "Eterne god, ... Why haue ye wrought this werke vnresonable," Arthur demands of Night, "What had th'eternall Maker need of thee, / The world in his continuall course to keepe, / That doest all things deface?" (iv.56). Arthur's despairing complaint is as impious within a biblical ideology as Dorigen's, but through its immediate affective motivation, loss of the fleeing Florimell, whom he had hoped to be his elf queen, it is made understandably so, and it is even given a comic cast, since his situation at this point twice allusively recalls that of Chaucer's Sir Thopas.[32] Transferred to a male, and an exemplary one at that, and treated sympathetically, the threat of Dorigen's questioning of God is thus contained: Spenserians have generally found Arthur's question unremarkable, by comparison thus highlighting both the problematical gendering of Dorigen's complaint and the more exclusively erotic focus of Britomart's.[33]

Between Britomart's and Arthur's complaints, the sea nymph Cymoent rushes to the side of her wounded son Marinell, whom she first thinks dead, and laments his demise inconsolably. If her complaint has a topical relation to either of Dorigen's in the *Franklin's Tale*, it involves the despairing instinct for death, submerged within Dorigen's "grysly rockes blake" and openly expressed in the extensive exempla of suicides in her second complaint. In canto iv, this instinct is also found within Britomart's "half-formed death-wish," which, "in the symbolic logic of the poem, ... directs her steps" to the stony seacoast in the first place.[34] The same instinct is *showcased* in Cymoent's complaint:

---

[32] For example, Spenser's III.iv.53, 61, and Arthur's intervening fantasy associating Florimell with his elf queen (iv.54), and *Tale of Sir Thopas*, vs. 778–803 (lineation of Benson [ed.], *The Riverside Chaucer*). But see also note 23. My argument is a close one spanning two pages, and it benefits from the larger context of discussion in my article. Relevantly, one of these memories of Sir Thopas simultaneously recalls the Redcross Knight when he disarms in Book I, an action soon followed by Orgoglio's capture of him.

[33] I did find it of interest in *The Growth of a Personal Voice: "Piers Plowman" and "The Faerie Queene"* (New Haven, 1976), pp. 110–13. What is especially notable about the passage is its representing a movement from affective personal experience to the mythologizing imagination.

[34] Quotations from Daniel S. Murtaugh, "The Garden and the Sea: The Topography of *The Faerie Queene*, III," *ELH* 40 (1973): 336.

O what auailes it of immortall seed
   To beene ybred and neuer borne to die?
   Farre better I it deeme to die with speed,
   Then waste in woe and wailefull miserie.
   Who dyes the vtmost dolour doth abye,
   But who that liues, is left to waile his losse:
   So life is losse, and deathe felicitie.
   Sad life worse then glad death: and greater crosse
To see friends graue, then dead the graue selfe to engrosse. (III.iv.38)

My use of the word *showcased* is meant to underline exactly what is special about Cymoent's complaint: its artfulness is on exhibit. A sea nymph, even to Spenser's readers, is a creature of the feigning fancy at its freest, and Cymoent is a figure in idyllic pastoral, of which a whole piscatory subgenre exists. The sea nymph's affecting lines, we might say, are well done. But again and again, they are undercut by the narrator, as happens in the immediate, comic sequel to her complaint. Right after two stanzas of her affective outpourings, reinforced by her companion nymphs', we get "Thus when they all had sorrowed their fill, / They softly gan to search his griesly wound" (iv.40). The arias completed, pressing matters of life and death now claim attention. If this effect were isolated, we might prefer to ignore it—Homer nodding or some such. But there is an instance of it just before (iv.35) and a still stronger one in the stanza immediately after the comic sequel just quoted:

Tho when the lilly handed *Liagore*,
   (This *Liagore* whylome had learned skill
   In leaches craft, by great *Appolloes* lore,
   Sith her whylome vpon high *Pindus* hill,
   He loued, and at last her wombe did fill
   With heauenly seed, whereof wise *Paeon* sprong)
Did feel his pulse. (III.iv.41)

Between the lily-handed Liagore's introduction and her actually feeling the severely wounded Marinell's pulse, there is time for a leisurely parenthesis of five lines to review her medical and mythological credentials. This is a form of timing and ironical juxtaposition—a tonal effect, if you will—associated repeatedly, distinctively, and memorably with Chaucer's writing. Perhaps the most notorious instance of it occurs in the description of the Prioress in the *General Prologue*: "But for to speken of her conseyence"—her conscience sandwiched between ten lines about her table manners and another eight about her kindness to animals. Such *irony of duration and position* finds a point of reference not only in Chaucerian practice generally, but specifically in the length and sequencing of Dorigen's complaint about threatened and virtuous women.[35]

---

[35] Mark Rasmussen, having read this essay, in personal correspondence interestingly

This second complaint by Dorigen is long, and its many exempla, while at first clear instances of her desire to keep her chastely married body undefiled, become increasingly less relevant to her situation, with the result that for many readers the complaint begins to take on a self-generating, virtuoso life of its own.[36] The narrator's laconic comment after roughly a hundred lines of lamentation, "Thus playned Dorigene a day or twey, / Purposyng euer that she wolde dey," is characteristically Chaucerian and ironic, implying, as it does, that Dorigen's prolixity efficiently defers any danger of action (f.lxiiii^r-v). This undercutting and trivializing of Dorigen's emotion is all the more effective coming right after the most seemingly irrelevant exempla of all to Dorigen's choice between infidelity to her word or to her marriage:

> Oh Thenta quene, thy wifely chastyte
> To alle wiues may a myrrour be.
> The same thing I saye of Bilia,
> Of Rodogone, and eke Valeria. (f.lxiiii^r)

In the words of Robert Burlin, "Lest there be any question of tone here, one need only recall [Germaine] Dempster's description of the magnificent irrelevance … to Dorigen's situation" of the three histories breathlessly bundled into one couplet: "'Valeria's glory had consisted in refusing to remarry, Rhodagune's in killing her nurse, and Bilia's in never remarking on the smell of her husband's breath.'"[37]

How to interpret Dorigen's second complaint has predictably become controversial in Chaucer criticism. Most earlier critics see the complaint as parody,

---

suggests that the "excessive, or willful, grief" of Cymoent and her companions "may be in part self-parody." He has in mind the echo of "The Teares of the Muses," vs. 229–32, in *The Faerie Queene*, III.iv.35.

[36] I disagree with Stephen Knight here, who finds Dorigen's initial examples irrelevant to her case since they concern virgins who choose death over defilement (27). Perhaps I am being too Spenserian in seeing the possibility of chaste love within marriage—that is, faithful love or "wifely chastyte" in Dorigen's words—and not identifying the *chastity* of Dorigen's exemplary virgins only with virginity, but a corrective Spenserian perspective does appear apposite.

[37] Robert Burlin, *Chaucerian Fiction* (Princeton, 1977), p. 200: Burlin cites Dempster's "Chaucer at Work on the Complaint in the Franklin's Tale," *Modern Language Notes*, 52 (1973): 22. Burlin speaks of the "bathetic inconsistency" (p. 199) of the exempla with Dorigen's immediate dilemma. Rhodogone killed her nurse for suggesting that she marry again; Valeria was faithful to her husband's memory in refusing to remarry. Trying to justify Dorigen's use of Bilia as an example, Gerald Morgan explains that Bilia's endurance of "her husband's bad breath is merely one reason she acquired so great a reputation (the other is her unawareness of the fact that not all men have bad breath)" ("A Defence of Dorigen's Complaint," *Medium Aevum* 46 [1977]: 93). Morgan seems to be saying that Bilia's heroic defense of womanly honor was to endure her husband's unspeakable halitosis in uncomplaining *ignorance* of other men.

whether of rhetorical exempla, of Dorigen, or of the Franklin. Knight, followed by Hansen, finds in it a self-denying cancellation of Dorigen's earlier assertion of a distinct and "critical feminine viewpoint," as when she reproached God for the destructiveness of nature and deflated Aurelius' illicit desire for her married body. Knight argues that her exempla of virgins who prefer suicide to defilement indicate her recoil from sexuality, and since the wives she invokes are predominantly nameless or widowed, she "projects her sense of isolation into non-marriage and unnaming." The notorious exempla in the final lines of her speech (Bilia and company) offer "the same mixture of relevant and urgently irrelevant cases." In support of masculine "hegemony," her earlier challenging viewpoint is thus "foreclosed as she imagines that very viewpoint as manless, nameless, lifeless." In contrast, an exceptional reading of Dorigen's lament is Gerald Morgan's. Invoking classical rhetorical tradition and medieval morality, Morgan mounts a spirited defense of the "truth, propriety and appositeness" of Dorigen's exempla, but he tends to discount their original contexts and disregards the tonal effects of duration and sequencing.[38] Perhaps most tellingly of all, Knight observes that a number of medieval scribes found Dorigen's long complaint "as boring as many critics have, and so cut its length."[39] From the medieval period to our own, the critical consensus at least acknowledges the problematical character of her complaint, which is too long to ignore and simply too insistent to forget.

Even without regard to the relation between Dorigen's despairing complaint about the rocks and Britomart's and Arthur's paired complaints, Spenser's treatment of Cymoent's complaint in itself is thus suggestively Chaucerian. Like Chaucer, Spenser is inclined to indulge but also to feminize and in some way to distance emotional effusions of the sort Cymoent utters, and if only by way of analogue to or tonal memory of Chaucer's ironical undercutting of Dorigen, as we have seen, he does so as a sequel to Cymoent's lament. When the *Franklin's Tale* is glimpsed among the texts informing all three complaints in Spenser's fourth canto (Britomart's, Cymoent's, and Arthur's), however, its relation to this canto indicates a dimension of meaning beyond those of localized rhetoric, theme, and source. This is a formal, structural dimension of signification that appreciably modifies our sense of the whole. Recreatively imaginative, idyllically pastoral, indulgent, and comic, the portion of Spenser's fourth canto that belongs to a sea nymph "of immortall seed ... ybred and neuer borne to die" is not merely self-containing; it also serves to contain the emotional excess on both sides of it, the real suicidal threat of despairing *tristitia* (joylessness, depression). It deflects their very real dangers. Sung in Cymoent's key, the poignant yet nonetheless self-indulging despair of Britomart, linked to Arthur's as well, is at once showcased in a recreatively artful form and ironized and thus safely contained and deflected. For an analogous moment, Spenser's Anacreontics come to mind: recreative, erotic,

---

[38] Knight, 27; Morgan, p. 84.
[39] Knight, 26, 34n46.

impatient, spiteful, and comic, they are an interlude in contrasting form between the *Amoretti* and *Epithalamion*, more serious business both.[40]

Like much of Spenser's Book I, his fourth canto in Book III, read with the *Franklin's Tale*, becomes in still another, larger way an intertextual and meta-originary reading of Chaucer and a text in the history of interpretation and form. The *relatively* more lifelike forms in which Chaucer writes Spenser typically reduces, then refocuses and magnifies, essentializing (or further essentializing) them to various degrees. He separates a single plight or character into several different but related ones, dividing to probe, analyze, clarify, and plumb. In the instance of the *Franklin's Tale*, his reading appears to recognize and respect what is at stake in Chaucer's, implicitly endorsing its ideological requirements in the ironizing of emotional effusion and the containment of religious doubt. At the same time, however, by dividing the whole of Dorigen's emotional plight into parts, his reinterpretation at least gets free enough of it to follow Britomart, the major figure and central signifier in Book III, beyond despair. This difference is a *result* of such refocusing and magnifying or, in other words, of a process of thought *embodied* in form.

---

[40] Janet Levarie Smarr's article on "Anacreontics" in A.C. Hamilton et al. (eds), *The Spenser Encyclopedia* (Toronto, 1990), p. 39, provides useful background to Spenser's use of this poetic form.

Chapter 5

"Les langues des hommes sont pleines de tromperies"
Shakespeare, French Poetry, and Alien Tongues

William J. Kennedy

Nobody wants to go there. Shakespeare, allegedly the most "English" of dramatists and poets, contrived richly imagined foreign settings for most of his plays and shaped them with a view to the European world beyond England. Among his literary sources, several appear in Italian, French, and Spanish texts for which no known English translations survive.[1] And at least some of his poems, including *Sonnets* and occasional lyrics in the plays, recall continental forms. Yet the scholarly establishment routinely slights the problem of Shakespeare's access to these languages and the poetry written in them.[2] The poet-playwright might easily

---

[1] These include *Two Gentlemen of Verona* from Montemayor's *Diana enamorada* (translated by B. Yonge around 1582 but not published until 1598, rather late for Shakespeare's use of it); *Merchant of Venice* from story 4.1 of Giovanni Fiorentino's *Il Pecorone* (1558) or possibly story 14 of Masuccio di Salerno's *Il Novellino* (1476); *Merry Wives of Windsor* from story 1.2 of *Il Pecorone*; *Hamlet* from Belleforest's *Histories tragiques* (1572), 5.3; *Twelfth Night* from the Sienese play *Gl'Ingannati* (1538, translated into French as *Les Abusez* by Charles Estienne in 1548; see Robert C. Melzi, "*Gl'Ingannati* and Its French Translation," *Kentucky Foreign Language Quarterly* 12 [1965]: 180–90); *Othello* from story 3.7 of Giraldi Cinthio's *Hecatommithi* (1566); and *Cymbeline* from story 2.9 of Boccaccio's *Decameron* (translated into French by Antoine Le Maçon in 1545). The lost *Cardenio* perhaps evokes Cervantes's *Don Quixote* (translated by Skelton in 1612). *Measure for Measure* may refer to Gabriel Chappuys's French translation (1584) of story 8.5 from Giraldi Cinthio's *Hecatommithi*, or alternately to George Whetstone's adaptation of the latter in *Promos and Cassandra* (1578); but Claudio's pre-figurement of hell (III, I, 116–31) seems an uncanny précis of Dante's *Inferno* that an Italian-reading acquaintance might have recounted in outline. References to Shakespeare are from G. Blakemore Evans et al. (eds), *The Riverside Shakespeare* (Boston, 1974).

[2] Hyder Edward Rollins, for example, admirably surveys scholarship on foreign sources for *Sonnets*, but dismisses those sources as "accidental," "incidental," and "based on Renaissance commonplace" in *A New Variorum Edition of Shakespeare: The Sonnets* (2 vols, Philadelphia, 1944), 1.125–32 and *passim*. Sympathetic general assessments of

have studied grammar or phrase books such as those composed by Jacques Bellot for French and John Florio for Italian, many of which include examples of—and commentary on—poetry in their respective foreign tongues. He might likewise have consulted such rhetorical manuals as those of Abraham Fraunce and George Puttenham, or adaptations of French and Italian poems in such volumes as Thomas Watson's *Hekatompathia*, many with touchstone quotations from foreign language texts. Doubtless, too, he might have deepened his insights by conversing with foreigners residing in London, chiefly Huguenot refugees, French and Italian merchants and artisans, and Dutch businessmen, some of whom would comment on their enthusiasm (or lack of it) for their native poetry. As such intermediaries filtered Shakespeare's encounters with vernacular European literary culture, their attitudes inflected the texts he heard about. These attitudes surely meant a great deal to the developing poet in the literary London of the early 1590s, animated by the worldly satire of the so-called "University Wits," and at the turn of the century, charged by the Horatian precepts of Jonsonian classicism.

In the following pages I am going to argue that Shakespeare knew a decent amount of French and other European languages and probably something of their literatures, too, and that he displays this knowledge against provocations set first by the University Wits and later by Ben Jonson. I begin with three factual observations. First, in 1604 (and possibly earlier) Shakespeare lodged at the house of M. Christophe Montjoy, a French Huguenot refugee and luxury artisan (of women's ornamental headdresses) who resided in Cripplegate ward near the north-west corner of the city walls. One of Shakespeare's six authenticated signatures bears witness to this relationship as it records his deposition for a lawsuit concerning his landlord's alleged withholding of his daughter's dowry.[3] The playwright's lodging *chez Montjoy* suggests some contact with London's alien community and implies some encounter with native-spoken French. Second, the printed texts of his plays display considerable use of foreign languages for dramatic effect, chiefly in French and Italian, but also in Spanish, Dutch, and a

---

Shakespeare's familiarity with Italian culture appear in Murray J. Levith, *Shakespeare's Italian Settings and Plays* (New York, 1989), pp. 87–90; Robin Kirkpatrick, *English and Italian Literature from Dante to Shakespeare* (New York, 1995), pp. 277–310; Alistair Fox, *The English Renaissance: Identity and Representation in Elizabethan England* (Oxford, 1997), pp. 83–91, 180–217; and Jack D'Amico, *Shakespeare and Italy* (Gainesville, 2001), pp. 14–20.

[3] See the spirited account of this discovery in Samuel Schoenbaum, *Shakespeare's Lives* (new edn, Oxford, 1991), pp. 464–72; and the analysis of Shakespeare's match-making efforts to recruit Montjoy's son-in-law in Samuel Schoenbaum, *William Shakespeare: A Compact Documentary Life* (New York, 1977), pp. 260–64. The complete documentation appears in E.K. Chambers, *William Shakespeare: A Study of Facts and Problems* (2 vols, Oxford, 1930), vol. 2, pp. 87–95.

vague Portuguese.[4] Perhaps more significantly, because more casual and indicative of ingrained mental habits, Shakespeare's rich vocabulary displays a considerable number of loan words from French (for example, Hamlet's "bourn," III, i, 78; Othello's "antres," I, iii, 140; Macbeth's "gouts of Blood," II, i, 46) and Italian (for example, "gundello [gondola]," *As You Like It*, IV, i, 38; "carbinado," *Coriolanus*, IV, v, 187; "banditti," *Timon of Athens*, IV, iii, 397).[5] Third, Shakespeare lived and worked in a polyglot London. A few thousand Huguenot refugees from France and the Low Countries, a mix of merchants and professionals from Italy and Spain, and visitors and resident aliens from abroad all provided opportunities for the English to hear, learn, speak, and read various European languages. Early characters such as Holofernes (who has been "at a great feast of languages, and stol'n the scraps," *Love's Labor's Lost*, V, i, 37) and later ones such as Parolles, "the manifold linguist" (*All's Well That Ends Well*, IV, iii, 236), personify such an environment.

With few biographical impediments to trip over, we can survey this linguistic environment where a gifted writer could encounter Europe's cultural diversity in even routine contacts. We have here what Anne Lake Prescott has called an "energy field," an "historically mobile and culturally pressured" milieu in which continental texts came to England (or, more precisely, came to the overlapping social worlds inhabited by English writers, scholars, lawyers, professional people, and courtiers) conditioned by attitudes and expectations that could only complicate their reception.[6] I take it as axiomatic that in this milieu Shakespeare was both a practical man of the theater and a professional poet and that he worked in

---

[4] Important (but admittedly inconclusive) passages include the following. From *Taming of the Shrew*: Sly's "paucas pallabris [pocas palabras]" and "sessa [cesa]" (Induction, i, 5–6), Tranio's "mi perdonato" (I, i, 25), Lucentio's "Basta" (I, i, 198), Petruchio's and Hortensio's Italian greeting (I, ii, 24–6, 280), and Gremio's appropriate renaming of Lucentio as Cambio (1.2.83). From *Love's Labor's Lost*: Armado's florid Mediterranean-style syntax (esp. I, ii, 1–185 and IV, i, 60–87) and "fortuna de la guerra" (V, ii, 530); Holofernes's Italian proverb (IV, ii, 97–8), "bien venuto" (IV, i, 257), and "sans question" (V, i, 86); and Berowne's "allons!" (IV, iii, 380) and "sans 'sans'" (V, ii, 416). From *Merry Wives of Windsor*: Pistol's "fico" (I, iii, 30), Caius's *franglais* (I, iv, 45–87), Falstaff's "Via!" (II, ii, 153), and Mistress Quickly's "Honi soit" (V, v, 76). From *Henry V*: Pistol's "couple a gorge" (II, i, 71), Katherine's long English lesson (III, iv), the French Constable's "dieu de battailles" (III, v, 15), Pistol's "figo" (III, vi, 57), the Dolphin's "cheval volant" and "Le chien est retourné" (III, vii, 14–15, 165), the Dolphin's call for his horse (IV, ii, 2–6), Pistol's encounter with the French soldier and the boy-interpreter (IV, iv), the outbreak of disorder among French troops (IV, v, 1–5), and Henry's wooing of Katherine (V, ii, 98–342). From *All's Well That Ends Well*: the Clown's pun on "Charbon [chair bonne]" for 'Puritan' and "Poysam [poisson]" for Papist' (I, iii, 52), Lafeu's "Lustik!" and Parolles's "mort du vinaigre" (II, iii, 41, 44), "capriccio" (II, iii, 293), and "coraggio" (II, v, 93).

[5] For other examples, see Sidney Lee, *The French Renaissance in England* (Oxford, 1910), pp. 243–5.

[6] Anne Lake Prescott, *Imagining Rabelais in Renaissance England* (New Haven, 1998), pp. vii–viii.

association with other playwrights, drafting and redrafting plays singly and in concert, as was the contemporary norm.[7] I also take it as axiomatic that as a poet— particularly in *Sonnets*—he drafted and periodically revised his texts as did other poets of the time, adjusting his attitudes at different stages in the process. The most convincing study of the chronology of the sonnets (based on the statistical distribution of their early and late rare words) concludes that at an early date (before 1595) Shakespeare composed sonnets 1–60, and that he revised them before their publication in 1609; that at an early date he also composed sonnets 61– 103 and sonnets 127–54, but left them largely unrevised for publication; and that he composed the remaining sonnets 104–26 around the turn of the century.[8] This chronology distributes *Sonnets* over various phases of Shakespeare's engagement with foreign languages and literatures.

Shakespeare's sonnets pointedly represent their speaker's awareness of differences in age, rank, and social status among himself and others; machinations associated with rivalry for aristocratic patronage and commercial success; and the evolution of a poetic style apt for expressing a challenge to shifts in the writer's *status quo*. They depict their speaker as a would-be contributor to a cultural milieu where sonnets and other elite continental art forms figure prominently. As a writer he appears a *parvenu*, though paradoxically he represents himself as old, or at least as older than the Young Man who soon becomes his sexual rival in a *menage à trois* with the Dark Lady. As a writer, too, he appears in various sorts of associations with and competition against other writers and their literary practices, whether as coterie poets seeking aristocratic patronage or as entrepreneurial dramatists working for an expanding market in the public theater. Shakespeare sees in the rambunctious Young Man a simulacrum of his own profession—playing— and its dangers and rewards. He also sees in the Young Man an embodiment of the leisure and conspicuous consumption of the noble and aristocratic ranks. In the London of his day, Shakespeare must have encountered a polyglot, multiclass, increasingly mobile society of transient merchants, immigrant artisans, and alien businessmen who met the demands of the upper classes for luxury goods and leisure activities. In this environment, contact with immigrants and foreign-language speakers from other cultures who specialized in such goods and activities was inevitable.

---

[7] For Shakespeare's self-conscious shaping of his career in relation to Spenser's as a poet and Marlowe's as a dramatist, see Patrick Cheney, *Shakespeare: National Poet-Playwright* (Cambridge, 2004), esp. pp. 108-40 and 207-66. For evidence that Shakespeare wrote plays not just for the theater but also for the printed book and sought a reputation as a "literary" author, see Lukas Erne, *Shakespeare as Literary Dramatist* (Cambridge, 2003), pp. 56–77.

[8] A. Kent Hieatt, Charles W. Hieatt, and Anne Lake Prescott, "When Did Shakespeare Write *Sonnets* 1609?" *Studies in Philology* 88 (1991): 69–109.

London had long proved a magnet for immigrants from the continent.[9] The Reformation brought Protestant refugees from the Low Countries (in large numbers after persecution by the Duke of Alva in 1567) and from France (especially after the St. Bartholomew's Day Massacre in 1572).[10] Periodic anti-alien riots disturbed the peace in London between 1586 and 1595, but on the whole the newcomers assimilated with ample evidence of close friendship, intermarriage among offspring, and long-term settlement.[11] The educated local elite welcomed the immigrants' fine craftsmanship in textiles, tailoring, metals, and glass-work, along with the scientific and medical expertise and musical and artistic talent that they brought from abroad.[12] The census of 1593 records 5,450 aliens in the City, Westminster, and Southwark, comprising about five percent of the total population.[13]

---

[9] For patterns of immigration, see Laura Hunt Yungblut, *Strangers Here Amongst Us: Policies, Perceptions, and the Presence of Aliens in Elizabethan England* (London, 1996), pp. 29–35, 51–60.

[10] See Thomas Wyatt, "Aliens in England before the Huguenots," *Proceedings of the Huguenot Society of London* 19 (1953): 74–94, which points out that the London census of 1567 recorded 2,730 aliens, of whom 2,030 were Dutch; the census of 1573 recorded 5,315 aliens, of whom the majority were French. The statistics for this study and for those by Scouludi and Finlay that follow are derived from *Returns of Aliens Dwelling in the City and Suburbs of London from the Reign of Henry VIII to That of James I*, eds R.E.G. Kirk and Ernest F. Kirk, in *The Publications of the Huguenot Society of London*, vol. 10, no. 2 (for the years 1571–1597) and no. 3 (for the years 1598–1625) (Aberdeen, 1902–1907). Shakespeare's landlord "Christofer [or 'Xp'ofer'] Monioye" is mentioned at vol. 10, no. 3, p. 55 and vol. 10, no. 3, p. 101.

[11] For contemporary complaints against "beastly" Belgians, "drunken" Flemings, and "fraudulent" Frenchmen in April–May 1593, which led to a search for libelous authorship by Thomas Kyd, who implicated Christopher Marlowe shortly before the latter's death, see *The Elizabethan Journals*, ed. G.B. Harrison (2 vols, Garden City, 1965), vol. 1, pp. 188–96; for the riots of apprentices in June 1595, see vol. 1, pp. 301–4.

[12] See Irene Scouludi, "Alien Immigration into and Alien Communities in London, 1558–1640," *Proceedings of the Huguenot Society of London* 16 (1937): 27–50; and Irene Scouludi, "The Stranger Community in London," *Proceedings of the Huguenot Society of London* 24 (1987): 434–42. For the Huguenot's growing economic power and increased social prestige from their work in such crafts and trades as textiles, printing, and goldsmithing and in such professions as education and the arts and sciences, see Robin D. Gwynn, *Huguenot Heritage: The History and Contribution of the Huguenots in Britain* (2nd edn, Brighton, 2001), pp. 74–117. For the dominance among them of the merchant elite and their contacts with international Calvinism, see Ole Peter Grell, *Calvinist Exiles in Tudor and Stuart England* (Aldershot, 1996), pp. 98–119.

[13] For the growth of London's population, see Roger Finlay, *Population and Metropolis: The Demography of London, 1580–1650* (Cambridge, 1981), pp. 50–69. For a close study of the population of Southwark in the same period, see Jeremy Boulton, *Neighborhood and Society: A London Suburb in the Seventeenth Century* (Cambridge, 1987), with reference to occupational involvement on pp. 60–73.

Contemporary drama reflects this cosmopolitan ambiance. The popular Estates Morality satires of the 1580s represent foreigners as sometimes clumsy contributors to the civic mix, as in Robert Wilson's *Three Ladies of London* (1581), where the Italian merchant Mercatore's lapses into accented English foreground his stereotypical pomposity: "A good a my frend doe axa me no shush a question."[14] Educated writers such as the Oxford-trained John Lyly, Thomas Lodge, and George Peele, and the Cambridge graduates Robert Greene, Christopher Marlowe, and Thomas Nashe displayed their polyglot competence as a measure of rhetorical facility and worldly wisdom. Greene, for example, uses Latin naturally enough for the clerical characters in *Friar Bacon and Friar Bungay* (1589–92), some Italian for the titular hero of *Orlando Furioso* (1588–92), and a bizarre macaronic for the would-be assassin Jaques ("Come, say you pater noster, *car vous estes morte*") in *The Scottish Historie of Iames the fourth* (1590–91).[15] Marlowe establishes the academic setting of *Doctor Faustus* (1588–92) with Latin and some Greek, and his protagonist speaks some Spanish in scene 1; Marlowe also assigns some Spanish and French to his title character Barabas in Act II, scene 1, and Act II, scene 5 of *The Jew of Malta* (1589–90). Although he was not university educated, Thomas Kyd in *The Spanish Tragedy* (1585–89) outdoes his contemporaries with Hieronimo's fourteen-line Latin dirge in dactylic hexameter (II, v), and for local color he assigns some Spanish to Hieronimo (III, xiv) and some Italian to the treacherous Lorenzo (III, iii; and III, iv).

These University Wits (to whom Kyd belongs by association) exemplify a breed of secular humanists preening for appointments in the emergent bureaucratic state.[16] Most came from humble backgrounds and ventured to parlay their classical training into profitable secular and administrative careers.[17] Soon alienated from the worldly arena by their own self-conscious intellectual appetites, they found themselves banded in literary pursuits on the margins of commercial venture. Shakespeare entered their professional world upon his arrival in London, and his early career can be understood in terms of his sometimes willing, sometimes

---

[14] See *Three Ladies of London*, ed. H.S.D. Mithal (New York, 1988), line 378.

[15] See *The Scottish Historie of Iames the fourth* (1593), sig. H1ʳ. Eight lines of imperfect Italian hendecasyllabic verse appear in *The Historie of Orlando Furioso* (1599), sig. D3ʳ⁻ᵛ.

[16] See the characterization of them in G.K. Hunter, *English Drama, 1586–1642* (Oxford, 1997), pp. 22–39; for the aspirations of Lyly in particular, see G.K. Hunter, *John Lyly: The Humanist as Courtier* (Cambridge, 1962), pp. 89–158.

[17] About 700 students matriculated annually at Oxford and 500 at Cambridge, representing about 1.6 percent of the fifteen to sixteen-year-old male population among the country gentry and urban professional class, a relatively high age-population rate by comparison with continental universities; about 44 percent of the matriculants received a B.A. degree, among whom some 12 percent remained for the M.A. degree, nearly all in theology, destined for ecclesiastical careers; see James McConica, *The History of the University of Oxford: Vol. 3, The Collegiate University* (Oxford, 1986), pp. 1–68, 645–732.

ambivalent collaboration with or competition against their skills.[18] Despite his apparent lack of a formal higher education, the socially striving newcomer transacted from the start whatever classical and rhetorical training he had. In this context, his debut effort to insert himself into the University Wits' cosmopolitan milieu betokens his enterprise, just as his avoidance of their subversive satiric edge hints at his wary and marginalized status in this avant-garde circle.[19] In the later 1590s, his tempered approach to social behavior would prompt him to reject newer satirical forms promoted by Jonson, Dekker, Marston, Chapman, and Middleton, and to concentrate instead on his preferred forms of festive comedy, personal tragedy, and mixed-mode romance.[20] And for the greater part of the decade, his evident interest in the distinctive work of Edmund Spenser, an author more high-reaching than the University Wits and later playwrights, would have led Shakespeare toward the French lyric and Italian epic poetry so formative for England's uncrowned laureate.[21]

Seen from this perspective, Shakespeare's tolerance for alien characters in English settings as well as for foreign characters in their continental settings contrasts with the xenophobia found in other writers.[22] Instead of tarring such characters with reproachable behavior (or conversely demeaning his English

---

[18] For Shakespeare's arrival in London and his association with the University Wits, see Jonathan Bate, *The Genius of Shakespeare* (London, 1997), pp. 5–26, and Stephen Greenblatt, *Will in the World* (New York, 2004), pp. 149–74.

[19] He would later confirm this enterprise by purchasing shares in his theatrical company, amassing substantial real estate at Stratford, and gentrifying himself with an approved coat-of-arms. See Katherine Duncan-Jones, *Ungentle Shakespeare: Scenes from His Life* (London, 2001), pp. 54–81; and James Shapiro, *A Year in the Life of William Shakespeare* (New York, 2005), pp. 230–49. For a review of such practical considerations impinging upon Shakespeare's publication of his plays, see David Scott Kastan, *Shakespeare After Theory* (New York, 1999), pp. 71–92.

[20] See James P. Bednarz, *Shakespeare and the Poets' War* (New York, 2001), esp. pp. 105–33 on *As You Like It* and *Sonnets* as Shakespeare's attempts to shape his literary reputation by answering Jonson's challenge. For Jonson's response as recorded in his prefaces, prologues, inductions, and critical prose, see James Shapiro, *Rival Playwrights: Marlowe, Jonson, Shakespeare* (New York, 1991), pp. 133–90.

[21] For Spenser's "intercareerist" interest in the French Pléiade poets, see Anne Lake Prescott, "Spenser (Re)Reading du Bellay: Chronology and Literary Response," in Judith H. Anderson, Donald Cheney, and David A. Richardson (eds), *Spenser's Life and the Subject of Biography* (Amherst, 1996), pp. 131–45; and Anne Lake Prescott, "The Laurel and the Myrtle: Spenser and Ronsard," in Patrick Cheney and Lauren Silberman (eds), *Worldmaking Spenser: Explorations in the Early Modern Age* (Lexington, 2000), pp. 63–78. For traces of Spenser's translations in Shakespeare's sonnets, see A. Kent Hieatt, "The Genesis of Shakespeare Sonnets in Spenser's *Ruines of Rome*," *PMLA* 98 (1983): 800–814.

[22] See A.J. Hoenselaars, *Images of Englishmen and Foreigners in the Drama of Shakespeare and His Contemporaries* (Rutherford, 1992), pp. 26–75, 108–43; and G.K. Hunter, *Dramatic Identities and Cultural Tradition* (Liverpool, 1978), pp. 3–30.

characters by having foreigners expose their folly or vice, as Jonson would do), Shakespeare folds their discourse into a rounded and humane portrayal of various attributes. The language-lesson scenes in *Taming of the Shrew* (III, i, in which Lucentio teaches Latin to Bianca), *Merry Wives of Windsor* (IV, i, in which Evans teaches Latin to William), and *Henry V* (III, iv, and V, ii, in which Katherine studies English), typify Shakespeare's upwardly mobile respect for learning and for acquiring the assets of a cultural sophistication.[23] They also typify what Katherine discovers (and what Henry represses) in *Henry V*, that "les langues des hommes sont pleines de tromperies" (V, ii, 115)—human tongues are full of deceits, or, alternatively, human languages are full of tricks, a more inclusive lesson that concedes the hollows of one's own native language as well as those of acquired foreign languages.

How, then, might Shakespeare have polished his own foreign-language skills in multicultural London after having acquired Latin at Stratford grammar school? A good elementary education at the time emphasized the classical languages but usually precluded any comparable study of modern vernaculars.[24] According to Drummond of Hawthornden, for example, Ben Jonson who had studied Latin and Greek at Westminster School "neither doeth understand French nor Italiannes."[25] A Londoner who moved in the shadow of such circles during the early 1590s could nonetheless acquire some skills through life experiences, through self-study, or through association with the city's alien community. Textbooks were available, tutoring was at hand, and one might practice one's repertoire with a friend, perhaps read a foreign-language poem or story and discuss it with a bilingual acquaintance, engage in a sight translation and oral commentary on it with the latter, or even peruse some text-*cum*-partial-translation being circulated in manuscript among the

---

[23] For possible sources of double-entendre in these scenes, see M.L. Radoff, "The Influence of French Farce in *Henry V* and *Merry Wives of Windsor*," *MLN* 48 (1933): 427–35.

[24] Formal instruction in reading and writing was done through the study of Latin and occasionally Greek, the former a gateway to understanding modern foreign vernaculars. To be literate therefore meant to have a command of Latin that provided some skills for decoding other foreign languages. See Peter Mack, *Elizabethan Rhetoric: Theory and Practice* (Cambridge, 2002), pp. 11–75, with notice of modern foreign language teaching on pp. 49–51; Joan Simon, *Education and Society in Tudor England* (Cambridge, 1966), pp. 316–32, 363–8, 383–6; and Kathleen Lambley, *The Teaching and Cultivation of the French Language in England during Tudor and Stuart Times* (Manchester, 1920), pp. 127–30. Lambley points out that many young students supplemented their grammar school instruction with lessons from private tutors, and that French refugees established a strong network for offering such lessons (pp. 145–52).

[25] *Ben Jonson's Conversations with William Drummond of Hawthornden*, ed. R.F. Patterson (London, 1923), p. 8. For textbooks available to Shakespeare, see T.W. Baldwin, *William Shakspere's small Latine and lesse Greeke* (2 vols, Urbana, 1944), vol.1, pp. 464–531.

sophisticated elite.[26] A popular French grammar published in England at the height of the University Wits' literary activity, G. De la Mothe's *The French Alphabet* (1592), urges language learners to do precisely that. The author, a Huguenot émigré from Normandy, advises mature students to discuss "with some French man by dayly conference together, in speech and talke, what you haue learned. And if you be in place, where Frenchmen haue a Church for themselves, as they haue in London, get you a French Bible, ... some French Dictionarie, and the hardest booke you can finde, then translate it."[27] Such advice invites the study of continental literature.[28]

What sort of continental literature might have been available in England at the time? Inventories of some 16,000 volumes in sixteenth-century Cambridge libraries allow a glimpse of the canon in modern vernaculars. The vast majority of books are written in Latin on topics concerning grammar, rhetoric, history, philosophy, medicine, law, theology, and the ancient classics, but De la Mothe would have been pleased to find eleven French Bibles, along with a dozen other translations into German, Italian, Dutch, and Spanish.[29] Petrarch is represented by four volumes of his *opera* (chiefly the Basel editions of 1554 and 1581, and likely the 1501 Aldine edition of *Le cose volgari*, inventoried between 1550 and 1593),

---

[26] A good example of such coterie literature is the unpublished poetry of Spenser's friend, Arthur Gorges, replete with dozens of translations from Italian and French, no doubt meant to be pointed out and discussed within his circle of readers; see *The Poems*, ed. Helen Estabrook Sandeson (Oxford, 1953). Of the 111 poems in Gorges's MSS, 11 draw palpably upon Du Bellay's *Olive*, six upon *Les Regrets*, 14 upon Desportes's *Amours de Diane*, and eight upon *Amours de Hippolyte*; 22 of these poems are in sonnet form; poems 46 and 75 draw upon Ronsard's *Amours* 20 and 106; other borrowings are from Marot (three elegies), Tessier (three chansons), and Peletier du Mans. See Sandeson (ed.), pp. 183–222; and Anne Lake Prescott, *French Poets and the English Renaissance* (New Haven, 1978), pp. 52–6, 108–9, 138–42. Among translations published in the sixteenth century, see John Soowthern, *Pandora*, facsimile of the 1584 edition, with notes by George B. Parks (New York, 1938). Soowthern's twenty-eight-line elegies are actually expanded translations of sonnets whose lines have been doubled, as elegies 1, 2, and 3 adapt Du Bellay's *Olive* 24, 27, and 50; the prefatory ode echoes Ronsard's "A Caliope" and several sonnets and odelettes follow Ronsardian models; sonnets 3, 9, and 13 draw upon Desportes's *Hippolyte* 29 and *Diane* 1.61 and 1.34. See Prescott, *French Poets and the English Renaissance*, pp. 105–14, 137–51 on Soowthern and other translators of Ronsard and Desportes.

[27] *The French Alphabeth* (1592); see Lambley, pp. 161–8.

[28] In a supplement to *The Annales, or a generall chronicle of England, begun first by Iohn Stow* (1615), pp. 961–3, George Buc argues that London's cultural and linguistic diversity allows opportunities for continental learning in the city as "a *Third Universitie of England*" on a par with the intellectual diversity of Oxford and Cambridge; see also "Of Languages," chapter xxxvii.

[29] See E.S. Leedham-Greene, *Books in Cambridge Inventories: Book Lists from the Vice-Chancellor's Court Probate Inventories in the Tudor and Stuart Periods* (2 vols, Cambridge, 1986), vol. 1, pp. 100, 120, with detailed index in vol. 2.

three editions of *De Remediis* (inventoried between 1579 and 1596), and three unidentified editions of the *Rime sparse* (inventoried between 1589 and 1593). Other authors include Boccaccio, one *Decameron* (1578) and nine Latin texts (1540–93); Sannazaro, one *opera* (1588); Castiglione, two *Cortegiano* (1588–90); Bembo, two *opera* (1565–89) and one *Gli Asolani* (1592); Ariosto, one *Orlando furioso* (1592) and one translation of the latter by Harington (1593). There is no edition of Dante. French authors are represented by Marot, one *oeuvres* (1546); Rabelais, one *Gargantua* (1546); and Du Bartas, two *Semaines* (1589–1601). There are no editions of any Pléiade poets. Spanish texts are represented by two copies of *Amadis de Gaula* (1578, 1593) and three copies of Montemayor's *Diana* (1592–1611). English authors are represented by Chaucer, eight volumes of *Works* (1542–91); Lydgate, one *Works* (1559); Gower, four *Confessio amantis* (1542–89); Skelton, three *Poetry* (1556–91); More, fourteen *Utopia* (1542–91); Tottel, three *Songs and Sonets* (1566–88); and Painter, one *Palace of Pleasure* (1589).

Private book collectors had different aims. Tudor and Stuart inventories of over 11,000 volumes distributed among 137 estates list several Vulgate Bibles and polyglot editions but no vernacular translations other than English.[30] Petrarch fares poorly with only one copy of *De Remediis*, one of the *Epistole familiares*, and no *Rime sparse*.[31] Comparing the other vernacular authors listed above, we find two copies of *Decameron*, eight *Cortegiano*, one *Orlando furioso*, one *Amadis de Gaula*, one Chaucer, and one Tottel. Among English texts, we find Marlowe's *Hero and Leander* and, in the Stuart period, Shakespeare's Folio *Works*, neither of which appear in the Cambridge inventories.[32] By the 1590s, Gabriel Harvey had assembled an (admittedly exceptional) personal library. A catalogue of 192 volumes in it includes copies (most of them with extensive annotations) of Aretino's comedies, Castiglione's *Cortegiano* and Guazzo's *La civile conversatione* (both in Italian and in English translations), Dolce's *Medea*, Domenichi's *Facitie*, Guarini's *Il Pastor fido*, Porcacchi's *Motti diversi*, Rabelais's *Oeuvres*, Straparola da Caravaggio's *Le notti*, Tasso's *Aminta*, and translations of *Lazarilo de Tormes*, Machiavelli's *Art of War*, and Du Bartas's *Canticle of Victorie* and *Triumph of Faith*.[33]

---

[30] See R.J. Fehrenback and E.S. Leedham-Green (eds), *Private Libraries in Renaissance England: A Collection and Catalogue of Tudor and Early Stuart Book Lists* (5 vols, Tempe, 1992–98).

[31] The *Familiares* is listed in the estate of the scholar Robert Bryan, 1508; *De Remediis* is listed in the estate of Robert Dering, Baronet of Kent, 1613 (Fehrenback and Leedham-Green [eds], vol. 2, p. 21; vol. 1, p. 235).

[32] See Fehrenback and Leedham-Green (eds), vol. 1, p. 87 for Marlowe; vol. 1, pp. 256–7 for Shakespeare.

[33] See Virginia Stern, *Gabriel Harvey: A Study of His Life, Marginalia, and Library* (Oxford, 1979), pp. 193–255. The catalogue also includes the Spanish grammar of Antonio de Corro, the Italian grammars of Claudius Holyband and Scipio Lentulo, Florio's *First Fruites*, and Eliot's *Ortho-epia Gallica*. Surprisingly, there are no French poets, nor any

We know that several major poets owned copies of Petrarch's *Rime Sparse*. Both George Gascoigne (though without evidence that he used it much) and Ben Jonson (despite Drummond's earlier claim) possessed Giovanni Andrea Gesualdo's edition of *Il Petrarca*, first published in 1533, which offers the most extensive rhetorical commentary on the poetry published in the sixteenth century.[34] Internal evidence in *Astrophil and Stella* suggests that Philip Sidney used the same edition.[35] In *Hekatompathia* (1582), Thomas Watson appears to have used Alessandro Vellutello's edition of *Il Petrarcha*, first published in 1525 and subsequently the most widely reprinted edition in the sixteenth century, notable for rearranging Petrarch's original sequence in order to narrate a story that parallels the poet's biography.[36] Fractional evidence in the *Amoretti* (1595) suggests that Edmund Spenser consulted a 1532 edition of *Il Petrarcha* with commentary by Fausto da Longiano, a Modenese humanist accused of Lutheran heresy, who represents the poet as an honest lover, a beleaguered courtier, and a proto-Protestant critic of the Avignon papacy.[37]

Other examples of foreign-language competence and the Elizabethan reception of continental literature can both astonish and disappoint us. In his *Arcadian Rhetorike* (1588), Abraham Fraunce illustrates rhetorical ornaments of style with examples drawn from the Greek and Latin classics, but more remarkably from the lyric poetry of Boscán and Garcilaso; from Marot, Belleau, Du Bellay (erroneously attributed to Belleau), Jodelle, and some minor French poets; from Du Bartas's *La*

Petrarch, Ariosto, or other Italian poets. English literature is represented by the *Mirror for Magistrates*, Chaucer's *Works* (Speght's 1598 edition), Gascoigne's *Posies*, Barnes's *Parthenope and Parthenophil*, Philip Sidney's *Countess of Pembroke's Arcadia*, and Jonson's 1616 *Works*.

[34] *Il Petrarcha, colla spositione di Misser Giovanni Andrea Gesualdo* (Venice, 1533). Gascoigne's autographed title page of a 1553 reprint appears as the frontispiece of Charles Prouty, *George Gascoigne: Elizabethan Courtier, Soldier, and Poet* (New York, 1942). George W. Pigman III (ed.), *A Hundreth Sundrie Flowres* (Oxford, 2000), reports that the volume, now in the Cudahy Library of Loyola University, Chicago, shows no signs of active use (p. 465n). For Jonson's ownership of the 1581 Basel *Opera* with Gesualdo's commentary, now in the Folger Library, see Christopher Martin, "Retrieving Jonson's Petrarch," *Shakespeare Quarterly* 45 (1994): 89–92.

[35] Sonnet 71 echoes Petrarch's sonnet 248, except for its figuration of the nightbird, which appears as an illustrative example in Gesualdo's commentary; see William J. Kennedy, *The Site of Petrarchism: Early Modern National Sentiment in Italy, France, and England* (Baltimore, 2003), pp. 174–6, 339n63.

[36] Watson translates four of Petrarch's sonnets, referring to the Italian originals with numbers that correspond to their placement in Vellutello's reordered edition, *Le volgare opere del Petrarcha con la espositione di Alessandro Vellutello da Lucca* (Venice, 1525).

[37] "Most goodly temperature" in sonnet 13 echoes "si mirabil tempre" from Fausto's commentary on the poem's Petrarchan analogue, sonnet 215, in *Il Petrarcha col commento di M. Sebastiano Fausto da Longiano* (Venice, 1532); see William J. Kennedy, *Authorizing Petrarch* (Ithaca, 1994), pp. 210–14.

semaine, La Judit, and "Le trionfe de la foi"; and from Tasso's *Aminta, Gerusalemme liberata,* and *Il re Torrismondo.*[38] Fraunce's knowledge of the Spanish poets is broad (registered in 59 quotations); his citation of Du Bartas is precocious (both James VI of Scotland and Philip Sidney had translated parts of his work earlier, but no references appeared in print until 1589); and his familiarity with *Gerusalemme liberata* is exceptional (its definitive Italian edition was published only seven years before). But his quotations from French lyric poetry derive from a popular and not very distinguished miscellany: "Who so desireth to see more of that kinde, let him reade *Accords Bigarrures.*"[39] The advice points to an anthology of fragments, *Les Bigarrures* (1582), compiled by Etienne Tabourot, Seigneur des Accords. Except for one quotation from Belleau, all of Fraunce's Gallic examples come from this mediocre volume. The sources remind us that an Elizabethan's access to continental publication remained inconsistent at best.

How might a contemporary Englishman hone foreign-literacy skills? By the mid-sixteenth century a broadly popular interest in such skills had emerged for businessmen, lawyers, and other professionals, whether through manuals designed for school use or through printed books intended for self-instruction. Some had a distinctly literary emphasis. William Thomas's *Principal Rules of the Italian Grammar, with a Dictionarie for the better understanding of Boccace, Petrarke, and Dante* appeared in 1550 as the first of eventually twelve Italian grammars and four Italian dictionaries published in England during the Tudor–Stuart period.[40] The anonymous *A plaine pathway to the French tongue, Very profitable for Marchants and also all other, which desire the same* (1571) aims at a commercial readership by inscribing conversational repartee among tailors, shoemakers, linen drapers, and booksellers along with sample letters of purchase and exchange.[41] Peter Erondelle's *French Garden For English Ladyes and gentlewomen to walke in* (1605) summons a female readership with its 13 facing-text dialogues on menu-planning, child-rearing, and shopping excursions ("Quelle boutique est cecy!"), including a visit to a jeweler and goldsmith where a Jacobean Lorelei Lee would have learned that "un beau diamant" could be thought of as "le meilleur ami d'une jeune fille qu'on peut avoir."[42]

---

[38] See Abraham Fraunce, *The Arcadian Rhetorike,* facsimile of the 1588 edn, intro. and notes by Ethel Seaton (Oxford, 1950), with analytic introduction (pp. xxiv–li) and index of quotations (pp. 131–6).

[39] Fraunce, p. 63.

[40] See the facsimile reprint, intro. R.C. Alston (Menston, 1968); the grammar is based on Alberto Accarigi's *Grammatica de la lingua volgare* (1543) and the dictionary is derived from Francesco Alunno's glossary for the Tuscan literary classics, *La Richezze della lingua volgare* (1543).

[41] See the facsimile reprint, intro. R.C. Alston (Menston, 1968).

[42] See the facsimile reprint, intro. R.C. Alston (Menston, 1969), with quotations drawn from sig. K6ʳ.

For Italian language instruction, *The Second Fruites ... of diuers but delightsome tastes to the tongues of Italiens and Englishmen* (1591) by John Florio, later the translator of Montaigne, projects serious literary intentions upon the author's earlier pedagogical effort, *First Fruites* (1578).[43] The latter offers bilingual dialogues on such topics as playgoing ("Vi piacciono le Comedie à voi?" sig. A1ʳ), tennis, hunting, and civilized chit-chat as well as a manual of "Necessarie Rules for Englishmen to learne to reade, speake, and write true Italian."[44] *Second Fruites* offers bilingual dialogues on courtiers and court-life along with discourses on the *pronostici* or "studenti delle matte lettere" (translated as "foolosophers," pp. 140–41) and beautiful or ugly women associated with them, and on love, both *celeste* and *volgare* (p. 166). Here Florio quotes proverbs (the title page advertises "six-thousand Italian Prouerbs," one of which on page 106 is recited by Holofernes in *Love's Labor's Lost*, IV, ii, 97–8), misogynist doggerel (p. 174), verse in praise of women (p. 176), a poem about vanity (p. 196), and five tercets from Petrarch's *Trionfo della castità* (pp. 196–9). Florio paraphrases bits of "il buon Tasso" (p. 166, called "il piu diuino moderno Poeta" on p. 186), "il diuino Ariosto" (p. 182), Boccaccio (p. 182), and Aretino ("il flagello de' prencipi," p. 188). Finally, the author's English and Italian dictionary, *Queen Anna's New World of Words* (1611), provides a list of books from which the entries are derived. They include editions of Dante with commentaries by both Landino (1481) and Daniello (1568) and of Petrarch with Gesualdo's *Vita del Petrarca* and his commentary *sopra il Petrarcha*.[45]

Shortly after *First Fruites* appeared, Claudius Holybande, a Huguenot refugé from Moulins who had anglicized his name from Claude Desainliens, issued his *Campo di Fior, or flowery field of four languages* (1583), a set of dialogues in Latin, Italian, French, and English based on Vives's *Linguae Latinae*

---

[43] See the facsimile reprints: *His First Fruites (1578)* (New York, 1969) and *Second Fruites (1591)*, intro. R.C. Simonini, Jr. (Gainesville, 1953). All further references are to these editions. For Shakespeare's complicated relationship with Florio based on their associations with the earl of Southampton see Frances A. Yates, *John Florio: The Life of an Italian in Shakespeare's England* (Cambridge, 1934), esp. pp. 334–6.

[44] Florio's subsequent praise of Lombardy, "Lombardia è il giardino del mondo" (*First Fruites*, sig. H3ᵛ) finds an echo in Shakespeare's "Lombardy, / The pleasant garden of great Italy" (*Taming of the Shrew*, I, i, 3–4). For Shakespeare's use of *First Fruites* and *Second Fruites*, see Naseeb Shaheen, "Shakespeare's Knowledge of Italian," *Shakespeare Survey* 47 (1994): 161–70.

[45] The latter both refer to Gesualdo's 1533 edition of Petrarch. See the facsimile reprint, *Queen Anne's New World of Words (1611)*, intro. R.C. Alston (Menston, 1968), sig. ¶5ᵛ-¶6ᵛ; and David O. Frantz, "Florio's Use of Contemporary Italian Literature in *A Worlde of Wordes*," *Dictionaries* 1 (1979): 47–56.

Exercitatio (1539).[46] His earlier *French Littleton* (1576), a textbook widely used in the grammar schools, provides a brief sampler of contemporary Gallic culture, though less sophisticated than Florio's guide to Italian culture.[47] It includes a short *Traicte de danses* (expressing sober disapproval of lewd gestures while dancing) and a handful of Christian prayers (sigs. H2ʳ–G4ᵛ). Four years later, *Le Maistre d'Ecole Anglois* (1580) of Jacques Bellot, an émigré from Caen who tried to capitalize upon an interest in French affairs during Elizabeth's marriage negotiations with the duc d'Alençon, includes an inert *Ballade sur la devise des couleurs* (sig. H1ʳ⁻ᵛ) and six bland sonnets on such moral themes as "De la verité" and "De la justice" (sigs. H2ʳ–H3ᵛ).[48] Bellot's subsequent *French Methode* (1588) offers commendatory French sonnets by William, John, and Richard Wroth, demonstrating how well they learned the target language and assuring students of the delights that await them in reading Marot, Beze, Du Bellay, Froissard, Ronsard, Colletet, Jodelle, and Herberay des Essarts, the French translator of *Amadis of Gaul*.[49] A thirty-page anthology of such outdated Marotic forms as chant royal, ballade, rondeau, dizain, huitain, and chanson (sigs. 2a1ʳ–2d3ʳ) concludes the volume.

The most ambitious French grammar came from John Eliot, an Englishman who had studied on the continent for five years. His *Ortho-epia Gallica* (1593) presents an extensive discourse on the excellence of various ancient and modern writers, awarding first place in French poetry to Clément Marot, "vn Poëte naturel" who "fit passer les monts aux Muses, & les a habillés à la Françoise."[50] Second is Ronsard, maker of "toutes sortes de vers, & d'arguments tantost en style bas, ores en moyen & sublime" (sig. e1ʳ). Third is Du Bartas, "homme d'autant grand esprit qui onques en nasquist en France" (sig. e1ʳ). Eliot also admires Rabelais, "that merrie grig" (sig. B3ʳ), whom he takes as a model for his own prose style "in a merrie and phantastical vaine" (sig. B1ᵛ).[51] Among Italian poets who inspired his French authors, Eliot features Petrarch, who "a inventé de tres-beaux mots" (sig. d3ʳ); Ariosto, "plaisant au possible à cause de la diuersité des choses qu'il

---

[46] The book was published by the Huguenot refugee Thomas Vautrollier, whose apprentice was Richard Field, a native of Stratford who might have befriended Shakespeare during his early days in London. See Lambley, pp. 134–45.

[47] See the facsimile reprint, intro. R.C. Alston (Menston, 1970). The title refers to a major textbook on law by Sir Thomas Littleton upon which Desainliens models his approach to the laws of French language; the volume begins with a commendatory sonnet by George Gascoigne (sig. *4ʳ).

[48] The authorship of these poems is anonymous, and their lack of poetic distinction betrays pedestrian origins. See the facsimile reprint, intro. R.C. Alston (Menston, 1967).

[49] See the facsimile reprint, intro. R.C. Alston (Menston, 1970), sigs. ¶¶2ᵛ–¶¶4ʳ.

[50] See the facsimile reprint, intro. R.C. Alston (Menston, 1968), sigs. d4ᵛ-e1ʳ.

[51] One of Eliot's dialogues is titled "Le Banquet des Yvrongnes" (pp. 35–54), with a lusty exhortation: "chantons, beuuons, entonnons" ["Let's sing, lets drinke, lets poure it in"] (p. 46).

recite" (sig. d3^v); and Tasso, "où toutes les richesses des grecs & latins sont recueillies" (sig. d4^r). Eliot offers only a few snatches of verse to support his claims, but his convictions about the literary canon of France and Italy convey a sense of order and coherence based on wide reading and broad appreciation. Such convictions stand out.

The "energy field" opened by these texts suggests an Elizabethan view of European literature at a time when Spenser and the University Wits were brandishing their continental sophistication, when poets such as Daniel, Drayton, Constable, and Giles Fletcher the elder (under the spell of the posthumous publication of Sidney's *Astrophil and Stella* in 1591) were adapting French and Italian models of sonnet writing, and when Shakespeare in his late twenties was publishing his narrative verse, *Venus and Adonis* and *Rape of Lucrece*. Shakespeare had compelling motivation to enhance his reputation as a serious author familiar with French, Italian, and other continental texts and forms. In 1592 Robert Greene had smeared his public image by alluding to him as an "vpstart Crow."[52] To counter the insult and regain some credit, the poet-playwright would have wanted to display his linguistic competence, literary refinement, and cultural awareness of writerly achievements beyond provincial England. And again at the turn of the century, after Spenser's demise and the decline of the University Wits, he would find it opportune to display such talents when Ben Jonson set a new standard for combining the discursive crosscurrents of classical satire, humanist form, and moral understanding.

How might French, Italian, and other continental models illuminate Shakespeare's development? If we grant that foreign-speaking acquaintances might have coached Shakespeare through readings of *novelle* and poems unavailable in published translations, then we can grant that they might have imparted to him at least some of their literary preferences and critical attitudes toward texts in their native languages. This scenario would explain the tenuous relationship of such plays as *Merchant of Venice, Measure for Measure*, and *Othello* to untranslated sources by Fiorentino and Giraldi Cinthio. It would be nice to know what Italian-speaking friend might have guided Mercutio's taunt about "the numbers that Petrarch flow'd in" (*Romeo and Juliet*, II, iv, 39), and nicer still to know the continental models, if any, for the "palmers' kiss" sonnet that introduces the lovers to each other (I, v, 93–106), or for such lyrical passages as "But soft, what light" (II, ii, 1–32), "Gallop apace" (III, ii, 1–31), and "Wilt thou be gone" (III, v, 1–36). Equally teasing are the possible French or Italian models for Berowne and his company's sonnets and songs in *Love's Labor's Lost* (IV, ii, 105–18; and IV, iii, 25–40, 58–71, 99–118); or, more speculatively, for such lyric set-pieces as Adriana's complaints in *Comedy of Errors* (II, i, 87–115; and II, ii, 110–46), Julia's anacreontic and Valentine's soliloquy in *Two Gentlemen of Verona* (I, ii, 102–26; and V, iv, 1–12), the parodies read by Rosalind and Celia in

---

[52] *Greenes Groatsworth of Witte* (1592), sig. F1^r.

As You Like It (III, ii, 88–154), and the exchange of vows between the principals in *Troilus and Cressida* (III, ii, 158–96).

These plays sketch a trajectory from early ones (*Two Gentlemen of Verona, Comedy of Errors*) through those cementing Shakespeare's dramatic reputation in 1594–95 (*Love's Labor's Lost* and *Romeo and Juliet*) to those reflecting his dramaturgical struggle with Ben Jonson in 1599–1601 (*As You Like It, Troilus and Cressida*). What about traces of his engagement with models of French poetry in sonnets composed during this period? Among such models for late Elizabethans, the frequently adapted yet rarely mentioned Philippe Desportes appears a prominent candidate, and Shakespeare offers some analogies with him.[53] In sonnet 88, the Young Man drives the speaker to self-disparagement ("When thou shalt be disposed to set me light, ... / Upon thy side against myself I'll fight"), just as Desportes's beloved does in *Les Amours de Hippolyte* 20: "Bref, je vous aime tant que je ne m'aime pas, / De moi-même adversaire, ou si je m'aime, hélas! / Je m'aime seulement pour ce que je vous aime."[54] Stronger analogies evoke a dark-complexioned lady. In *Love's Labor's Lost*, Rosaline is "black as ebony" (IV, iii, 243), prompting Berowne to declaim that she was "born to make black fair" (IV, iii, 257, *passim* in lines 244–67), while in sonnet 127, "my mistress' brows are raven black ... / Sland'ring creation with a false esteem." Both passages recall Desportes's beloved in *Hippolyte* 19: "L'arc de vos bruns sourcils mon coeur tyrannisant, / C'est l'arc même d'Amour, dont traître il nous martyre."

Desportes's moral situations offer some parallels as well. The lover of *Hippolyte* 5 assents to self-deception, and he even exhorts his beloved to deceive him: "Puisque vous le voulez, demeurez inhumaine, / Et, me faisant mourir, feignez de n'en rien voir." So does the lover of Shakespeare's sonnet 140: "If I might teach thee wit, better it were, / Though not to love, yet, love, to tell me so." The lover of *Hippolyte* 55 responds by berating his own eyes for allowing such deception to occur: "Vous n'êtes point mes yeux, ô trompeuse lumière / Par qui le trait d'Amour dans le coeur m'est venu." The speaker of Shakespeare's sonnet 148 attributes similar deceit to his eyes for drawing him to the Dark Lady: "O me, what eyes hath Love put in my head, / Which have no correspondence with true sight!" Shakespeare's sonnet 149 registers a further complaint, "Canst thou, O cruel! say I love thee not, / When I against myself with thee partake?" Both poems recall worldly-wise protestations of Desportes's lover, cognizant of his beloved's propensity to feign self-serving motivations: "Je me plains seulement de voir que

---

[53] For Desportes's paradoxical reception in England based on frequent imitation yet scarce mention, see Prescott, *French Poets and the English Renaissance*, pp. 132–66.

[54] References to Desportes are to *Les Amours d'Hippolyte*, ed. Victor E. Graham (Geneva, 1960); for traces of Desportes in *Sonnets*, see Fernand Baldensperger, *Les Sonnets de Shakespeare traduits en vers français et accompagnés d'un commentaire continu* (Berkeley, 1943), pp. 255–7, 271, 297, 341.

la cruelle / Ne croit pas que je l'aime, et m'appelle inconstant, / Ou dit que mes ennuis viennent d'autres que d'elle" (*Hippolyte* 74).

In a different vein, lesser counterparts of Desportes in France took special delight in issuing backhanded compliments. The aptly titled sonnets *Contr'amours* by the Pléiade's youngest member, Etienne Jodelle, offer taunting prototypes for Shakespeare's "Black is the badge of hell" (*Love's Labor's Lost*, IV, iii, 254) and "In the old age black was not counted fair" (sonnet 127): "Combien de fois mes vers ont-ils doré / Ces cheveux noirs dignes d'une Méduse?" (*Contr'amours* 7).[55] The last poem, a palinode in the manner of Shakespeare's "My mistress's eyes are nothing like the sun" (sonnet 130), inverts the idealized figuration of standard Petrarchism with a breezy indifference to convention: "Combien de fois ce teint noir que m'amuse, / Ai-je de lis et roses coloré? / Combien ce front de rides labouré / Ai-je aplani?" *Contr'amours* 6 presents the beloved as a striking conjunction of both "the better angel" and "the worser spirit" that Shakespeare would parcel out in sonnet 144: "Jà si longtemps faisant d'un Diable un Ange, / Vour m'ouvrez l'oeil en l'injuste louange, / Et m'aveuglez en l'injuste tourment." The banal Petrarchism regnant among Elizabethan sonneteers cried out for a challenge such as Shakespeare's. Jodelle is of course intensifying tropes that his Pléiade elders had supplied, correcting through spoof the hyperbolic tendencies of their outmoded forms.

According to Hieat, Hieat, and Prescott's chronological analysis, the poems that I have just cited date from 1592–95, a period ending with the composition of *Love's Labor's Lost* and *Romeo and Juliet*. The following scenario emerges: Shakespeare, like the University Wits a young careerist eager to maximize his fortunes in London in the early 1590s, but (unlike them) without the benefit of a formal undergraduate education, sought to attract attention and make a living with his writing. Just as they had capitalized upon their linguistic skills and cosmopolitan temper by spicing their plays with foreign languages and by basing their poetry upon continental models, so would he. Shakespeare turned to a widely imitated, yet rarely acknowledged French poet, Desportes, and to a lesser, largely ignored Pléiade poet, Jodelle, each reasonably current yet sufficiently *recherché* for the rising poet to display his own smart refinement. His allusions to these poets are gossamer at best, and nowhere direct, but they affirm his dialogue with sophisticated forms and his aim to reprove Greene's slur in 1592. We might wonder whether Greene's friend, Thomas Lodge, had this "vpstart Crow" in mind when in *A Margarite of America* (1596) he dismissed Desportes (and those

---

[55] References to Etienne Jodelle are to *Poètes du seizième siècle*, ed. Albert-Marie Schmidt (Paris, 1969) pp. 707–36. For possible echoes in Shakespeare, see Baldensperger, pp. 263, 291, 297; and Lee, pp. 270–75.

contemporaries who echoed him) as "alreadie for the most part englished, and ordinarilie in everie mans hands."[56]

What about the major Pléaide poets, especially Du Bellay and Ronsard? Du Bellay looms as a possible model for Shakespeare's early figurations of the beloved as a rising sun.[57] Sonnet 10 of *Olive* represents her as a rival of that orb in its journey from east to west: "Quand le Soleil lave sa tête blonde / En l'océan" (which Ronsard rivaled with his own version in "De ses cheveulx la rousoyant Aurore / Eparsement les Indes remplissoyt" in sonnet 95 of *Les Amours*).[58] Using this trope, Berowne extols Rosaline "like a rude and savage man of Inde / At the first op'ning of the gorgeous East" in *Love's Labor's Lost* (IV, iii, 220). In the same play the Princess of France mocks Boyet's pretensions in honoring her with such invention: "My beauty, though but mean, / Needs not the painted flourish of your praise" (II, i, 13). It is as though she had taken a retrospective leaf from Du Bellay's mock-earnest disavowal of this style in *Contre les Pétrarchistes*: "Je veux d'amour franchement deviser / Sans vous flatter et sans me déguiser." But the latter's promotion of this style tells a more appealing story in *Olive*, just as it does with respect to the Young Man in Shakespeare's sonnet 7, "Lo, in the Orient when the gracious light / Lifts up his burning head," and sonnet 21, "Making a couplement of proud compare / With sun and moon."

Du Bellay's discrepant attitudes toward the excesses of Petrarchism would be replicated by his Huguenot readers (if any) at home and abroad. Those in England might decry Du Bellay and his anti-Calvinist satire in *Les Regrets* (especially in sonnet 136, "J'ai vu dessus leur front la repentance peinte"), but they could share his sense of exile registered in that sequence. The figure of wandering Ulysses in sonnet 31, "Hereux qui, comme Ulysse, a fait un beau voyage," captures a sense of longing echoed distantly in Shakespeare's later sonnet 56, "Let this sad int'rim like the ocean be / Which parts the shore." Such readers could also share Du Bellay's critique of a depraved Rome in sonnet 82: "Rome est de tout le monde un public échafaud, / Une scène, un théâtre." Jaques is no Huguenot, but he too views the world as a Du Bellayan theater of folly (*As You Like It*, II, vii, 139 and *passim*), as does the speaker of Shakespeare's sonnet 15 ("When I consider ... / That this huge stage presenteth nought but shows").

---

[56] *The Complete Works of Thomas Lodge*, ed. Edmund Gosse (4 vols, Glasgow, 1883), vol. 3, p. 79.

[57] References to Joachim Du Bellay are to *Oeuvres poétiques*, eds Daniel Aris and Françoise Joukovsky (2 vols, Paris, 1993–1996). For critical study see Prescott, *French Poets and the English Renaissance*, pp. 44–52; Kennedy, *Site of Petrarchism*, pp. 77–159. For traces of Du Bellay in *Sonnets*, see Balsensperger, pp. 109, 125, 229, 335.

[58] References to Pierre de Ronsard are notoriously difficult to coordinate because of his revisions and additions in successive editions. I have used the superb new Pléiade edition, *Oeuvres complètes*, eds Jean Céard, Daniel Ménager, and Michel Simonin (2 vols, Paris, 1993–94), with cross-references to the definitive *Oeuvres complètes*, eds Paul Laumonier, Raymond Lebègue, and Isidore Silver (20 vols, Geneva, 1914–1974).

English as well as Huguenot attitudes toward Ronsard were even more conflicted, partly because of the poet's patronage ties to the Catholic Guise faction and his sentimental devotion to Mary Stuart, the young widow of François II.[59] Still, Ronsard was the most highly praised French poet of earlier decades, celebrated by his compatriots as both "prince des poètes" and "poète des princes."[60] Some readers have heard reverberations of his *Hynne de la mort* ("Recevans sans repos maux sur maux, à milliers ... / Lors la mer des ennuis se desborde sur nous," lines 150, 225) in the "thousand natural shocks" and "sea of troubles" of Hamlet's fourth soliloquy (III, i, 58–61).[61] These are distant echoes, but distinctively Ronsardian turns of phrase do recur in Shakespeare's poetry. Not the least of them build upon Ronsard's exuberant neologisms ("crevasser" *Les Amours* 127, and "enmannée," *Les Amours* 140), coinages from Greek ("parangonne," *Les Amours* 5), and such compound word-formations as "chasse-nue," "esbranle-rocher," and "irrite-mer," all from *Les Amours* 206. Shakespearean analogues include "world-without-end hour" (sonnet 57), "my all-the-world" (sonnet 112), "dear-purchased right" (sonnet 117), and "short-numb'red hours" (sonnet 124). In depicting the mock-comic consequences of enslavement to the beloved, as in sonnet 1.7 of *Les Amours*, Ronsard has much to offer Shakespeare: "Mais si le Ciel m'a fait naître, Madame, / Pour ta victime, en lieu de ma pauvre ame, / Sur ton autel j'offre ma loyauté." Shakespeare's mordantly ironic sonnet 57 projects a similar abjection: "Being your slave, what should I do but tend /Upon the hours and times of your desire?" Ronsard's play on the noun *oeil* and verb *oeillader* from sonnet 1.8 of *Les Amours*, "Lors que mon oeil pour t'oeillader s'amuse," echoes in the second line of Shakespeare's sonnet 104, "For as you were when first your eye I eyed," suggesting that the English poet's eye eyed the French poet's text with tantalizing care.

Ronsard's *Sonnets pour Hélène* carry the motif of abjection further in presenting a witty skirmish between a woman of talent and intelligence and a poet who has already played every trick in the book of seduction. The latter's ironic riposte ("Vous aurez en mes vers un immortel renom: / Pour n'avoir rien de vous, la recompense est grande," *Hélène* 1.55) resonates with Shakespeare's sonnet 57, "I have no precious time at all to spend, / Nor services to do till you require." The beloved's reaction ("Mais vostre oeil cauteleux, trop finement subtil, / Pleure en chantant mes vers," 1.33) forecasts the heroine's self-defense in *Troilus and Cresside*: "The error of our eye directs our mind" (*Troilus and Cressida*, V, ii, 110). Arming himself with caution, Ronsard calculates the mismatch between the

---

[59] See Prescott, *French Poets and the English Renaissance*, pp. 76–131.

[60] He was proclaimed as such by Maclou de la Haye in 1553 upon the publication of the second edition of *Les Amours*; see Fernand Desonay, *Ronsard, pote de l'amour* (3 vols, Brussels, 1952), vol. 1, p. 73.

[61] See Hugh M. Richmond, "Ronsard and the English Renaissance," *Comparative Literature Studies* 7 (1970): 141–60.

beloved's youth and his own weather-beaten years ("Comme un viel combatant, qui ne veut plus s'armer," *Hélène* 2.40), and he fantasizes a time, "Quand vous serez bien vielle," when Hélène will say with regret, "Ronsard me celebroit du temps que j'estois belle" (*Hélène* 2.43). So, too, Shakespeare's speaker acknowledges the mismatch ("My glass shall not persuade me I am old," sonnet 22) and he fantasizes a time, "If thou survive my well-contented day," when the Young Man will wish with regret, "Had my friend's Muse grown with this growing age" (sonnet 32). Hélène's stubborn virtue prompts the speaker's retreat, "Adieu, cruelle, adieu, je te suis ennuyeux: / C'est trop chanté d'Amour sans nulle recompense" (2.74), in a gesture that anticipates Shakespeare's sonnet 87, "Farewell, thou art too dear for my possessing." Finally, Ronsard's willingness to compromise ("Aimez moy, s'il vous plaist, grison comme je suis, / Et je vous aimeray quand vous serez de mesme," 1.22) forecasts Shakespeare's "On both sides thus is simple truth suppressed" (sonnet 138).

The plays that I have just cited—*As You Like It, Hamlet, and Troilus and Cressida*—date from 1599–1601, and the poems (except for sonnets 86, 87, and 138) qualify as revisions or compositions around 1600 according to Hieatt, Hieatt, and Prescott. In these last years of Elizabeth's reign, Shakespeare faced the challenge of a new generation of dramatists led by Jonson, Marston, and Dekker. In response, he tried his hand at mordant satire associated with the new playwrights, but he also reverted to older, popular forms of festive comedy and revenge tragedy associated with the University Wits and Thomas Kyd. In poetry, he revised his work in the now out-of-favor sonnet form, latterly distinguished by Spenser in *Amoretti* (1595). In the context of Spenser's death in January 1599, Shakespeare might plausibly review the work of canonical Pléiade poets who had attracted his predecessor's attention, chiefly Du Bellay and Ronsard. At the very end of the sixteenth century, as Jonson labored to shift the imitative standard from French and Italian models to Latinate classicism via Horatian theory, Shakespeare returned to the register of an older generation. When finally, in 1609, he acquiesced to the publication of his *Sonnets*, he did so with the confidence of a body of work composed over a long period and brought to a finish in an era of divergent literary tastes. Its deliberate echoes of Elizabethan forerunners, and possibly of some continental poets, proclaim the poet's deepest literary values and his recurrent aesthetic convictions.

Shakespeare's curiosity about European languages and literary forms imbues his poetry and drama with a reaction to the provocation set by his contemporaries. Upon his arrival in London, the celebrity of Marlowe, Greene, Lodge, Nashe, and above all, Spenser, had prompted his inquiry into continental models. At the very end of Elizabeth's reign, Jonson's turn to classicism prompted Shakespeare to think harder about modern vernacular influences in an earlier era. Aids to understanding the European canon in the foreign-language textbooks of Florio, Bellot, and Eliot; in the rhetorical handbooks of Fraunce and Puttenham; in the translations of Watson, Gorges, Swoothern, and the young Spenser; and in the advice of G. De la Mothe about associating with resident émigrés in London all narrowed cultural gaps between England and the continent. That Shakespeare legally resided at the home of M. Christophe Montjoy in 1604 adds a lively garnish: how better to augment a tutorial in the languages of continental literature than by conversing with a native speaker who had dispatched the poet as a go-between in the marriage of his daughter and son-in-law? With his relish for shape-shifting irony and his penchant for hiding within his own inventions, Shakespeare sported a tincture of aplomb by assaying his facility with "les langues des hommes." As for his forays into French and Italian literary practices, who ever imagined that these transactions could be anything but "pleines de tromperies"?

Chapter 6

Joining the Conversation
David, Astrophil, and the Countess of Pembroke

Margaret P. Hannay

Mary Sidney Herbert, Countess of Pembroke, boldly entered into literary conversation with the two central poetic discourses of early modern Europe, the discourses that clustered around the authorizing voices of Petrarch and of David. She addresses the Psalm tradition directly, by completing the metrical *Psalmes* that her brother Philip had begun: he metaphrased Psalms 1–43; she completed the remaining 128 poems. In her metrical *Psalmes* she draws on virtually every Psalm version and commentary available to her in English, French, and Latin, but her primary sources are the French *Psaumes*, Coverdale's Psalms in the Book of Common Prayer, the Geneva Bible, and the Psalm translations and commentaries of John Calvin and Theodore Beza (in Latin and in English translation). In her *Psalmes*, she also enters into dialogue with others who composed English metrical Psalms—including Anne Lock, Sternhold and Hopkins, Matthew Parker, and of course her brother Philip. She addresses the Petrarchan sonnet tradition more obliquely, translating *The Triumph of Death*, which gives the silent Laura a voice after her death, and rendering Psalms 100 and 150 in two different sonnet forms, Sidneian and Spenserian (or Scottish). For her, as for many sixteenth-century English poets, the voice of Petrarch is largely mediated through the voice of Astrophil. She not only enters individual conversations with these voices that cluster around Astrophil and David, but also draws them into conversation with each other in her *Psalmes*.

Psalm translation and meditation were highly valued as devotional practices, and undoubtedly the Sidney *Psalmes* did fulfill a devotional function for their authors and many of their original readers. Nevertheless, Pembroke's direct allusions to English lyric poets—notably Wyatt, Spenser, and Sidney—signal that her work is also a deliberate effort to enter the lyric tradition. She alludes to Wyatt in Psalm 57, as we shall see, but her debt to Edmund Spenser is more profound. Her *Psalmes* demonstrate an extensive stylistic debt to Spenser, and she makes extended allusions to his works in Psalms 78, 104, and 107, as I have argued elsewhere. She was, in many ways, one of the first Spenserian poets.[1] And yet her most important literary conversation is with her brother Philip's works, both secular and sacred. Like her Spenserian echoes, the Countess of Pembroke's Sidneian echoes are not merely an act of homage, but a strategy to position herself in the mainstream of the English poetic tradition. The Psalms are, like Petrarch's *Rime sparse*, "a mastertext through which the writers of the age tested their capacities, in this case not only as worshippers and theologians but as poets and critics," as Roland Greene observes.[2] She thus makes a bid to enter the literary conversation by engaging the two central poetic discourses of sixteenth-century Europe—Petrarch and Psalms—particularly as both were addressed by her brother.

It has long been recognized that Pembroke "in a devotional sense, *meditated* on the text," recreating the Psalms as "Elizabethan poems," and that the Sidneys together "create a new persona for the Psalmist," that of "an Elizabethan poet, expressing a contemporary religious sensibility with rare and delicate artistry," thus contributing to the development of the seventeenth-century religious lyric "in the biblical and psalmic mode."[3] Pembroke herself, however, disclaims originality, stressing that her poems simply transmit the biblical text. In "Angel Spirit," she says that the Sidneian *Psalmes* are not "transform'd / in substance," but only in "superficiall [at]tire," thus drawing on the traditional metaphor of translation as reclothing to dispel any anxieties (including, perhaps, her own) that their splendid rhetorical dress alters their sacred content.[4] Similarly, her dedicatory poem to Queen Elizabeth declares that "the Psalmist King" would be "undispleased" by this reclothing, "Oft having worse, without repining worne."[5] Such a gesture is necessary because metrical Psalms raise in a particularly acute form the problems inherent in all scriptural translation. Because Christians normally read, recite, and sing the Psalms in Latin or in their own vernacular, there is already a gap between

---

I am grateful to Michael G. Brennan, Noel J. Kinnamon, and Debra K. Rienstra for their insightful comments on this essay.

[1] Steven May, *The Elizabethan Courtier Poets: The Poems and Their Contexts* (Asheville, 1999), pp. 208–9; Margaret Hannay, "The Countess of Pembroke as a Spenserian Poet," in Sigrid M. King (ed.), *Pilgrimage for Love: Essays in Early Modern Literature in Honor of Josephine A. Roberts* (Tempe, 1999), pp. 41–62.

[2] Roland Greene, "Sir Philip Sidney's *Psalms*, the Sixteenth-Century Psalter, and the Nature of Lyric," *Studies in English Literature* 30 (1990): 19.

[3] J.C.A. Rathmell (ed.), *The Psalms of Sir Philip Sidney and the Countess of Pembroke* (New York, 1963), p. xx; Barbara Lewalski, *Protestant Poetics and the Seventeenth-Century Religious Lyric* (Princeton, 1979), p. 241.

[4] "To the Angel Spirit," lines 8–9, in *The Collected Works of Mary Sidney Herbert, Countess of Pembroke*, eds Margaret P. Hannay, Noel J. Kinnamon and Michael G. Brennan (2 vols, Oxford, 1998), vol. 1, p. 110 (unless otherwise noted, references are to this edition); Debra K. Rienstra and Noel J. Kinnamon, "Revisioning the Sacred Text," *Sidney Journal* 17 (1999): 53–77.

[5] "Even Now that Care," lines 29–32.

the sacred original and the words they use, as there is for any biblical text. This worried the Geneva translators, who stress in their very title their translation from the original biblical languages (*The Bible and Holy Scriptures ... Translated According to the Ebrue and Greke*), and reassure their readers that "whereas the necessitie of the sentence required any thing to be added" they have put the interpolations in italic type.[6] Metrical Psalters are by definition freer translations, since a looser paraphrase (or, more technically, metaphrase) was required by rhyme and meter. Yet those composing metrical Psalters, including Pembroke's father's friend and correspondent Matthew Parker, Archbishop of Canterbury, confronted some of the same problems as any biblical translator.[7] While Parker does not use italic type, he does believe it necessary to justify his poetic expansion of the text:

> Who more will searche: how here it goes,
>   let him the Hebrew trye:
> Where wordes were skant: with texts or glose
>   that want I did supplye.[8]

The responsibility was the greater because for many readers the translator (or poet) became invisible, and they read the metrical Psalms as, quite simply, the Word of God. In England, this is perhaps most obvious in the Sternhold and Hopkins Psalter, which was sung by all social classes both in church and in the home. But even the elaborate Sidney *Psalmes* could be received as sacred text, as in the two early seventeenth-century manuscripts (MSS *I* and *K*) rubricated for Morning Prayer and Evening Prayer.[9] John Donne, writing after God had "translated those translators," says that "in formes of joy and art" the Sidneys "re-reveale" the Psalms.[10] He thereby "lends the *Psalmes* a quasi-inspired status" that might have gratified—but also worried—those "translators."[11] This would be particularly true if Pembroke, as Michael Brennan suggests, did at one time consider publishing the Sidney *Psalmes* for use in public worship.[12]

---

[6] "To Our Beloved in the Lord," *The Geneva Bible* (1560), facsimile edn, ed. Lloyd E. Berry (Madison, 1969), sig. 3*4[r]. All scriptural quotations are from this edition.

[7] Sir Henry Sidney to Archbishop Matthew Parker, 1 December 1574, De L'Isle and Dudley MS 1475 C7/15. Cited with the kind permission of the Viscount De L'Isle MBE.

[8] Matthew Parker, *The Whole Psalter Translated into English Metre* (1567), sig. B3[r].

[9] *Collected Works of Mary Sidney Herbert*, vol. 2, pp. 317–22.

[10] John Donne, "Upon the Translation of the *Psalmes* by Sir Philip Sydney, and the Countess of Pembroke His Sister," in *John Donne: The Divine Poems*, ed. Helen Gardner (1952; Oxford, 1978), pp. 34–5.

[11] Debra K. Rienstra, "Mary Sidney, Countess of Pembroke, *Psalmes*," in Anita Pacheco (ed.), *A Companion to Early Modern Women's Writing* (Oxford, 2002), p. 122.

[12] Michael G. Brennan, "The Queen's Proposed Visit to Wilton House in 1599 and the 'Sidney Psalms'," *Sidney Journal* 20 (2002): 27–54.

In their role as transmitters of sacred text, the Sidneys had to be primarily concerned with accuracy to the biblical original, but as poets they would also find metrical Psalms problematic. As Anne Prescott asks, "Whom does a translator of the psalms imitate? God? If the Lord favors such poetry, does he also lend a hand? If so, does the help travel through tradition and exegesis? Perhaps it works through the power of scripture itself, or maybe the aid comes directly from the Spirit." If the translator does well, that voice will be "intensely personal, yet he may hope (or fear?) that it also belongs to David and Christ, his cospeakers, and to God, his coauthor and patron."[13] On the one hand, to stray from the biblical text is theologically perilous. On the other hand, "except for the crucial disability of his divine inspiration and authority," David may indeed "make a very presentable right poet" in the terms used by Sidney in his *Defence of Poetry*.[14] But where does that leave Sidney himself? If David imitates the excellency of God in an original, although inspired, act of creation, how can a non-inspired poet achieve a similar result? And if this is problematic for Philip Sidney, how much more for his sister, who adds the authorizing voice of her brother to those of David and of God?

Psalms did solve one persistent problem for English women writers. By making God's praise the subject of her verse instead of some male lover, real or imagined, she could circumvent gender restrictions on women's speech while winning accolades for godly virtue. That praise for the beloved often employs the same language as religion is a commonplace. Sidney's words to Stella, "Not thou by praise, but praise in thee is raisde: / It is a praise to praise, when thou art praisde" (*Astrophil* 35.14), or "To you, to you, all song of praise is due / Only in you my song begins and endeth" (*First Song*.3–4), could as easily be applied to God, as Pembroke's words to God, "I will heape thy praise with praise" (Ps. 71.45) could as easily be applied to a human lover.[15] So closely are the two traditions intertwined that it would be difficult to say whether Pembroke follows Astrophil or David in her words of praise.

The genre of complaint is similarly entwined. When the Psalmist pours out his heart before God, Pembroke will have the speaker "plaine." In Psalm 50.36, for example, God instructs the people to bring their "praying plaints," and Psalm 88 asks, as did Astrophil, why the beloved (God, in this case), rejects those plaints. Psalm 77.35–6 introduces a formal complaint in words almost indistinguishable from those of the disappointed lover: "my silent hart / distracted thus did plaine."

And as the courtier's desire to receive "favor"—in some tangible form like a title, estate, grant, or monopoly—might be recast into the Petrarchan complaint to a

---

[13] Anne Lake Prescott, "Musical Strains: Marot's Double Role as Psalmist and Courtier," in Marie-Rose Logan and Peter Rudnytsky (eds), *Contending Kingdoms* (Detroit, 1990), p. 48.

[14] Anne Lake Prescott, "King David as a 'Right Poet': Sidney and the Psalmist," *ELR* 19 (1989): 134.

[15] *The Poems of Sir Philip Sidney*, ed. W.A. Ringler (Oxford, 1962), pp. 182, 196.

mistress, so petitions to God can be recast in the language of the courtier. Departing from the Geneva phrasing ("Heare the right, o Lord, consider my crye"), Sidney uses this technique in opening Psalm 17: "My suite is just, just lord to my suite hark" (17.1). Pembroke develops it at more length throughout Psalm 86. The speaker refers to herself as "this Client ... this servant," praises the Lord, appeals to past favors as the basis for new favor, reminds the Lord that not only has the speaker herself been at court, "who in thy service have attended," but also is the child of those who have attended in the past, "and of thy handmaid am descended."[16] She pleads for "some token of thy love ... some Cognisance" to show others "that thine I am, that by thee graced" (86.39–43).

In these three parallel modes of encomium, complaint, and petition, the poet addresses the beloved (whether God or Stella). A fourth, and perhaps most interesting parallel mode, is the poet's exploration of the divided self. Such a connection is natural, for, as Debora Shuger reminds us, in this period "The language of introspection, desire, and inner struggle migrates from devotional *praxis* ... to literature."[17] Not surprisingly, Pembroke's conversation with David and Astrophil is most audible in her Psalms that explore inwardness, an essential feature of both the sonnet and Psalm traditions. Wyatt's treatment of "Inward Sion, the Sion of the ghost" and the "heart's Jerusalem" is extended in Anne Lock's sonnet sequence on the penitential Psalm 51.[18] As in those and other previous metrical English versions of the Psalms, the Sidney Psalms have a strong emphasis on inwardness. For example, Pembroke echoes the "restlesse rest" of the frustrated lovers who sigh with "armes crost" (*Eighth Song*.19–20), but expands it with the "sleepie sleeplesse eies" of the Psalmist in Psalm 77.19. The speaker, assaulted by "Whole troupes of busy cares," cannot find rest, and in a striking instance of self divided between the mind and heart says that she sent "my thoughts abroade ... to search the truth" while yet "my silent hart / distracted thus did plaine" (77.17, 33–6).

Other Sidney allusions abound in her *Psalmes*. She even uses some of Sidney's more unusual rhymes for the Psalms, such as "notorious" / "glorious" (22.77–8; 76.2, 4), "containeth" / "raigneth" (24.1, 3; 119V.29–30); "fetches" / "wretches" (37.102–3; 112.33, 35), and "bequeathing" / "breathing" (42.39–40; 87.14, 16). Although some of these may be derived from a common source, there are enough

---

[16] Pembroke's Psalmist is carefully non-gendered, but to distinguish the voices of Sidney and Pembroke in their *Psalmes*, I will use gendered pronouns.

[17] Debora Kuller Shuger, *The Renaissance Bible: Scholarship, Sacrifice, and Subjectivity* (Berkeley, 1994), p. 165.

[18] Stephen Greenblatt, *Renaissance Self-Fashioning: From More to Shakespeare* (Chicago, 1980), p. 115; *The Collected Works of Anne Vaughan Lock*, ed. Susan M. Felch (Tempe, 1999), pp. liii–lviii; Hannibal Hamlin, *Psalm Culture and Early Modern English Literature* (Cambridge, 2004), ch. 3; Danielle Clarke, *The Politics of Early Modern Women's Writing* (London, 2001), ch. 4.

to indicate that she is remembering, even if unconsciously, his rhymes—and few enough to indicate that she made a deliberate attempt to avoid repeating them too often. (She makes a similar effort to avoid repeating rhymes, especially for the same Psalms, in other Psalters she knew well, like those by Sternhold and Hopkins and Matthew Parker.) Phrases from Sidney occur so frequently in her poems that they indicate how thoroughly his works had permeated her thoughts, but she rarely uses Sidney's phrases in unjustified contexts; rather, that wording tends to be legitimized by biblical translations or commentaries. For example, she uses Sidney's phrase "Eternal Essence" for God (25.24, 68.7). But her usage is also based on the Geneva note (verse 4), which says that God's name Jehovah does "signifie his essence and maiestie incomprehensible." Similarly, in Psalm 143.26, her phrase God's "hand-writyng" is a subtle reworking of Sidney's description of God's "handworking" (19.4) that makes the skies His book: "Their Words be set in letters great / For ev'ry body's reading" (19.15–16). Yet it is justified by the biblical "workes of thine hands" (143:5). And in Psalm 51, her phrase "trewand soule" (51.21) may recall *Astrophil* 1.13, "my trewand pen," as a reference to a novice learning a poetic craft, as Rivkah Zim suggests, but the idea of truancy is also brought to mind by the conceit of the womb as God's "hid schoole," which Pembroke develops from Calvin's comment on 51:8 that David has been "taught by God as one of his household" and has "become a froward scholer."[19]

Two of Pembroke's Psalms give a more extensive insight into her recasting of Sidney's words: Psalm 53, which revises Sidney's Psalm 14; and Psalm 73, which interweaves references to Sidney's Psalm 37 and to *Astrophil* 5. Psalm 53, which, except for verse 6, is the same as Psalm 14 in the Hebrew Psalms, illustrates how she directly addresses her brother's work.[20] Her first version (in Samuel Woodforde's transcription of what he says was the authors' working copy, MS *B*, Bodleian MS Rawl. poet 25) is much closer to Sidney than is the more polished version in the Penshurst manuscript, where she demonstrates her growing self-confidence as a writer by deliberately moving away from Sidney's version in form, wording, and rhyme.

In her early draft, she retains Sidney's twenty-four lines in six-line groupings, though hers are 12-line stanzas with the two parts connected by the rhyme in lines 6 and 12 (*aabbbcddeeec*). She covers the same verses as he does in each grouping

---

[19] Rivkah Zim, *English Metrical Psalms: Poetry as Praise and Prayer, 1535–1601* (Cambridge, 1987), p. 200; John Calvin, *The Psalmes of David and others. With M. John Calvins Commentaries*, trans. Arthur Golding (1571). Cf. Beth Wynne Fisken, "Mary Sidney's *Psalmes*: Education and Wisdom," in Margaret P. Hannay (ed.), *Silent but for the Word: Tudor Women as Patrons, Translators, and Writers of Religious Works* (Kent, 1985), p. 178. Less obviously connected is her allusion in Psalm 114.20 to "purling spring" from *Astrophil* 15.1.

[20] The verse division and numbering of Psalms 14 and 53 vary in the Book of Common Prayer and Geneva. Like MS *B*, I follow the Geneva numbering.

(except for verse 6 in Psalm 14, omitted in Psalm 53). In her first version of Psalm 53, where she repeats his rhyme words "eye" and "bread" in rendering the same verses, she carefully varies them, so that where Sidney has "ey" / "espy" (lines 7–8), she has "pry" / "eye" (lines 7–8), and where he rhymes "led" / "bread" (lines 13–14), she has "bred" / "fedd" (lines 13–14). In her revised Psalm 53, she avoids Sidney's rhyme words altogether, but her first version continues to be close to his in wording.

For verse 1, for example, both Sidney and Pembroke's first version render the line to encapsulate the Geneva note: it is not atheism that makes them say, "There is no God," but rather that they have "no regarde" of "vertue nor of vice." Sidney works that interpretation into the stanza, explaining that the "foolish man" has reassured his "guiltie heart" with the "fond thought" that "There is no God that raigneth," and so therefore he and "all his Mates / Do works which earth corrupt and Heaven hates" (14.1–5). Pembroke expresses the same idea by having the fool say, "There is no God that marks mens wayes." He and "all the Witless train" do not believe God will pay attention to what they do, and so they think they are completely free to do evil—"Such deeds both do, and don maintain," or justify. In verse 2, "God loked downe from heaven" is rendered by Sidney as God's "piercing ey" and by Pembroke as God's "searching eye."

Subsequent verses are given similarly close interpretation and, as we have seen, two rhyme words are repeated at the same place in the text. Pembroke also uses Sidney's descriptive noun "Canibals" for the wicked who eat God's people "as if they were bread" (14.14), though she amplifies their bestiality by terming them "Wolvish Canibals" (53.15). The adjective shows her careful biblical scholarship, for Calvin's commentary on this verse refers to the vivid description of the wicked in Micah 3, "They eat also the flesh of my people, and flay of their skinne from them, and they break their bones, and chop them in pieces, as for the pot." Calvin says nothing about wolves (and Geneva nothing about Micah), but the Geneva note on this passage in Micah compares the "wicked governers" to "wolves, lyones, and most cruel beasts."

Pembroke also uses Sidney's term "astraying" where the Book of Common Prayer has "gone out of the way" and Geneva "gone backe" (verse 3). She expands the description of God's destruction of the wicked to fill in for the three lines that Sidney uses to render verse 6 which, as we have seen, is missing from Psalm 53. Then, like Sidney, she begins the concluding desire for the coming of Christ to comfort Israel with the exclamatory "Ah," although her term "Saviour" makes the Christological interpretation (explicit in Beza and other commentaries) even more evident than Sidney's "saver."[21] Geneva has a note on Romans 3 (and Beza and Calvin emphasize this passage), which quotes Psalm 14.1–2. This section of Romans declares that since "all have sinned," justification can come only by

---

[21] The difference between "saver" and "Saviour," however, could have been scribal, since we do not have an autograph manuscript.

"grace, through the redemption that is in Christ Jesus" (3: 23–4). For the Sidneys, the application of this passage in Romans was therefore present in the text on the Psalm. Like Sidney, Pembroke renders the conclusion with an emphasis on the long time before redemption will come, although it is somewhat clearer in her phrase, "Ah! when shall time away be worne."

Except for such subtle changes, this early version of Psalm 53 therefore looks like a deliberate imitation of Sidney's Psalm 14—except that she makes two radical changes, alterations that evince considerable rethinking of the text. Her first change is to add questions and exclamations, restructuring the Psalm as a dialogue. "Who good among them?" she asks, and supplies the answer, "None" (line 6). When God searches for one righteous person, "What finds he? All astraying go" (10). She cries out, "O Fury! Are Gods people bred" for the wicked to devour? Even more striking is her decision to recast verses 4–5 as direct address to those "Wolvish Canibals." There is no such direct address in Sidney, and her closest biblical parallel for this seems to be the brief switch to "you" in verse seven of some versions of Psalm 14.[22] Her switch to direct address adds considerable drama to the Psalm as the speaker confronts these "Canibals" with God's coming vengeance—and thereby adopts the psalmist's authorized voice even more boldly than does her brother.

In her revision of Psalm 53, in the Penshurst manuscript Pembroke demonstrates her entrance into the poetic tradition by her metric innovation. She changes the poetic form to three eight-line stanzas rhymed *aabbcdcd* and alters the meter to iambic tetrameter. In this more independent version, she also eliminates the repeated rhyme words and almost all of the phrasing from Sidney, including the memorable "Canibals." The only place where she comes somewhat closer to Sidney is in the reference to the coming of the Messiah, where she uses Sidney's term "saver" instead of her former usage "Saviour." She replaces the rhetorical questions with dialogue, beginning with the statement of the fool, "There is noe god," and turning the second stanza to God's words (rather than the Psalmist's) that describe (rather than directly address) "this cursed brood." Just one question remains, placed in her rendition of verse 4, as it is in the original. Then she alters her concluding lines to dramatize the joy of the former captives: "The lord his folk will one daie free: / then Jacobs house shall daunce and sing." Such a note of joy is characteristic of many of her Psalm versions, as in Psalm 68.5–6: "the just meane while shall in Jehovahs presence / play, sing, and daunce."[23] She may have found justification for these joyful additions in Sidney's Psalm 30.34, wherein the forgiven sinner can "now daunce for joy," or in Psalm 42.15–16, wherein the Psalmist remembers leading God's people, "his prayses singing, / Holy daunce to God's house bringing." Her lyrics maintain what Coburn Freer aptly terms

---

[22] Geneva and Book of Common Prayer 14:7; both Geneva and the Book of Common Prayer use the third person in 53:7.

[23] Cf. *Psalmes* 51.27–8, 75.12, 96.36, 149.10.

"devotion as a joyful game."[24] Pembroke, like her brother, may often have begun with the Geneva Bible as the basis of the poetic metaphrase, and she certainly turned often to the commentaries of Calvin and Beza (all of which suppress biblical references to dance), but the Sidneys' use of Genevan sources was leavened with the more liberal and joyful tradition of worship and psalmody that grew up around Matthew Parker.

Parker's prefatory poem to his own Psalter explains that the psalms are intended for singing:

> [The] princepall thing: your lute to tune,
>   that hart may sing in corde:
> Your voyce and string: so fine to prune,
>   to love and serve the Lord.[25]

Pembroke, who was celebrated for her lute-playing, may have likewise intended at least some of her *Psalmes* for singing, whether congregational or private song. She may even have sung the settings for lute and soprano voice of her own Psalms 51 and 130, preserved in British Library MS 15117.[26] She frequently adds the lute where her usual sources have harp.[27] More strikingly, her metaphrase of Psalm 57: 8 draws on both Parker and Wyatt, once again joining the sacred and secular poetic traditions: "wake my tongue, my lute awake" (57.34). Her echo of Wyatt's famous lyric, "Awake my lute," is justified by Parker's phrase, "awake my tonge ... awake both harpe and lute" (verse 8). (Parker, of course, had also read Wyatt.) She has tuned her lute as Parker admonishes, and declares: "prepared is my hart / to spread thy praise / with tuned laies" (57.31–3).[28] As Danielle Clarke suggests, "the joyous consolation of the Psalm demands to be read against the corrupt, courtly, existential despair of Wyatt's 'My lute awake.'"[29]

But many other Psalms strike a minor key—lamentation, complaint, and inward struggle against doubt and despair. An opportunity to compare the treatment of inwardness by Sidney and Pembroke is provided by the parallel Psalms 37 and 73. Although they are not, like Psalms 14 and 53, virtually identical in the Hebrew Psalms, they do both treat the same problem. Both are Wisdom Psalms, meditating on the problem of the prosperity of the wicked and the suffering of the godly. Psalm 37 is the voice of an elder issuing both assurances

---

[24] Coburn Freer, *Music for a King: George Herbert's Style and the Metrical Psalms* (Baltimore, 1972), p. 25.

[25] Parker, sig. A2ᵛ.

[26] Linda Austern believes that this manuscript collection may have been a woman's choice for her own use, although not necessarily Mary Sidney herself (private correspondence).

[27] See, for example, *Psalmes* 81.6, 87.22, 92.9, 98.15, 144.36, 150.6.

[28] Lewalski suggests a comparison with George Herbert's "Easter" (pp. 246–7).

[29] Clarke, p. 142.

and imperatives to a troubled younger believer, whereas Psalm 73 reads like the testimony of that younger believer. Psalm 37, an acrostic in the original, is structured more like a jazz improvisation on this theme rather than a progressive argument. Sidney makes the structure clearer by highlighting the admonition to "Frett not" followed by an assurance that the godly will be rewarded and the wicked punished in lines 1–16 (verses 1–6); a repeated admonishing "Chafe not" followed by a similar assurance in lines 17–60 (verses 7–24); concluded by the personal testimony of the elder, lines 61–104 (verses 25–40), who says, "I have been younge now old I am." He declares that he has never seen God's "Holy ones" forsaken, although he has seen the wicked destroyed.

Unlike Psalm 53, we do not have an early draft of Psalm 73 in manuscript *B*, transcribed by Woodforde (before he rescued the manuscript, his brother had used that section to put up coffee powder), but in the Penshurst manuscript, Pembroke adapts some of Sidney's phrasing. Both add the pride of the wicked (37.26, 73.8), and both add the idea of sliding; Sidney's speaker promises that the godly "shall not slide" (37.80), and Pembroke's more hesitant speaker points to an experiential paradox, "when most I slide, yet still upright I stand" (73.69). Both speakers are able to "stand" because they are upheld by God's hand. Both say that the godly will be rewarded and the wicked shall be "consumed," but for the speaker of Psalm 73, this conviction is hard won.

As the anguished cry of the believer torn by doubts, Psalm 73 already participates in the tradition of inwardness expressed by both the metrical Psalm and the Petrarchan poetic traditions.[30] Psalm paraphrase and meditation could thus become a form of life writing, exploring the self divided between what it should choose and what it wants (virtue and desire in Sidney), or between what it should think (faith) and what it does think (doubt).

Pembroke's rendition of this Psalm is particularly interesting because it signals her deliberate effort to enter the lyric tradition by its extensive references to Sidney's secular lyrics. She uses the Psalm to express the same kind of subjectivity that is present in the lyric tradition—wherein the poet can "superimpose the subjectivity of the scripted speaker on the reader," as Greene notes.[31] Yet the Psalms were a special case, for the devout were told to make the words of the Psalms their own, as explained in words attributed to Athanasius in the opening of the Sternhold and Hopkins Psalter: "It is easy ... for every man to finde out in the

---

[30] On the English tradition, see particularly Thomas P. Roche, *Petrarch and the English Sonnet Sequences* (New York, 1989); Heather Dubrow, *Echoes of Desire: English Petrarchism and Its Counterdiscourses* (Ithaca, 1995); and Roger Kuin, *Chamber Music: Elizabethan Sonnet-Sequences and the Pleasure of Criticism* (Toronto, 1998).

[31] Roland Greene, *Post-Petrarchism: Origins and Innovations of the Western Lyric Sequence* (Princeton, 1991), pp. 5–6.

Psalmes, the motion and state of his owne soule."[32] The Psalter frequently also included a chart of applications of the Psalms to specific conditions, offering additional encouragement for readers to superimpose their own subjectivity on that of the scripted speaker. "David's infolded voices express Christ and ourselves as well as his own circumstance," as Anne Prescott reminds us.[33]

In Psalm 73, Pembroke interweaves these two traditional expressions of inwardness with interlocked quotations from Sidney's poems and from Psalm versions and commentaries. Both poems begin with a reasonable proposition, but both poems are skeptical of the power of reason to solve life's problems: in the sonnet, reason is undercut by desire, but in the Psalm, reason is—eventually— surpassed by faith. This Psalm vividly portrays what Shuger calls the "decentered and complex subjectivity" of "the Calvinist saint," who struggles with doubt and with the divergence between the desire to be godly and the reality of sin.[34]

The opening lines closely parallel biblical phrasing, which is rendered "yet God is good to Israél: *even*, to the pure in heart" in the Geneva Bible (73: 1). Christian interpreters saw those two phrases not as a parallel restatement, as in the Hebrew, but as a definition. For their purposes, the term "Israel" was allegorized as the "godly" or, as some translators (but not Pembroke) occasionally say, the "church." Her statement is closest to Beza ("it must needes be true and inviolable, that God can not be but favorable unto Israel; that is, to them that worship him purelie and devoutlie" [verse 1]), but her phrasing is a quotation from *Astrophil and Stella* 5 in the words that open each quatrain, "It is most true," in what Zim terms "sacred parody."[35]

Pembroke's decision to use language from *Astrophil* 5, with its struggle between Reason and Desire, may well have been inspired by Beza's Argument for Psalm 73 on "the strife betwixt reason and the affections," which is also a concise summary of the *Astrophil* sequence in general and this sonnet in particular. Man's reason is incorrect, Beza argues, when it says that "their paines and travel is in vaine which seeke vertue" because the wicked prosper while the godly suffer adversity. Beza first proposes two common—and unsatisfactory—answers to the

---

[32] *The Whole Booke of Psalmes Collected into English Meter by Thomas Sternhold, J. Hopkins and Others* (1562), sig. *7^v; see also Parker, sig. C1^r.

[33] Prescott, "King David as a 'Right Poet'," p. 134; see also Lewalski, pp. 301–2; Zim, pp. 6, 43–79.

[34] Shuger, p. 105. See also Louise Schleiner, *Tudor and Stuart Women Writers* (Bloomington, 1994), pp. 72–3.

[35] Zim, pp. 199–200. Pembroke repeats the phrase in Psalm 126.9, where it is also justified by Beza, "and surelie so it is" (verse 3). These two poems teach particularly well together. See Margaret Hannay, "Incorporating Women Writers into the Survey Course: Mary Sidney's Psalm 73 and *Astrophil and Stella* 5," in Patrick Cheney and Anne Lake Prescott (eds), *Approaches to Teaching Shorter Elizabethan Poetry* (New York, 2000), pp. 133–8. For additional verbal echoes of Sidney, see *Collected Works of Mary Sidney Herbert*, vol. 1, pp. 71–2.

problem: the godly suffer because "they stand in neede of chastisement," an answer rejected in the book of Job, and the godly suffer so that "they may learne to hope for better things" in heaven, an answer that may be more theologically sound but remains emotionally inadequate. He concludes that the appearance of injustice is illusory, "for unto the evil men, good things are turned to evil" and for the good, "even evil things turne to good," an answer that Pembroke presents in her opening lines:

> It is most true that god to Israell,
>> I meane to men of undefiled hartes,
>> is only good, and nought but good impartes.

Thus Pembroke's first stanza directly parallels the opening of *Astrophil* 5 and makes a similar argument about the danger of straying from reason, although the problem presented in Psalm 73 appears quite different from Astrophil's desire for Stella. Yet Sidney structures the sonnet on what Susanne Woods terms a "submerged equation" that "Stella is true beauty and true beauty is virtue." The reader, Woods argues, first sees a contrast between love of Stella and love of virtue, then realizes that the two terms should be congruent, and finally realizes that two orders of truth are being addressed: the human, subject to Cupid, and the divine, subject to God. The religion of love is at best secular and at worst "dangerous to the Christian soul."[36] Pembroke may have had such a parallel in mind, for her phrase "scourging plagues" (line 14) echoes Sidney's "Beautie's plague, Vertue's scourge" from *Astrophil* 78.6, a phrase that, like Sonnet 5, conflates beauty and virtue.

Pembroke's speaker, however, is not concerned about the connection between beauty and virtue, but about justice and virtue. She grew angry when she "first … saw the wicked proudly stand, / prevailing *still* in all they tooke in hand." All the speaker's anger is supposedly in the past, but the prosperity of the ungodly is constantly present, highlighted by the repeated use of *still*: they are "prevailing *still*," their "horne of plenty" is "Freshly flowing *still*," their riches increase while "our wealth" is "*still* growing lesse."[37] So distressing is this that "ev'n godly men" are likely to turn "from their better will" to question God (Ps. 73.8, 9, 29, 36, 28).

Pembroke's emphasis on subjectivity becomes clearer in the next stanza, "Nay ev'n within my self, my self did say" (73.37). As Gary Waller suggests, the opening of that third stanza may adapt *Astrophil* 33.9, "But to my selfe my selfe

---

[36] Susanne Woods, *Natural Emphasis: English Versification from Chaucer to Dryden* (San Marino, 1985), pp. 164–5.

[37] Lyn Bennett suggests that the "past seems conflated with the present" in this "cathartic reenactment" of the speaker's rage (*Women Writing of Divinest Things: Rhetoric and the Poetry of Pembroke, Wroth and Lanyer* [Pittsburgh, 2004], p. 88).

did give the blow."[38] In this passage the repeated personal pronouns stress internal struggle, a conflict that the speaker works to keep contained "within my self." As the repeated *still* emphasizes the continuing good fortune of the wicked, the speaker's repeated use of the words *in vaine* emphasizes the apparent futility of godliness in wording that once again quotes Sidney. Translating verse 13, "Certainly I have clensed mine heart in vaine, and washed my hands in innocencie" (Geneva), she uses the phrases "In vain my hart" from *Arcadia* (II.14.5) and "filthy stayne" from Sidney's Psalm 32.1: "*In vain* my hart I purge, my hands *in vain* / in cleanes washt I keepe from filthy stayn" (73.38–9). Then the speaker steps back to consider the implications of her thoughts. Is it legitimate to articulate such doubts, even though they are common to the godly? In her effort to express her own subjectivity, the speaker is impeded by a traditional feminine desire to nurture others. Whereas the Geneva note says that such statements would offend against God's providence, Pembroke's speaker here, with almost motherly care, is concerned about God's children. Because of her responsibility to others she decides to remain silent. The poem thus paradoxically expresses the very doubt it resolves to suppress—and hints at the deliberate erasure of a woman's anger.

To avoid giving "such offense," the speaker alters direction. Turning her *thoughts* another way, she seeks an answer within, "but combrous cloudes my inward sight did blynd" (73.44–5). It is only when she turns her *feet* another way, directing her steps to God's house that she finds the answer. That is, as the problem is both personal and communal, so is the answer.[39] It is only by redirecting her feet to God's house that she learns the fate of the wicked who are in a high but "slippery place" (73.52), a biblical phrase also used in Sidney's description of ambition in *Astrophil* 23.10. That is, only as a member of the community can she find the answer, that it is the wicked who are "most vaine," who will vanish like a dream. Similarly, Pembroke repeats "still" in stanza 6 to underline the contrast between the continued prosperity of the wicked that she had outlined earlier and her continued reliance on God: "but as I was yet did I *still* attend, / *still* follow thee … when most I slide, yet *still* upright I stand." She prays, "then guide me *still*, then *still* upon me spend / the treasures of thy sure advise" (73.67–71).

Looking back on her former struggle with her new understanding of God's presence, she asks a new question—not why the wicked prosper while the godly suffer, but why she was so distressed: "Then for what purpose was it? to what end? / for me to fume with malecontented hart, / tormenting so in me each inward part?" The question is another restatement of Sidney's metaphrase of Psalm 37.1: "Fume not, rage not, frett not I say." The speaker in Pembroke's Psalm has fumed,

---

[38] Gary Waller, *Mary Sidney, Countess of Pembroke: A Critical Study of Her Writings and Literary Milieu* (Salzburg, 1979), p. 199.

[39] Neither the "combrous cloudes" nor the feet are in the biblical original. She may well be recalling Sidney's Psalm 18.60–61.

an emotional reaction that she now disavows. Like Astrophil, she concludes, "I was a foole" (73.61–4).

Whereas the wicked presumptuously "pronounce as from the skies" at the beginning of the poem, the speaker in the conclusion prays for someone to teach her to "clyme the skyes" (73.23, 73). This may be an allusion to Sidney's role as her poetic mentor as Zim suggests, or, in his current state as an "Angell Spirit," even as a spiritual guide, with a reference to the spiritual pilgrimage that Astrophil (not Philip Sidney) knew he should take, but refused.[40]

In this search for subjectivity by Pembroke's speaker, there are thus several differences from the divided self in *Astrophil*, most of which are present in the original Psalm but are amplified by Pembroke and underscored with quotations from Sidney. The struggle is put safely in the past tense, whereas Astrophil uses the present, and an attempt is made to externalize the inner struggle as between the "godlesse Crue" and "godly wee." Whereas Astrophil rejects reason to choose desire and thus Stella, Pembroke's speaker rejects reason to choose faith and thus God. Both have chosen to love and both have chosen to write of that love. Pembroke characteristically expands the final reference to the poet. As Hannibal Hamlin notes, she "not only acknowledges her brother's model but asserts its supercession by her own more serious psalm."[41] Sidney has chosen to speak of the struggle between desire and reason through the comic persona of Astrophil; Pembroke overgoes that model by speaking through the voice of the Psalmist. Hamlin also suggests that her use of the "erected face" of the kneeling believer awaiting God's blessing in her quantitative rendering of Psalm 123 may allude to Sidney's description in the *Defence of Poetry* of our "erected wit" that allows us to "know what perfection is," underscoring that her quantitative Psalms "derive from her brother's practice" in the *Arcadia* "and yet take his practice a step further toward that 'perfection' he describes" by combining "classical and biblical poetic models."[42]

Pembroke's speaker enfolds herself in the godly community and positions herself within God's house; from that secure haven, she is empowered to speak both for herself and for the community. The conclusion of the Psalm provides an opportunity to consider her poetic vocation. Whereas the Geneva text reads simply, "that I may declare all thy workes," Pembroke vows "to sing his workes while breath shall give me space." Authorized by her brother's voice and empowered by the traditional identification of the Christian reader with the voice of the Psalmist, Pembroke makes her most open statements on her craft in her metaphrases of the Psalms. She frequently expands, or even adds, a personal statement by the Psalmist/poet. For example, her rendition of Psalm 104 concludes with the poet's "resolute decree" to sing God's praise and a prayer that "my song might good

---

[40] Zim, p. 201.

[41] Hamlin, p. 99.

[42] Hamlin, p. 127.

acceptance finde." Similarly, Psalm 106 concludes, "lett all the Earth with praise approve my word." In Psalm 111, she calls attention to the "skill" that is necessary to praise God, as Suzanne Trill notes.[43] Psalm 119 portrays the poet as God's "scholer" composing "a holy hymn of praise" (119Y.10–11), using Petrarchan paradox: "esteeming it but pleasing paines / to muse on that thy word containes" (119T.15–16).[44] Even more striking is the conclusion she adds to Psalm 75:

> And I secure shall spend my happie tymes
> in my, though lowly, never-dying rymes,
>   singing with praise the god that Jacob loveth.

The combination of humility and self-assertion in those "lowly" yet "never-dying rymes" is characteristic of the Countess of Pembroke, a woman who had found a culturally acceptable way to enter the English poetic tradition. The immortality traditionally sought by the poet here blends with praise of the eternal God as she gives us a brief glimpse of her "happie tymes" spent working on the *Psalmes*, surrounded by her copies of the Book of Common Prayer, the Geneva Bible, Calvin, and Beza—with other Psalm versions and commentaries no doubt on shelves nearby (or perhaps on a book wheel) for easy reference. And always present in her mind were the English poets whom she sought both to emulate and to join—Wyatt, Spenser, and particularly her brother Philip.

---

[43] Suzanne Trill, "Sixteenth-Century Women's Writing: Mary Sidney's *Psalmes* and the 'Femininity' of Translation," in William Zunder and Suzanne Trill (eds), *Writing and the English Renaissance* (London, 1996), p. 151.

[44] Helen Wilcox suggests that Pembroke's opening of Psalm 45 expresses her own desires as a writer in "the comparison with other writers—the wish to point out that her writing is 'as swift' as that of any other (presumably male) writer" ("'Whom the Lord with Love Affecteth': Gender and the Religious Poet, 1590–1633," in Danielle Clarke and Elizabeth Clarke [eds], *"This Double Voice": Gendered Writing in Early Modern England* [New York, 2000], p. 190).

PART 3
Technologies of Conversation

Chapter 7

The Puzzling Letters of
Sister Elizabeth Sa[u]nder[s]

Betty S. Travitsky

Ruminating in 1522 about letter writing, Desiderius Erasmus remarked in his *De conscribendis epistolis*, "if there is something that can be said to be characteristic of this genre, I think that I cannot define it more concisely than by saying that the wording of a letter should resemble a conversation between friends."[1] More than a century later, in perhaps the earliest consideration of the genre by a woman, Madeleine de Scudéry, the "first of a series of women in the seventeenth century to ... adapt rhetoric to women's circumstances," defined letter writing as "conversations between absent persons."[2] In 1587, at about the halfway mark

Many gracious and learned persons provided me with suggestions and information at a time when I was unable to leave New York City to conduct my researches first-hand and nevertheless ventured into unfamiliar intellectual territory. My deep thanks to Reverend Mother Anna Maria O.Ss.S. (Syon House), Professor Electa Arenal (Graduate Center, CUNY), Ms Charlotte Berry (Old Library, University of Exeter), Mr Peter Paul Bogan (Archivist [Hon] St. Peter's Parish, Winchester), Dr Andrea Clarke (British Library), Dr Carolyn Bowden (St. Mary's College), Dr. Susan Dinan (William Patterson University), Professor Jane Donawerth (University of Maryland), Father Terry Drainey (Ushaw College, Durham), Dr Jessica Gardner (Old Library, University of Exeter), Professor Ann M. Hutchison (Pontifical Institute of Medieval Studies), Sister Theresa Lamy (College of Notre Dame of Maryland), Professor Elizabeth Lehrfeldt (University of Minnesota), Mr. David (Jack) Norton (University of Minnesota), Ms Julie Packard Hunter (College of Notre Dame of Maryland), Father John Pardo (English College, Valladolid), Dr. Javier Burrieza Sánchez (Archivist English College, Valladolid), Dr Colleen Seguin (Valparaiso University), and Reverend Monseignor Michael Williams (English College, Valladolid). The mistakes that remain, despite their kind and expert assistance, are, of course, my own.

[1] Quoted from *Collected Works of Erasmus* (84 vols, Toronto, 1974), vol. 25, p. 20, by Laurel Carrington, "Women, Rhetoric, and Letter Writing: Marguerite d'Alençon's Correspondence with Bishop Briçonnet of Meaux," in Molly Meijer Wertheimer (ed.), *Listening to Their Voices: The Rhetorical Activities of Historical Women* (Columbia, 1997), p. 217.

[2] Jane Donawerth's comment and the quotation from de Scudéry's *Conversations*

between the appearance of these texts, two puzzling exemplars of such a written "conversation" were penned in the little-noted, extraordinarily action-packed, and surprisingly problematic letters by a sixteenth-century Bridgettine nun, Sister Elizabeth Sa[u]nder[s]. These letters were written at the behest of the staunchly Catholic Sir Francis Englefield (c. 1522–1605) of Berkshire, an aristocrat who was a longtime supporter of Sa[u]nder[s]'s family and of her convent and who was then living in Valladolid, Spain.[3] The remarks that follow describe this steadfast Bridgettine and her letters, as well as a number of related texts by and about her, and outline some puzzles surrounding them.[4]

Details, regrettably, are sparse about the life of Sister Elizabeth Sa[u]nder[s] (d. 1607).[5] We do know that she was one of the twelve children of a prominent family

---

Nouvelles sur Divers Sujets, Dediées Au Roy (1685), sig. B8[v], are from Donawerth's "'As Becomes a Rational Woman to Speak': Madeleine de Scudéry's Rhetoric of Conversation," in Wertheimer (ed.), pp. 306, 312. I thank Professor Donawerth for a very helpful conversation on early modern women and rhetoric, and for sharing with me a pre-publication copy of the translation she has co-edited with Julie Strongson (*Selected Letters, Orations, and Rhetorical Dialogues* [Chicago, 2004]).

[3] A.J. Loomie, "Englefield, Sir Francis (1522-1596), courtier and Roman Catholic exile," *Oxford Dictionary of National Biography*, online at http://www.oxforddnb.com, article 8811; Thompson Cooper, "Englefield, Sir Francis (d. 1596?), catholic exile," *Dictionary of National Biography* (London, 1917–), vol. 6, pp. 790–93. Once a key officer of the household of Princess and then Queen Mary I, Englefield left England following the accession of Elizabeth, settling in Valladolid. He took an active part in supplying the wants of other English Catholic exiles, and though his estates were later seized by Elizabeth, he was granted a pension by the King of Spain. Some recent biographers give Sir Francis's death date as 1605; see, for example, David Nash Ford, "Royal Berkshire History," at http://www.berkshirehistory.com.

[4] These include two texts by Sister Elizabeth and a cipher, now housed among the Englefield Correspondence at the English College, Valladolid.

[5] The spelling of her name is given variously as Sander[s] and Sa[u]nder[s]. Henceforward, for simplicity's sake, I will spell it 'Sanders,' the usual spelling given her brother, Nicholas Sanders. Sister Elizabeth's death date, and that of her sister, are given by Joseph Gillow in his *Literary and Biographical History, or Bibliographical Dictionary of the English Catholics from the breach with Rome, in 1534, to the present time* (5 vols, 1885; New York, 1961), vol. 5, p. 475 and in BL MS Add. 22285 (to which I was referred by Professor Ann M. Hutchison and which was checked for me by Dr. Clarke). Three essays by Professor Hutchison shed a great deal of light on Sister Elizabeth's experiences: "Three (Recusant) Sisters," in Anne Clark Bartlett et al. (eds), *Vox Mystica: Essays on Medieval Mysticism In Honor of Professor Valerie M. Lagorio* (Rochester, 1995), pp. 147–58; "Beyond the Margins: The Recusant Bridgettines," in *Studies in St. Birgitta and the Brigittine Order*, vol. 2, *Analecta Cartusiana: Spiritualität Heute und Gestern* 35: 19 (Salzburg, 1993): 267–84; and "Eyes Cast Down, But Self Revealed: Letters of a Recusant Nun," in Bonnie Wheeler (ed.), *Representations of the Feminine in the Middle Ages* (Dallas, 1993), pp. 329–37. Professor Hutchison has prepared an edition, published in *Birgittiana* (vol. 13 for 2002) in two parts, of a manuscript concerning Sister Mary Champney, a nun

in Surrey, at least three of whom (herself and her siblings Margaret and Nicholas) entered holy orders, and that her father, William Sanders of Charlwood, at one time served as high sheriff of that county.[6] At a time when the English were forbidden, under increasingly stringent laws, to practice as Roman Catholics in England or to move to the Continent where they could practice their faith openly, the Sanders family was staunchly Roman Catholic; Sister Elizabeth's mother, Elizabeth (Mynes) Sanders, was reported in 1565 to be among the Catholic exiles in Louvain,[7] and Elizabeth Sanders followed her older sister, Margaret (d. 1576), in joining the Bridgettine order as a nun at Syon (Sion) Abbey.[8] The sisters' birth dates and the dates of their professions do not seem to be recorded, and so it would seem impossible to know whether they were among the nuns who were relocated from the original foundation.[9] Traditionally, they were said to be far older than their more prominent brother, Dr. Nicholas Sanders (c. 1530–81),[10] the Roman Catholic historian and controversialist,[11] though Canon John Rory Fletcher

---

sent to England at the same time as Sister Elizabeth ("Mary Champney a Bridgittine nun under the rule of Queen Elizabeth I," pp. 3–32 and—the text—"The life and good end of Sister Marie," pp. 33–89). I thank Professor Hutchison for reading and commenting on this essay, for bringing several important sources to my attention, and for telling me about her edition.

[6] T.F. Mayer, "Sander [Sanders], Nicholas (c. 1530–1581), religious controversialist," *Oxford Dictionary of National Biography*, article 24621; Thomas Graves Law, "Sanders or Sander, Nicholas (1530?–1581)," *Dictionary of National Biography*, vol. 17, pp. 748–51.

[7] John Hungerford Pollen (transcribed by Joseph E. O'Connor), "Nicholas Sander (Sanders)," *Catholic Encyclopedia Online* at http://www.newadvent.org/cathen/.

[8] Syon Abbey, a Bridgettine Monastery founded in 1415 by Henry V at Twickenham and moved in 1431 to the royal manor of Isleworth, was relocated in the time of Henry VIII, restored under Mary Tudor, and moved from place to place in Belgium after Elizabeth ascended the throne. In 1572, the community moved to Mechlin, where the events narrated by Sister Elizabeth would begin. By the time of her return to Syon Abbey, it had relocated to Rouen. In 1594, the community moved to Lisbon, where it remained until 1861, when it returned to England. In 1925, it moved to South Brent, Devon, its present location. For its sixteenth-century history, see Peter Guilday, "The Bridgettines of Syon," in his *The English Catholic Refugees on the Continent, 1558–1795* (London, 1914), pp. 56–61. Professor Hutchison kindly supplied me with a time line that refines details of the movements of the community.

[9] I thank Ms Charlotte Berry, archivist at University of Exeter, for checking the "Obituary catalogue," "Syon Abbey notebook 1," and the "Alphabetical list: Syon necrology," held in the Old Library at University of Exeter.

[10] Alfred Frederick Pollard, "Sanders, Nicholas (c. 1530–1581)," *Encyclopaedia Britannica* (11th edn, Cambridge, 1911), vol. 24, p. 138.

[11] Sanders may be best known for circulating—though not originating—the story that Anne Boleyn was the daughter of Henry VIII. In England, in fact, his efforts in *De Origine ac Progressu schismatis Anglicana* (1585) "obtained for its author the evil name of Dr. Slanders" (Law, "Sanders," p. 750).

plausibly attributes the genesis of the dramatic ordeal recounted in Sister Elizabeth's texts to her relative youth in 1578, the date at which her exile from the convent began (and by which time Margaret—who perhaps had been older—had died).[12] In a pattern familiar from contemporary references to many early modern Englishwomen (both Roman Catholic and Protestant),[13] and even in self-references by them,[14] Sister Elizabeth is customarily identified or designated not in her own right but as Sanders's sister.[15]

Of course, Sister Elizabeth Sanders's texts claim our attention simply as recovered—though, as we shall see, problematic—letters by an early modern Englishwoman.[16] There are further reasons, however, for which these letters and some related documents deserve our scrutiny. The most intriguing, to my mind, is that they epitomize what is proving to be one of the most abundant—but also the most difficult to recover—of all forms of early modern Englishwomen's texts: the writings, and especially the manuscript writings, of recusant Englishwomen. Among the cogent explanations for these difficulties provided by Dr Caroline Bowden, two seem particularly relevant. The first is the invisibility of learned *Catholic* women to mainstream scholars because of the consensus "that

---

[12] "Probably another reason ... was the anxiety of the Abbess to place the younger Sisters in a place of safety ... already a community of nuns had been paraded naked through a Calvinist camp" (John Rory Fletcher, *The Story of the English Bridgettines of Syon Abbey* [Devon, 1933], p. 52). Hutchison agrees with this interpretation ("Eyes Cast Down," p. 330).

[13] For example, William Browne's epitaph for Mary Sidney Herbert, possibly the most outstanding sixteenth-century woman writer in England: "Sidney's sister, Pembroke's mother" (BL MS Lansdowne 777, f 43^v).

[14] Perhaps most outstandingly in Margaret Cavendish's attempt at the end of her autobiography to differentiate herself from William Cavendish's first wife: "My Lord having had two Wives, I might easily have been mistaken, especially if I should dye, and my Lord Marry again" (*A True Relation of My Birth, Breeding, and Life* [1656], pp. 390–91).

[15] For example, in a letter dated November 18, 1580, from "John Watson, Bishop of Winchester, Sir Henry Radeclyff, and others to the Council. Have apprehended and examined Elizabeth Saunders, sister of Dr Saunders, with whom they found certain lewd and forbidden books, and a protestation or challenge of the Jesuits" ("Reign of Elizabeth, 1558–1580," *Calendar of state papers, domestic series, of the reigns of Edward VI, Mary, Elizabeth [and James I] 1547–1625: preserved in the State Paper Department of Her Majesty's Public Record Office*, ed. Robert Lemon [12 vols, London, 1856], vol. 1: 688).

[16] For recent light on letters by early modern Englishwomen, see James Daybell: "Women's Letters and Letter Writing in England, 1540–1603," Ph.D. dissertation, University of Reading, 1999; James Daybell, "Women's Letters and Letter Writing in England, 1540–1603: An Introduction to the Issues of Authorship and Construction," *Shakespeare Studies* 27 (1999): 161–86; James Daybell, *Early Modern Women's Letter Writing, 1450–1700* (Basingstoke, 2001); and James Daybell, *Women Letter-Writers in Tudor England* (Oxford, 2005). I thank Dr Daybell for generously copying and posting to me a copy of his dissertation.

Protestantism had led to a significant expansion of educational opportunities for English women" with the "obverse [effect of leaving] *Catholic* women out of serious consideration as producers of documents."[17] The second is "the practical difficulty in locating and accessing relevant material relating both to Catholic families and to women religious," because of the difficult circumstances attendant on early modern English Catholics at home and the "traumatic events" attendant on the religious communities established for English nuns in exile on the continent, all of which led to the dispersal and destruction of many documents (quite apart from "the usual problems of fires, damp and rodent infestation faced by all archives").[18]

To these explanations, I would add that the modesty practiced by women religious sometimes renders attribution of their works problematic for later readers.[19] Also, the very erudition of the exiled English nuns conspires to make even their printed works less accessible to us today: frequently published abroad in Latin or at least in vernacular foreign languages, these printed works fall outside the scope of standard English-language bibliographical tools like the revised *Short-Title Catalogue* and therefore are invisible to anyone who does not examine supplementary sources of bibliographical information like Guilday, Allison and Rogers, and most recently, Walker.[20] And of course these difficulties complement the well-documented general tendencies—contemporary and traditional—to denigrate and minimize early modern female accomplishments,[21] tendencies, sadly,

---

[17] Employing an anthropological term borrowed by Diane Willen in her "Comment on Women's Education in Elizabethan England," *Topic* 36 (1982): 66–73 (where it is taken from Charles Hudson (ed.) *Red, White and Black: Symposium on Indians in the South* [Athens, 1966], vol. 6, p. 1), I would describe this difficulty as an instance of "structural amnesia," that is, the relegation to "historical oblivion" of the sub-sub-group—Catholic women—within the larger, barely visible sub-group—early modern Englishwomen.

[18] Caroline Bowden, "Biographies of women religious: a special case?," paper presented at "Early Modern Lives: biography and autobiography of the Renaissance and seventeenth century," Middlesex University, London, June, 2002, emphasis added. I thank Dr Bowden for very generously sharing this material with me and for graciously answering many questions that I put to her.

[19] The scant sources are divided, to take one example, in assigning the translations of *The history of the angelicall virgin glorious S. Clare* and *The Rvle of the Holy Virgin S. Clare* to Sister Magdalen of St. Augustine of the Poor Clares (Catharine Bentley) or to Sister Catherine of St. Magdalen of the Poor Clares (Elizabeth Evelinge). In his recent introduction to *The history* and in her forthcoming edition of *The Rvle*, Professor Dr Frans Korsten and Dr. Claire Walker judge the scant evidence to favor Elizabeth Evelinge (*Elizabeth Evelinge, I* [Aldershot, 2002]; *Elizabeth Evelinge, III* [Aldershot, 2006]).

[20] Peter Guilday, "Bibliography," in *The English Catholic Refugees*, pp. xxiv–liii; A.F. Allison and D.M. Rogers, *The Contemporary Printed Literature of the English Counter-Reformation between 1558–1640* (2 vols, Aldershot, 1989–94); Claire Walker, "Bibliography," in her *Gender and Politics in Early Modern Europe: English Convents in France and the Low Countries* (Hampshire, 2003) pp. 217–31.

[21] A case in point is discussed by A.F. Allison in "New Light on the Early History of the

that we can find internalized and expressed by early modern women writers themselves.[22]

Sister Elizabeth's letters also hold great interest as descriptions of a series of dangerous, if ultimately successful, adventures that are extraordinary, yet paradoxically typical, of the experiences of English recusants.[23] As noted earlier, Catholics who remained in Elizabethan England were subject to scrutiny and punishment for their observance, but as Sister Elizabeth's letters illustrate in detail, the exile communities were by no means secure. In 1578, the situation of Syon Abbey, then located in Mechlin, became precarious, for the city was taken over by Calvinists, and the Catholic religious communities there, already suffering abject poverty, were threatened by hostile raiders. In these by no means quiet times, it was decided that a dozen of the younger nuns, among them Sister Elizabeth Sanders, should be safeguarded by being sent back to England, where—as Fletcher noted—they might be placed out of harm's way, and where they also might be able to raise funds for their convent. While this removal was presumably the better course, Sister Elizabeth's stout and understated narrative demonstrates that it was by no means a simple one. Back in England, after all, this was the decade, as S.T. Bindoff has written, "which saw the Catholic assault at its height, and the government's defence at its fiercest."[24]

Indeed, Sister Elizabeth's letters hold particular interest as rare first-person narratives—even, it might be said without much exaggeration, as autobiographical narratives—by an English recusant nun. Ordinarily, as an enclosed Bridgettine, Sister Elizabeth Sanders would not have conducted any correspondence at all. Her

---

Breve Compendio: The Background to the English Translation of 1612," *Recusant History* 4.1 (1957): 4–17. As Allison explains, *Abridgment of Christian perfection*, the English translation from a 1598 French version (*Bref discours* ... [1598]) of *Breve compendio* ... (1585?)—a mystical work originally written in Italian—was done almost entirely by Lady Mary Percy, abbess of the English Benedictine convent in Brussels, who also composed one dedicatory preface to the work that she signed with her initials. One of the French prefaces in the 1612 edition was translated by the Jesuit Anthony Hoskins (d. 1615). Despite Lady Percy's work, two subsequent editions printed by John Wilson at the S. Omer Press in 1625 and 1632 dropped her preface and were ascribed by Wilson to Hoskins alone. Long misplaced, the unique copy of the 1612 edition was recently relocated at the Venerable English College (Rome); it will be reprinted in *Catherine Greenbury and Mary Percy* (Aldershot, 2006), with an introduction by Drs. Jos and Frans Blom.

[22] Anne Dowriche, for example, in a preface to her *French Historie* (1589) addressed to her brother, writes: "If you finde anie thing that fits not your liking, remember I pray, that it is a womans doing" (sig. A3ʳ).

[23] Such adventures are perhaps most familiar to students of early modern Englishwomen in the case of Elizabeth Cary, Lady Falkland, who managed to spirit her sons out of England, an achievement recounted in her daughter's biography, recently edited by Barry Weller and Margaret W. Ferguson (*The Tragedy of Mariam The Fair Queen of Jewry with The Lady Falkland Her Life by One of Her Daughters* [Berkeley, 1994]).

[24] Fletcher, pp. 52–3; S.T. Bindoff, *Tudor England* (Middlesex, 1980), p. 241.

life would have been defined by separation from worldly affairs. As Hutchison details, "Normally all correspondence with the outside world was—and today is still—handled by the abbess, the community's head and administrator."[25] Nor, needless to say, would she have been sent away from her convent under ordinary circumstances. Sister Elizabeth, whose accounts, as we will see, provide graphic testimony to both her obedience to her vows and her willingness to beard even exalted Protestants, writes to Sir Francis Englefield,

> Thus w^t my hūble and dewtyfull comendatyons, I haue sett downe in wrightyng accordyng to your worshypps Desyre, that before writen, the w^{ch}, neyther I could sett downe my self (as you wor. knowyth I am no scriuener and yeat yf I could, I would haue byn very loathe to haue done, the matter beyng of my self, yeat to shew vnto yor wor. the prompt Dewty wch I am alwayse most ready to Þforme towards yow, (especially my Lady and our ffather wyllyng me) thys wch I haue byn very loathe to do, I haue most wyllingly done by an other scrybe, callyng to mynd, all in effect, and some of the Þtyculars.[26]

In conformity to early modern formulae and in further demonstration of her willingness to please her patron, Sister Elizabeth ends this letter with the evocative *conclusio*, "Your worshypps poore beadswomā S. Elyzabeth Sanders."

The first letter, headed "The coppy of S. Elyzabethe Sander^s letters vnto your wor. of her beyng in England" (1), seems to be a copy by another hand, thereby explaining Sister Elizabeth's otherwise cryptic statement that she has obeyed Sir Francis's wishes ("I haue most wyllingly done by an other scrybe" [3]). Although the letter is rhetorically unembellished, indeed, homely, Sister Elizabeth does begin with a *salutatio* ("Salutatyons most hūble and infynite Þmysed" [1]) and does end with a *conclusio* (quoted earlier); she also includes—mid-way through—an indirect *narratio* (cited earlier) in which she spells out her purpose (that is, to "sett downe in wrightyng accordyng to your worshypps Desyre" [3]). There is neither

---

[25] The typical enclosure and self-effacement undertaken by a sixteenth-century Bridgettine nun are clarified by Hutchison, "Eyes Cast Down," pp. 329–30. Hutchison surmises ("Three Recusant Sisters," p. 149) that Sir Francis requested an account of her experiences from Sister Elizabeth to ascertain the names of those in England who had been helpful to her and other Catholics. Hence her anomalous letters. Some forceful letters by early modern abbesses are included by Sir Henry Ellis in the first and third series of his *Original Letters Illustrative of English History* (3 vols, London, 1824: II 74–5; 1846: III 10–12, 50–53, 116, 232, 233–4) and by Mary Anne Everett Wood Green in her *Letters of Royal and Illustrious Ladies of Great Britain* (4 vols, London, 1846: II: 49–51, 52–3, 53–6, 56–7, 57–9, 60, 150–53, 154–5, 156–8, 181–2, 183–4, 184–6, 213–15, 215–16, 216–18, 265–6, 288–91; III: 69–70, 71–2, 72–4, 85–7, 87–9).

[26] I transcribe this excerpt and other quotations from Sister Elizabeth's first letter from the photocopy of Val. Ser. II, L. 5, no. 12 (first page), kindly searched out for me by David (Jack) Norton and sent to me by Dr Javier Burrieza Sánchez, archivist of the English College, Valladolid. The page numbers I supply are my own.

benevolentiae captatio nor *petitio.*[27] Held at the English College in Vallodolid, the home in exile of its recipient, the original (English) text was first published in 1894, in *Poor Soul's Friend and St. Joseph's Monitor,* the journal of Syon Abbey.[28]

Although space constraints allow me to include only a few excerpts, I believe that Sister Elizabeth's tale is best told in her own words. Initially, she writes, she arrived at "Grauel Inne" (Gravelines) from whence she removed to "byllingsgate" (Billingsgate) and to "Abbyngton" (Adingdon), remaining there "one yeere and half," though she had to leave "that place beyng in daunger of troubles." Alas, "troubles" nonetheless found Sister Elizabeth out, and she was "delyueryd ... vnto the offycers of the Towne" who "comaundyd me to be sent ... vnto the SuÞintendent of Wynchester" (Winchester). As we have noted, Sister Elizabeth was commonly regarded not in her own right but as the sister of Dr. Nicholas Sanders, a relationship that complicated her position in captivity; for example, in a familiar pattern, this officer "sayed ... that bothe I and others mo were sent by my Brother D. Saunders hyther into England, and put in hope, that ō Relygion and ordre should come upp agayne" (1).

In further sessions, "dyuers of the masters and scollers ... were sent vnto me, to Þswade wᵗ me, concludyng, that yf I would yeald, I should haue great ffavour shewyd me ...." (2). Since she remained steadfast, however, Sister Elizabeth "was sent strayght Prysoner vnto the Castle, callyd brydwell [Bridewell] ... wher I remayned close prysoner 23 weeks" (2). Following this initial incarceration, Sister Elizabeth "was sent for to come to the syces [assizes] ..." where she was "indyted 20ᶠ eũy monethe for not goyng to the churche. And so I was sent back agayne from whence I came, where I remayned styll, tyll I was callyd wᶜʰ was about 6 or 8 tymes to eũy syces" (2). This incarceration continued,

> full 6 yeers, duryng wᶜʰ tyme, besyds the sodayne and often searchyng and takyng away all my books and other stuff they could fynd, besyds I haue byn dyuers tymes three dayes together wᵗ out any meat browght vnto me by the keeÞ, and 9 dayes I was thrust

---

[27] These "elements" are summarized by Carrington (p. 216). Sister Mary Humiliata describes epistolary practices that seem closer to Sister Elizabeth's homely style in her "Standards of Taste Advocated for Feminine Letter Writing, 1640–1797," *HLQ* 13 (1950): 261–77, although her discussion of letter writing is culled from a slightly later period.

[28] They were republished in 1966: "The History of Syon (continued). Englefield Correspondence—English College Valladolid: The Coppy of S. Elizabethe Sanders Letter Unto Your Wor. of Her Being in England. The First Letter (Rouen 1587)," *Poor Soul's Friend and St. Joseph's Monitor* (January/February 1966): 11–22. This edition corresponds to a photocopy from the archive and to a typed transcription of the letter (Val. Ser. II, L. 5, no. 12) kindly sent to me by Father Terry Drainey, formerly Spiritual Director of the English College, Valladolid.

vpp in a chambre without eyther wyndow or ayer. And yet I thank god I lackyd neyther meate nor ayer, for good ffolks dyd helpe me by secreat meanes. (3)[29]

Sister Elizabeth follows this account of her initial imprisonment with "[t]he other part towchyng my returne home" (3), a return, we learn, that was attempted several times following her receipt of letters from the superiors of her Abbey,

> ... at dyuers and sondry tymes, as well vnto vs all ther in England, as allso vnto me in þrticular, as well wᵗ sweet entreatyng, as allso wᵗ expresse Comaundments vppon our obedyence to god, our Religion, and vnto them, chargyng vs, to seeke by all meanes possyble, well and convenyently to returne vnto them and theyr Covent agayne, euen as we would answere vnto god, ... dyschargyng them selfe, and laying the burden of our abode from them, vpon our owne necks, yf we dyd abyde there, after we could fynd any meanes possyble how to escape. (3)[30]

Despite these seemingly clear directions, several "prysts, verteowse and well learnyd" (3) to whom Sister Elizabeth showed these letters, "cōcludyd that I could not wᵗ good conscyence depart from pryson of my self" (3). Other, more worldly prisoners offered Sister Elizabeth money to buy her liberty, "but when yt came to the poynt, my name Sanders beyng knowen, neyther sutes, nor mony could at any tyme prevayle" (4) and it seemed that with stiff fines accruing at every session she would have "to lye in þpetuall prison" (4). However, in time she was "delyueryd of all my dett ... by reason that I was sent to an other pryson vndre an other keeÞ" (4) where the fines were annulled, and there she bribed the wife of the jailor to free her: "vppon her words I preparyd my self, and to depart downe by a rope ouer the castle wall" (4).

This daring nighttime escape did not end Sister Elizabeth's "troubles," however, for after just one night in a safe house she was advised by a priest who was her fellow lodger that she "was bownd to returne to the pryson agayne from whence I came, and ther to abyde, tyll god should delyuer me, by some better meane" (4). Despite Sister Elizabeth's counter-arguments, this priest and

> ... 2 other yong prysts to whom he shewyd the case ... agreeyd, that in conscyence I was bownd to returne to my pryson agayne, and there to remayne, tyll by some ordynary meanes, I myght come to lyberty, wᶜʰ when I heard them all agree vppon, I concludyd wᵗ

---

[29] Interestingly, and quite apart from the drama of these incidents, this language is reminiscent of the account by the Quakers Katherine Evans and Sarah Cheevers of their incarceration by the Inquisition in Malta; see *This Is A Short Relation of some of the Cruel Sufferings (for the Truths sake) of Katharine Evans & Sarah Chevers* ... (1662), for example: "The Room was so hot and so close, that we were fain to rise often out of our bed, and lie down at a chink of their door for air to fetch breath ..." (p. 13).

[30] Hutchison dates the letters from Syon "between late summer or early autumn 1580 and early 1583" ("Three Recusant Sisters," p. 157 n25).

my self, to go back agayne to pryson, and so the next mornyng by tymes, w^t horse and man, and a crowne in mony, he sent me back agayne to pryson (4).

As frustrating as we would imagine that her return to gaol (jail) must have been to her, it did gain Sister Elizabeth the respect of her captors, and once back, she relates, her fellow prisoners all advised her that "seyng my intent was only to returne to my Relygyon and Covent, and for no other respect ... [she] myght most saffly and w^t a most secure conscyence followe myne owne purpose and Determinatyon, in seekyng meanes, to returne to my Company" (4). Shortly thereafter, consequently, Sister Elizabeth again "went forthew^t out of pryson" (4). Unfortunately, however, she was retaken after "about a monethe" and bound over "to apeere w^{t}in 20 dayes next ensuyng" (4). After obtaining permission to go to London for further advice, she "was taken agayne by an other pursevant [pursuivant]" (4). A number of persons assisted her with money to pay her debt to the keeper's wife, and eventually one such person procured "a saffe passport [for her] but not vndre myne owne name but by the name of Elyzabethe neale" (5). Under that name, Sister Elizabeth returned to Syon Abbey.

I believe that these brief excerpts from her first letter demonstrate both the tendency towards understatement with which Sister Elizabeth describes her misadventures and daring and her deep commitment to her faith and to her vows. Another facet of Sister Elizabeth's personality communicates itself between her lines: a self-respect that is all the more interesting in conjunction with her self-effacement and obedience. In a passage that was written in the margin of her letter, she says:

> I had almost forgotten to tell yow, how one of the Iustices callyng on me, demaundyd, when I would paye the 20$^£$ a monethe for nott goyng to the churche, I answeryd, alas I could neuer paye ytt, then he badd me borrowe ytt of a Catholyque gentleman ther Þsent one m^r Travisse a prysoner, but I was nott dysposyd then to stretche my credytt by borrowyng to pay such detts beyng content w^t scylence to lett the dett rune vnpayed vnto such tyme as the Queene and I should meete att a masse, and ther rekon w^t her for how many monethes I was indettyd vnto her, the wch when ytt wyll please her to do, I shall not refuse any day she shall appoynt, ffor syns my comyng home, into the kychyne, I haue learnyd to cast an accompt, wch I neuer could do before, and therby I do assure my self sufficiently, yf she meete me att masse, she shall not deceyue me, or misrecon me (3).

We note no doubt on Sister Elizabeth's part as to the rightness and ultimate triumph, of her faith, no deference to earthly majesty, and no discomfort about her work at "home" in the "kychyne."[31]

---

[31] Staunch women of both the old and the new faiths! Sister Elizabeth's self-assurance is reminiscent of that of an earlier, Protestant woman, Anne Askew, who also did not flinch from asserting herself and also did so without self-dramatics. See *The first examinacyon ...*

By late May 1587, Sister Elizabeth had returned to Syon Abbey, then in Rouen.[32] In that year, from Rouen, at the behest of Sir Francis Englefield, she wrote the letter from which I have been quoting. Englefield was a very strong supporter of Nicholas Sanders and of Syon Abbey and an associate of Robert Persons, or Parsons (1546–1610), a Jesuit famous for his organization of missionary activity in England and on the continent, who was founder in 1589 of the seminary in Valladolid, and who would be connected to the later history of Sister Elizabeth's texts.[33] That Sister Elizabeth's first letter should have been preserved among the Englefield Correspondence at the English College, Valladolid, is not surprising, given this background information; its presence there suggests that the letter eventually did reach Englefield at Valladolid, though not immediately.

The delay in the post, it seems, led Sister Elizabeth to write a second letter to Sir Francis. The second letter, as published in 1966, lacks a *salutatio* and part of the *conclusio*, but the impression that her first letter went astray is stated in her first paragraph:

> In the long letter I wrote you some days ago, I told you what happened to me in England …, now having received yours, in which you say nothing of any letter received from me, but rather desire me to give you an account, not only of my imprisonment but of the way in which our Lord chose to guide me in leaving England, I will do both, recapitulating briefly what I had already written, and relating more fully how I came to leave that kingdom.[34]

(1546): "he bad me, saye my mynde without feare. I answered hym, that I had nought to saye. For my conscyence (I thãked God) was burdened with nothynge" (p. 23).

[32] A letter, dated 22 May 1587, from Dr Thomas Bayly, Vice President of Douai College, to Father Gibbons, states, "I hear that Sister Saunders is lately come out of England to Sion again." The letter is printed in Henry Foley (ed.), *Records of the English Province of the Society of Jesus: historic facts illustrative of the labours and sufferings of its members in the sixteenth and seventeenth centuries* (7 vols, London, 1877–83), vol. 4, p. 483. An extract is included in John Hungerford Pollen (ed.), *Unpublished Documents Relating to the English Martyrs, I (1584–1603)*, although Pollen gives the date as 21 May (*Catholic Record Society Publications* V [London, 1908], p. 140).

[33] Victor Houliston, "Persons [Parsons], Robert (1546–1610), Jesuit," *Oxford Dictionary of National Biography*, article 21474; Thomas Graves Law, "Parsons or Persons, Robert (1546–1610), jesuit missionary and controversialist," in *Dictionary of National Biography*, vol. 15, pp. 411–18; J.H. Pollen (transcribed by W.G. Kofron), "Robert Persons (also, but less correctly, Parsons)," *Catholic Encyclopedia Online*, http://www.newadvent.org/cathen/.

[34] "The History of Syon (continued). Englefield Correspondence—English College Valladolid: Sister Elizabeth Saunders 'Second Letter' to Sir Francis Englefield," *Poor Soul's Friend and St. Joseph's Monitor* (March/April 1966): 43–54. For the reasons behind the modernized spelling of this letter, see below.

Taking up her narrative from the time of her second arrest, Sister Elizabeth recounts her experiences more pithily and more angrily than in her earlier account:

> ... as if they had taken a great malefactor or thief, they brought me before more judges than Annas and Caiphas, Pilate and Herod .... They asked me many most impertinent questions, to all which I gave but one short answer, saying that I was a woman and a nun .... (43)

She also is much more chary about naming those who assisted her, for reasons that may be clarified by the afterlife of this letter.

It is with this second letter that we begin to touch on the intriguing propagation of Sister Elizabeth Sanders's texts. *Poor Soul's Friend,* alluded to above, reprints both her letters in two separate numbers, in January/February and in March/April 1966. We learn from a paragraph appended to the published transcription of the first letter, that the English language "original" of the second "seems irrecoverable," and therefore that the text to be published in the next issue of the newsletter comes from "a Spanish translation ... published by Yepez [sic] in his *Historia Particular* ... [and] its interest is such that it is well worth translating back from Spanish into English. The retranslation [is] by Dom Adam Hamilton, O.S.B., Buckfast Abbey" (22).[35]

It *is* true that the text printed in the March/April issue of *Poor Soul's Friend* is taken from Yepez (or Yepes),[36] and there is no reason to doubt that the retranslation is by the prolific Dom Adam Hamilton. Hamilton, however, does not mention that this version of the letter is the *second* extant (virtually identical) version put in print within Sister Elizabeth's lifetime. In fact, the appearance of Sister Elizabeth's second letter in Yepes' volume was no less than its *third* appearance, in Spanish, in print. The first, printed just a few years after she had

---

[35] "The History of Syon ... First Letter," p. 22; Dom Adam Hamilton, a prolific Benedictine monk, is known primarily for *The Chronicle of the English Augustinian Canonesses Regular of the Lateran, at St. Monica's in Louvain (now at St. Augustine's Priory, Newton Abbot, Devon)* (2 vols, London, 1904–1906).

[36] A member of the Hermits of St. Jerome, Diego de Yepes (before 1549–1613), was at one time the confessor of Philip II and is best known for his life of Saint Teresa of Avila; he was appointed in 1599 Bishop of Tarazona. Sister Elizabeth's letter is printed in his collection about the English Catholics (Allison and Rogers, vol. 1, p. 43, entry 284), *Historia particular de la persecucion de Inglaterra, y de los martirios que en ella ha auido, desde el año del Señor, 1570* (Madrid, 1599), under the heading, "Traslado de vna carta de vna monja Inglesa, llamamada Isabel Sandera, hermana del Do tor Nicolas Sandero, escrita vn Roan, ciudad de Francia, a Francisco Englefild, cauallero Ingles, residente en Madrid: en que le da cuenta de sus persecuciones, y trabajos que ha passdo nuestra santa Fê, en Inglaterra: y de la marauillosa prouidencia que Dios nuestro Señor vso en conseruarla, y lilbrrla dellos" (pp. 724–36). I thank Professor Electa Arenal, Sister Theresa Lamy, and Ms Julie Packard Hunter for their gracious and expert assistance with this Spanish material.

written it, seems not to be extant.[37] The second (but first extant) version, printed at about the same time as the first, was included in Persons's collection, *Relacion de algunos martyrios* (1590).[38] The association of the indefatigable Persons with Sir Francis Englefield, Nicholas Sanders, and Valladolid suggests clear channels through which he might have acquired Sister Elizabeth's letter; his purpose for publication of this private, indeed modest "conversation," would seem what D.M. Rogers calls an "extended attempt to make the situation of the Catholics in England known to readers of Spanish."[39]

Undoubtedly, it was this print afterlife that earned Sister Elizabeth's letters an extended synopsis in an entry in *A Biographical Dictionary of English Women Writers 1580–1720,* the closest they have come to recognition by students of early modern writings by Englishwomen, though the entry does not note the prior publication of the letter by Persons, the publication of Hamilton's retranslation, or discrepancies between the Spanish and English versions.[40] Despite this relative renown, however, there are two significant puzzles connected with the Spanish afterlife of Sister Elizabeth's letters.

The first is that while the two Spanish publications are virtually identical, both differ from the translation in *Poor Soul's Friend* in including some 900 words concerning "the captivity of the fathers of our religion, named Marsh and Vivian," who were seized on the high seas and taken as prisoners to England.[41] (In the

---

[37] Allison and Rogers report (vol. 1, pp. 134–5, entry 965) that they did not find a copy of what would appear to have been its earliest publication in Spanish: "Traslado de vna carta de cierta monia inglesa, llamada Isabel Sandera escrit en Ruan ciudad dee Francia a Francisco Englefild cauallero ingles residente en Madrid. 4° *Seuilla, Clementee Hidalgo, n.d.* [c. 1590]."

[38] "Traslado de Vna carta de vna monja Inglesa, llamada Ysabel Sandera, hermana del Do tor Nicols Sandero, escrit de Roan, cuidad de Francia, a vn cauallero Ingles, residente en Madrid; en que le da cuenta de sus persecuciones y trabajos que ha passado por nuestra santa Fê en Inglaterra: y de la marauillosa prouid cia que Dios nuestro Señor vsó en conseruarla y librarla dellos," in Robert Persons, *Relacion de algunos martyrios, que de nueuo han hecho los hereges en Inglaterra, y de otras cosas tocantes a nuestra santa y Catolica religion. Traduzida de Ingles en Castellano, por el padre Roberto Personio* (Madrid, 1590), pp. 42–61. See Allison and Rogers, vol. 1, pp. 122–3, entry 894.

[39] In his introduction to the 1971 facsimile of Yepes's *Historia particular,* D.M. Rogers goes on to style Persons's collection "a direct forerunner of the *Historia particular*" (*Diego de Yepes Historia Particular de la Persecucion de Inglaterra Madrid 1599* [London, 1971], p. 3).

[40] "Saunders, Elizabeth, *fl.* 1587" in *A Biographical Dictionary of English Women Writers, 1580–1720,* eds Maureen Bell, George Parfitt, and Simon Shepherd (Boston, 1990) 171–2. The entry reads, in part, "A second letter to Englefield, recounting her experiences in prison survives only in a Spanish translation published by Yepez [sic] in his *Historia Pecular*; a retranslation into English by Dom Adam Hamilton of Buckfast Abbey seems not to have been published" (p. 172).

[41] My deep thanks, again, to Ms Packard Hunter, who translated the passage for me (20

transcription in *Poor Soul's Friend*, the closing of the letters falls in the place of this passage in the Spanish translation.) Without examining the original, of course, it is impossible to say whether this passage was present in the original letter, was added by Persons and then Yepes, or was, for some reason, deliberately omitted from the version in *Poor Soul's Friend*, perhaps merely to conserve space.

The second is one that is known to me, and that I can report, only fortuitously: Father Drainey, who so kindly sent me the typed transcription of Sister Elizabeth's first letter, also sent me a transcription of some additional, stray pages (Val. Ser. II, L. 5, no. 13) that seem to be by her. However, these pages (headed, "A Note, of such Accidents as hath befallen vs in ffraunce") correspond neither to the transcriptions of Sister Elizabeth's letters in *Poor Soul's Friend*, nor to the additional narrative in Persons and Yepes. Rather they recount a different segment of Sister Elizabeth's experiences, not those that occurred in England.

At present, therefore, Sister Elizabeth's letters, which at first seem free of the enigmas that so often characterize early modern women's texts, in fact share a number of these qualities, requiring authentication and the establishment of provenance.

The most likely solution, I think, to the puzzles in this case, is that Sister Elizabeth (perhaps at the behest of Sir Francis Englefield) may have composed a longer narrative than the two letters traditionally ascribed to her. We are all cognizant of the dismayingly poor survival of many written records of the early modern period; in the case of correspondence, the letters from women to which we have (since) published responses by famous male recipients, seem often to have gone missing. One thinks immediately, among Protestant women, of the famously missing letters of Anne Vaughan Lok [Lock, Locke] to John Knox.[42] Recusant women seem to have attempted to keep their texts carefully, but their many forced removals—and especially the plight of the convents when they were forced out of France—led to a mass destruction and dispersal of materials, many of them unlocated to this day.[43]

I would hypothesize that at least portions of Sister Elizabeth's proposed narrative—or a partial typescript of it—may be extant, as the stray typescript sent me indubitably is, even though only one small portion of this narrative, the retelling of "the captivity of the fathers of our religion, named Marsh and Vivian," has ever reached print. I have ascertained, with the very kind assistance of the Abbess of Syon House, South Brent, and of a librarian and an archivist at the University of Exeter (repository of many of the convent's records), that this

---

November 2003); the phrase is hers.

[42] Knox's letters to Lok are printed in *Works of John Knox*, ed. David Laing (6 vols, Edinburgh, 1895). VI: 11–15, 21, 21–7, 30, 83–85, 100–101, 103–4, 107–9, 120–21, 140–41. In some of these letters, there are references to Lok's letters, now apparently lost.

[43] Walker, *Gender and Politics*, esp. ch. 5, "Active in Contemplation: Spiritual Choices and Practices," pp. 130–72.

hypothetical document is held neither in South Brent nor in the university's library.[44] Although I have been unable to travel to Valladolid, Mr. David (Jack) Norton and the Valladolid archivist, Dr. Javier Burrieza Sánchez, found the texts I discuss above among the Englefield Correspondence there, and both Father John Pardo, presently rector of the English College, and Reverend Monsignor Michael William, its former historian, have written that access to the archives is allowed "bona fide researchers who have the proper clearance and references to undertake this kind of work here."[45] I am in touch with a number of repositories holding the papers of Robert Persons, and hope that eventually it will be possible either to verify my hypothesis or to recover other materials that will otherwise explain these discrepancies, and so progress further in the explanation of Sister Elizabeth's presently puzzling letters.

---

[44] Reverend Mother Anna Maria, O.Ss.S, kindly took the time to look through the records herself. Both Archivist Charlotte Berry and Dr Jessica Gardner also responded meticulously to my questions.

[45] E-mail message from Father Pardo (20 November 2003). Monsignor Michael Williams, formerly historian of the college, has confirmed in a separate letter written from his retirement in England (20 November 2003) that "permission is sometimes given for visiting scholars to visit and consult."

Chapter 8

A Civil Conversation
Letters and the Edge of Form

Roger Kuin

Sur le sujet des lettres, je veux dire ce mot, que c'est un ouvrage auquel mes amys tiennent que je puis quelque chose. Et eusse prins plus volontiers ceste forme à publier mes verves, si j'eusse eu à qui parler. Il me falloit, comme je l'ay eu autrefois, un certain commerce qui m'attirast, qui me soutinst, et soulevast. Car de negocier au vent, comme d'autres, je ne sçaurois que de songes, ny forger des vains noms à entretenir en chose serieuse: ennemy juré de toute falsification.

[Touching this subject of Epistles, thus much I wil say; It is a worke wherin my friends are of opinion I can doe some-thing; And should more willingly have undertaken to publish my gifts, had I had who to speake unto. It had bin requisite (as I have had other times) to have had a certaine commerce to draw me on, to encorage me, and to uphold me. For, to go about to catch the winde in a net, as others doe, I cannot; and it is but a dreame. I am a sworne enemie to all falsifications.]

Michel de Montaigne[1]

Story

Thus Montaigne in his *Considérations sur Cicéron*, reminding us that if his friend La Boétie had not died, the *Essais* would have been a correspondence. From the earliest mentions of letters, in the treatise on style attributed to Demetrius of Phaleron, the "certain commerce" to which Montaigne regretfully refers has been seen as the essence of the *e)pi-stolh&*, the "sent thing" ("Isidore construes it as *missa*," says Lipsius[2]): letters are one side of a conversation, they are a conversation between friends, they are the heart's good wishes in brief, they are a

---

[1] Michel de Montaigne, *Essais* (Paris, 1953), p. 290; John Florio, trans., *The essayes ... of Lo: Michaell de Montaigne* (1603), sig. M3ᵛ.

[2] Justus Lipsius, *Principles of Letter-Writing: A Bilingual Text of* Justi Lipsi Epistolica Institutio, trans and eds R.V. Young and Thomas Hester (Carbondale, 1996), p. 5.

gift from one friend to another.[3] Yet almost at the same time and quite as durably, they are, as Montaigne reminds us, "un *ouvrage*," a "*forme à publier* mes verves" (my italics): as Luigi Morozzo put it in 1674, "La lettera è una Orazione in quinta essenzia" (*a letter is in its essence an oration*).[4] It is this perpetual tension, what I call the *edge* of epistolary form, between the murmured conversation of close friends and the public oration conferring glory which I should like to explore a little in the present essay. To limit an otherwise borderless field, I will concentrate on the correspondence of Sir Philip Sidney, a collection of around 300 letters that exhibit almost all the stylistic and other traits of the sixteenth-century familiar *litteræ*. I have chosen five letters from the 300 or so in Sidney's correspondence both because they are representative and, in various ways, interesting: a juvenile exercise in style, an extreme of rhetoric (tongue-in-cheek or no), the much-admired limpidity and unaffectedness of Languet, the brisk yet polite manner of Sidney's final year, and the moving scrawl of a dying young man.

Although the history of the letter is well known, the historical dimension is so much a part of the genre's ethos that it is worth briefly bringing it back. While Babylonian and Greek letters had existed, the Romans were the first great private correspondents of Antiquity. (Undoubtedly, the readier availability of paper had something to do with this, as had the geographic vastness of the Empire which increased the distance between a man and his friends even as good roads made communication easier.) The first monumental collection of letters we have is that of Cicero. These became the foundation of all later Western epistolography; yet the paradox of their early disappearance and their dramatic rediscovery in the Renaissance leads me to defer them here, and consider them rather in that context. The letters of Seneca and of Pliny the Younger were more "literary" and conformed at times to Montaigne's "negocier au vent ... je ne sçaurais que de songes."

More formal, in a monarchic age, were the letters of the Middle Ages. Written by and for Papal Chanceries and Royal secretariats, these required a strictly regulated style and form, graded according to the recipient's rank, and known by the generic term *dictamen*. The authors of the *artes dictaminis*, the handbooks for this kind of writing,[5] took from Cicero's prose certain stylistic features, notably the

---

[3] Cf. *Demetrius On Style*, §§223–35, trans. T.A. Moxon, in *Aristotle's Poetics, Demetrius on Style, Longinus on the Sublime*, ed. John Warrington (London, 1963), pp. 114–17.

[4] Luigi Francesco Morozzo, *Dell'arte delle Lettere missive* (Torino, 1674), quoted in Kathleen T. Butler, *The "Gentlest Art" in Renaissance Italy* (Cambridge, 1954), p. 18.

[5] The earliest known is Albericus of Montecassino (1075–1110); some others are Hugo of Bologna (ca. 1124), Bonum of Florence (ca. 1210), Boncompagno of Signa (ca. 1205), Thomas of Capua (ca. 1240), Johannes Angelicus (ca. 1270), and Brunetto Latini (ca. 1260).

rhythmic sentence- and clause-endings, and grafted these on to a simplified, formal Latin to produce a curious hybrid:

> Verum quia super aliis que proponebantur ex parte sepedicti Paris*iensis episcopi* nobis non potuit *fieri plene fides* causam ipsam vocis *duximus committendam* per apostolica *scripta mandantes.*

> [But because concerning the other matter proposed by the said Bishop of Paris, we could not entirely trust this, we have ordered the case to be debated, in accordance with the apostolic writings.][6]

Official letters written in this kind of prose were divided into parts according to the rules for the classical oration, with a *salutatio*, an *exordium*, a *narratio*, a *petitio*, and a *conclusio*. Their quintessence, in fact, *was* "una Orazione," and the nobler or more regal the addressee, the grander the style.

It was in May 1345 that Francesco Petrarca found, in the Chapter library of Verona, a manuscript of Cicero's letters to Atticus, Quintus Cicero, and Brutus. This momentous find, followed half a century later, in 1392, by Coluccio Salutati's instigating the discovery in the Cathedral library at Vercelli of Cicero's letters to various friends, the *Ad Familiares,* definitively changed European epistolography, essentially by bringing back the familiar letter as a recognized and respected form—by reintroducing, in other words, the civil conversation. The effect on European writing, and perhaps even on European manners, is impossible to overestimate.

Even today, and even in translation, Cicero's letters can be read with pleasure as sublime examples of the "conversation with an absent friend." Here he is, writing from Athens to Cælius Rufus, a friend in Rome, in October of 51 B.C.:

> Quid? Tu me hoc tibi mandasse existimas ut mihi gladiatorum compositones, ut vadimonia dilata et Chresti compilationem mitteres et ea quæ nobis cum Romæ sumus narra nemo audeat? Vide quantum tibi meo iudicio tribuum (nec mehercule iniuria: *poli>tikw&teron* enim te adhuc neminem cognovi): ne illa quidem curo mihi scribas quæ maximis in rebus rei publicæ geruntur cottidie, nisi quid ad me ipsum pertinebit … abs te … ut ab homine longe in posterum prospiciente, futura exspecto, ut ex tuis litteris, cum formam rei publicæ viderim, quale ædificium futurum sit scire possim.

> [Really! Is this what you think I asked you to do—send me pairings of gladiators, court adjournments, Chrestus' pilfering, all the trivia which nobody would dare tell me when I

---

[6] From a letter by Innocent III (A.D. 1199), quoted in A.C. Clark, *Fontes Prosæ Numerosæ* (Oxford: Clarendon, 1909), p. 45. The italics in the Latin text are mine: each italicized phrase represents a rhythmic unit or *cursus*, respectively a *cursus tardus* (/xx/xx), two *cursus veloces* (/xx/x/x), and a *cursus planus* (/xx/x).

am in Rome? Let me show you how highly I value your judgement—and right I am, for I have never known a better politique than you! I do not even want you to tell me day-to-day political developments in matters of major consequence, unless I am affected personally .... What I want from so far-sighted a fellow as yourself is the future. From your letters, having seen, as it were, an architect's drawing of the political situation, I shall hope to know what kind of building is to come.][7]

Cicero's range, of course, extended well beyond such familiarity, as we should expect from the foremost orator of his age. His famous letter to Lucius Lucceius, the politician and historian, of 12 April 55 (B.C.) shows a far more formal style, including the well-known exordium:

Coram me tecum eadem hæc agere sæpe conantem deterruit pudor quidam pæne subrusticus quæ nunc expromam absens audacius; epistula enim non erubescit.

[Although I have more than once attempted to take up my present topic with you face to face, a sort of shyness, almost awkwardness, has held me back. Away from your presence, I shall set it out with less trepidation. A letter has no blushes.][8]

Even here, however, the Latin prose never tips over into speech-making: Cicero is a master of tone, and preserves at all times in his letters a sense of (more or less reflective) immediacy and a real charm. It is scarcely surprising that only a few decades after their discovery, as early as 1419, these letters should have become part of Guarino Guarini's Verona school curriculum.

Another feature of their discovery by Petrarch, however, indicated, and indeed began, a different direction. Cicero had written his letters with a good deal of care, as he wrote all his prose, and their recipients not unnaturally treasured them, both for their pleasing memory of a good and interesting friend, and as the ephemera of a master wordsmith. The letters to Atticus were collected by Atticus himself; those to his other friends, probably by his own freedman Tiro; and these letters were not only collected, but—according to a plan of Cicero's own, not completed before he died—edited, "given out," published, *made public*, shortly after his death in 43 B.C.

This excellent idea had for effect an emphasis on the delicate balance between the letter as conversation and the letter as a literary product, and for consequence a fateful action of Petrarch's. Almost as soon as he had discovered Cicero's letters

---

[7] *Ad Familiares* II.8; no. 80 in Cicero, *Letters to Friends*, trans. and ed. D.R. Shackleton Bailey (3 vols, Cambridge, 2001), vol. 1, pp. 354–7. Unless otherwise noted, references are to this edition.

[8] *Ad Familiares* V.12.

(some say in the very same year[9]), Petrarch began to collect and edit his own—making sure that he would fulfil the same ambition as Cicero's, but during his lifetime. And while it is true that the publication of Petrarch's *Epistolæ de rebus familiaribus* made the *dictatores* and their rigid prescriptions seem old fashioned, his immense authority also kept very much alive the idea of the epistolary genre as a form of self-presentation and a potential source of glory.

On the other hand, Petrarch had learnt from Cicero that the language appropriate to a familiar letter is the *genus humile*, a simple, agreeable style. As Vives wrote in 1534, Cicero's "letters so faithfully reproduce his familiar domestic speech that I think that is exactly the way he spoke with his wife, slaves and relatives, in the forum, in the field, at the baths, in the bedroom or in the dining-room."[10] Or, as Petrarch characterizes his own style (following Cicero's), "hoc mediocre domesticum et familiare dicendi genus."[11] Moreover, he insists—and this he is the first, however glancingly, to theorize—that the style of each letter be adapted not to the rank and grandeur, but to the nature and character of the addressee. And as addressees' personalities are more numerous and varied than their possible ranks, this necessarily gave the letter-writer an almost limitless freedom in choosing his manner.

The first thoroughly to admit this was Desiderius Erasmus in his immensely influential *Opus de conscribendis epistolis* of 1522. The rediscovered Cicero and

---

[9] For example, Ugo Dotti, in the introduction to his edition of *Le Familiari I–IV* (Urbino, 1970), p. 61. The result was three collections of letters, from different periods of Petrarch's life, including some to historical persons: the most moving of these for the present purpose is the opening of his letter to Cicero (*Familiares* XXIV, 3, "written among the living, on the right bank of the Adige, in Verona ... on June 16 in the 1345th year of the Lord you never knew") in the lovely French translation of Pierre de Nolhac: "Tes lettres, que j'ai cherchées si longtemps et trouvées enfin dans le lieu le plus inattendu, je les ai lues avec une avidité extrême. Je t'ai écouté dire de toi-même beaucoup de choses, beaucoup gémir, beaucoup varier, de sorte qu'après t'avoir connu jadis comme maître des autres, ô Marcus Tullius, j'ai appris à te connaître tel que tu as été .... O âme toujours inquiète et anxieuse, ou, pour te faire reconnaître tes propres paroles, vieillard impétueux et disgracié (*o præceps et calamitose senex*), pourquoi as-tu cherché tant de luttes, excité tant de haines sans aucun profit? ... Hélas! oublieux des conseils de ton frère et de tes propres préceptes de sagesse, tu as été comme un voyageur portant un flambeau dans la nuit, et tu éclairais seulement pour ceux qui te suivaient le chemin où tu es misérablement tombé." Pierre de Nolhac, *Pétrarque et l'humanisme* (2 vols, 2nd rev. edn, Paris, 1965), vol. 1, p. 257. For a useful discussion of Petrarch and his several collections of letters, see also Marco Ariani, *Petrarca* (Rome, 1999), pp. 167–193.

[10] Juan Luis Vives, *De Conscribendis Epistolis*, in Lippi Brandolini, *De ratione scribendi tres ... adiecti sunt Io. Ludovici Vivis ... de conscribendis epistolis libelli* (Frankfurt, 1568), p. 310, sig. X5[v]. All further citations from this edition.

[11] Francesco Petrarca, *Le Familiari, Libri I–IV*, ed. Ugo Dotti (Urbino, 1970), p. 81 (I, 1, section 16).

his brilliant follower Petrarch had now been joined by a third giant, and this one had not only written and published hundreds of letters, but produced the genre's first major work of theory. Erasmus writes with his usual verve, never more than when he is demolishing real or imaginary opponents and defending liberty. As a modern scholar puts it:

> Il y a dans le relatif désordre de cette œuvre quelque chose d'inspiré, d'allègre, d'irrésistible, la délectation victorieuse d'un homme qui non seulement a fait de sa propre culture une seconde nature, mais qui a découvert dans ce naturel supérieur un principe de liberté propre à déchirer toutes les bandelettes de la *persona* officielle.

> [There is, in this work's relative disorder, something inspired, blithe, irresistible: the triumphant delight of a man who not only has made of his own culture a second nature, but who in this superior naturalness has discovered a principle of freedom capable of ripping off all the swaddlings of the official *persona*.][12]

What is crucial here is that while Erasmus celebrates the freedom conferred by the letter's close relationship with its addressee, he is careful to distinguish this freedom from license. The culture that has become second nature makes him stress that

> … ego eam Epistolam optimam judico, quæ a vulgato hoc & indocto literarum genere quam longissime recedat: quæ sententiis exquisitissimis, verbis electissimis, sed aptis constet: quæ argumento, loco, tempori, personæ, quam maxime sit accommodata, quæ amplissimis de rebus agens, sit gravissima: de mediocribus, concinna: de humilibus, elegans, & faceta …

> [I consider that epistle best which gets farthest away from that vulgar and unlearned kind of letters (that is, the strictly legislated): which consists of the most exquisite ideas and the most beautifully chosen yet appropriate words: which is maximally fitted to the argument, the place, the time, (and) the person; which in dealing with great matters is gravest; with middling matters, neat; with low things, elegant and witty.][13]

And in all this variety, he says, letters should still achieve a unity of tone: always elegant (*munda*), always educated (*erudita*), always healthy (*sana*). Clearly, Erasmus is not concerned to jettison the careful balance of what one might now

---

[12] Marc Fumaroli, "Genèse de l'épistolographie classique: rhétorique humaniste de la lettre de Pétrarque à Juste Lipse," *Revue de l'histoire littéraire de la France* 78.6 (1978): 889. This article is one of the finest pieces extant on the subject, for the mastery of its insights and the elegance of its writing.

[13] *De ratione conscribendi epistolas liber,* cap. VI, in Desiderius Erasmus, *Desiderii Erasmi Roterodami Opera Omnia*, ed. P. van der Aa (10 vols, Leiden, 1703–1706), vol. 1, col. 349.

almost call "private" and "public" aspects of the epistolary genre; and indeed, he gives a wealth of impeccably traditional and highly formal rhetorical advice, which has led some scholars to conclude that his intended audience consisted not so much of students but of teachers.[14]

There is, though, no contradiction between his stressing of freedom and this insistence on rhetoric. As Fumaroli puts it: "the choice of a style harmoniously fitted in each case to the numerous variables which rule the writing of a letter is an operation too complex and delicate to be left to spontaneity." Rhetoric here is the instrument for the training of instinct, in its strict considerations to be left behind upon the maturing of personal civilization and taste: it is "la pédagogie d'une culture, d'un goût, d'une liberté de la parole"(*the teaching of a civilization, of taste, of a [certain] freedom of speech*).[15] And this freedom once achieved, as the familiar letter at its best is a conversation between absent friends, the characteristics it loves are *simplicitas, candor, festivitas,* and *argutia* (simplicity, sincerity, gaiety, and what can best be translated as a lively sagacity).[16]

We shall have occasion to glance at Erasmus again; but it may be worth just mentioning the other two influential sixteenth-century texts on letter-writing. The Spanish humanist Juan Luis Vives published his work, which respectfully borrows Erasmus' title, in 1534; due to the large number of editions of the Dutchman's work, the two to a certain extent circulated at the same time. Vives abbreviates: instead of the many types of letters Erasmus enumerates, he makes his own categories—letters of information, petition, recommendation, and advice. He stresses not only the character of the recipient, as Erasmus had done, but the recipient's feelings, "*ut absit species omnis arrogantiæ*"—so that all semblance of arrogance may be avoided.[17]

Vives, in a way, kept Erasmus' ideas alive for a following generation. He too believed in the letter as a cultured freedom, the product of a mind and a skill trained in rhetoric; he, too, appreciates the ideal letter's varied qualities:

> There should be no letter in which there is not some virtue of the mind and some pleasing charm, and in which there does not appear, here some innocent modesty, there some reverence; now friendliness, now some kind and moderate dignity; then again trust toward a friend, faithfulness, goodwill, respect of integrity, serenity even to enemies, and a certain equanimity.[18]

---

[14] For example, Erika Rummel, "Erasmus' Manual of Letter-writing: Tradition and Innovation," *Renaissance and Reformation* 25.3 (1989): 299–312.

[15] Fumaroli, p. 890 (my translation).

[16] Erasmus, vol. 1, cap. VII, col. 350. Fumaroli sees in this liberty and simplicity an analogy with the qualities of the Christian soul saved from sin, in the theological view of Erasmus (p. 890).

[17] Vives, *De Conscribendis*, p. 286, sig. S7ᵛ.

[18] Vives, *De Conscribendis*, p. 305, sig. V1ʳ.

Finally, Vives recognizes, agrees with, and maintains the fine line, the delicate balance, the *edge*, of the great tradition. Not only is the letter "a reflection of daily conversation and continued dialogue, and it was invented for no other purpose than to report and represent the conversations of those who are absent from one another"; at the same time, "every letter should have some excellence to commend it, either in subject matter or diction, so that it will gladly be read by those to whom it is sent, *and also by posterity if it reaches them.*"[19]

The final work on epistolography I want briefly to remember here was written (though not published) during Sir Philip Sidney's lifetime by one of his correspondents. Justus Lipsius, the great Dutch scholar and thinker, had published a *Century* of his own letters with a preface in 1586; his *Epistolica Institutio* was printed by Raphelengius, Christopher Plantin's son-in-law, at the latter's printing-house in 1591. If Vives was more concise than Erasmus, Lipsius seems positively condensed. He drops most of the elements of rhetoric and virtually all the laborious examples that Erasmus had adopted and adapted from the *artes dictaminis* he so decried. He looks at the origin of letters and their nature, their beginnings and endings, all with admirable brevity, and then comes to the organization of content, where he divides letters into *serious, learned,* and *familiar.* "Serious" (*seria*) he calls a letter "which pertains to public or private matters, but also treats them fully and carefully"; a "learned" (*docta*) letter is one which "appertains to knowledge or wisdom" and "dresses up a non-epistolary subject in the garment of a letter."[20]

As always, though, such letters are in practice mentioned only for completeness' sake: like other authors, what Lipsius really wants to get to is the *familiaris*, the "familiar" letter, "quæ res tangit nostras aut circa nos, quæque in assidua vita"—which touches our affairs or those around us, and deals with our daily life. "This is the proper and most common subject of a letter; and, if we are willing to admit the truth, the only one belonging to it."[21] With his usual realism, he then goes on to say that the serious and the learned are often mixed with the familiar letter (as we see in the Sidney correspondence, where the *seria*, at least, is splendidly represented by his *Letter to the Queen, touching her Marriage with Monsieur*, and where the exchanges with Hubert Languet are continually larded with both serious and learned discussions of international politics and principles of government).

The qualities a letter needs, continues Lipsius, are *brevitas* (brevity), *perspicuitas* (clarity), *simplicitas* (simplicity), *venustas* (elegance or charm), and *decentia* (decorum). Clarity and simplicity are not the same—the former is about comprehensibility, the latter about unadorned forthrightness, "candorem liberæ mentis," the candor of a free mind. *Decentia* is the fittingness (translated from the

---

[19] Vives, *De Conscribendis*, p. 344, sig. X4ᵛ; p. 352, sig. Y8ᵛ, emphasis added.

[20] Lipsius, *Principles of Letter-Writing*, p. 21.

[21] Lipsius, *Principles of Letter-Writing*, p. 21.

Greek τό πρέπον) that adapts the whole of a letter to the subject and, especially, to the recipient. Brevity is a major quality (perhaps *the* major one), but—interestingly—only for adults: like simplicity, it is not to be attempted by the very young, nor to be expected of them, as they will get it wrong.[22]

I have ended this quick overview with Lipsius because he was a correspondent of Sidney's, of Sidney's time and, to some extent, of Sidney's mind. They knew each other in the Netherlands; Lipsius' treatise on Latin pronunciation was written in answer to a question of Sidney's, and dedicated to him.[23] Had Sidney written an *Institution of a Letter-Writer* as well as *Defence of Poesy*, it would probably have been wittier (in our sense) than Lipsius', but its ideas would in many ways have resembled his. It is, then, in one sense the best commentary to set beside Sidney's correspondence when looking at the particular edge that is my subject here.

The *Epistolica Institutio*, like the letters it praises, is deceptively simple and unadorned. Marc Fumaroli's beautiful expression of its implications may be allowed to lead us out of this historical review towards real letters, their writing and reading:

> Lipse découvre, ou du moins approfondit, la spiritualité de la situation épistolaire, deux solitudes méditatives qui se croisent dans le silence et l'absence, qui échangent des connivences dans la nuit du temps.[24]

> [Lipsius discovers, or at least deepens our sense of, the spiritual aspect of a correspondence: two thoughtful solitudes which meet in silence and in absence, exchanging affinities in the dark of time.]

Fumaroli then adds a comment that, although referring specifically to Lipsius, sums up the whole of Classical and Renaissance theory and practice of the letter, on its characteristic edge between public and private, between rhetoric and chat:

> Il en va de l'épistolier lipsien comme des comédiens de l'Art: son improvisation est un trompe l'œil qui cache les rouages d'une mnémotechnique et les roueries d'un art quotidiennement exercé.[25]

> [Lipsius' writer of letters is like the actors of the *commedia dell'arte*: his improvisation is a *trompe l'œil* which hides the machinery of memory training and the machinations of an art practiced every day.]

---

[22] Lipsius, *Principles of Letter-Writing*, p. 27.

[23] Justus Lipsius, *De recta pronunciacione Latinæ linguæ dialogus* (Leiden, 1586). On the relations between Sidney and Lipsius, see Jan A. van Dorsten, *Poets, Patrons, and Professors: Sir Philip Sidney, Daniel Rogers, and the Leiden Humanists* (Oxford, 1962).

[24] Fumaroli, p. 897.

[25] Fumaroli, p. 899.

Letters

Five letters from the copious Sidney correspondence will, I hope, illuminate the ideas coming from the Ancients and the Renaissance, some of which have been outlined here. The first is a piece of *juvenilia*: it is, in fact, the first piece of writing by Philip Sidney to have come down to us. Written to Sir William Cecil by a precocious fourteen-year-old, it beautifully shows both the careful learning of Ciceronian templates and the elaboration the theorists (Erasmus, Vives, and Lipsius) consider proper for a young man. (I give the Latin as well as my translation, since it is the working of the Latin language that is the essence, as well as in part the conscious subject, of the letter.)

Philip Sidney to Sir William Cecil, Oxford, 12 March 1569 (Feuillerat I)[26]

> Mirifica tua beneficia in me (nullo meo merito) cumulatissimè collata (egregie vir) faciunt ut (licet per tempus commòde et uti me decet non possim) hasce tame*n* ad te literas præscribam; Quod no*n* eò quidem facio, ut inde queas diiudicare qua*n*tos progressus in literis latinis habeam. Qua in re et verè et no*n* sine graui dolore meo fateor satisfacere me nullo modo posse, vel expectationi tuæ vel cupiditati meæ. Istas aut*em* consilio ad te nunc mitto, ne nomine negligenti*æ* ei suspectus sim, cuius in me tanta exta*n*t beneficia, ut si vitam pro eius dignitaté profunda*m*, nullam parte*m* videar tuoru*m* meritoru*m* assequutus. Hæc igitur me una causa impulit, hasce ut ad te nunc de*m* , et ut meis ineptiis te su*m*mis grauissimisq*ue* occupationibus distentu*m*, et implicatu*m* iam interpellem, ut qua possum ratione intelligas, beneficia in me tua quà*m* grata memoria cola*m*: et ea ex animo meo excidere quà*m* nullo modo sina*m*. Te vero etià*m* atq*ue* etiam rogo, ut quod ab optima voluntate, sit profectum, id in bonam partem accipias, nec tam audaciam et temeritate*m* mea*m* reprehendas, q*ui* tibi scribe*n*do molestus sim, qua*m* probes studiu*m* animu*m*que in te meu*m*, qui officii et obseruantiæ erga te meæ, quos possum libentissime velim, apud te testes deponere mihi quidem p*er*fecto, in om*n*i vitæ cursu, res ta*m* erit nulla proposita, qua*m* ut quotidiè veheme*n*tius, de me optime meritu*m* esse lætere. Vale. Oxonii 12° Martii a° 1568.
> Tui deditissimus,
> Philippus Sidneius

> [Your remarkable (and entirely undeserved) kindnesses to me, most copiously conferred, excellent Sir, urge me to write you this letter, even though time does not permit me to do so properly and as I ought. I certainly do not do it in order that from it you may judge my progress in Latin letters: on that score I must truly and not without much grief confess that I can in no way satisfy either your expectation or my desire. But I send you this now, so that I may not be suspected of negligence towards him who has

---

[26] The original is in the National Archives, State Papers Domestic, Elizabeth (SP12), vol. 49, no. 63, fols 135–6. In these transcripts, italics are used to expand scribal abbreviations.

shown me so many kindnesses that if I gave my life for his dignity I should not attain any part of your merits. So this one reason has impelled me: that I owe you this now, and that having in your exalted and most serious business distracted and entangled you with my fooleries, I may now interrupt you to let you understand as clearly as I can with how much gratitude I honour the memory of your kindnesses, and how determined I am never to let them be erased from my mind. I do however most earnestly implore you that as this letter proceeds from the best possible intentions you will accept it in good part; and that you will not disapprove my boldness and temerity in bothering you by writing, but rather recognize my duty and affection toward you. I should very much like to let you have it as the best possible testimony of my duty and service to you; and when I have run through the whole course of my life, nothing will possibly be able to have befallen me that will so utterly deserve my daily increasing joy and celebration. Farewell. From Oxford, 12 March 1568 (1569). Yours most devotedly,
Philip Sidney]

In an effort such as this, the fact and the form combine to make the letter: there is nothing in between. The letter, in the normal sense, is not *about* anything it actually says: it is about itself, about being a Latin letter, written in the approved mold by a young scholar. It is also—as the approved model stipulates—adapted to the addressee, who is a grand and very busy statesman, as well as an occasional friend of the family.

The next letter is an example of the degee to which rhetoric can rise (or sink) in an actual situation. It was written to Sidney in September 1574 by Matthäus Wacker, an acquaintance of Sidney's friend and mentor Hubert Languet. Wacker and Sidney had been students at Padua together: Wacker was still there, Sidney had gone on to Vienna to join Languet.

Matthæus Wacker to Philip Sidney, Padua, 27 September 1574[27]

Salve in Domino Iesv CHRISTO.

Sic me Deus benè amet, Illustris ac generose Domine Sydnaee; ut nihil mihi gratius accidere & jocundius potuit litteris tuis: quibus tu servulum tuum alloqui, & pro humanitate tua benignissime amplexari non es dedignatus. Itàne verò beatum Wackerum, ut a Sydneio litteras accipiat? ita me felicem, ut is, cujus ego iampridem seruitiis me totum addixi, sua manu amicissimam ad me epistolam exaret? Profectò (dicam enim quod verum est) cum litteras inspicerem; & cum tàm insignia annuli, quam manum ipsam agnoscerem; immò cum totas jam secundo perlegerem; vix tamen adduci ut crederem potui, eas ab Illustri tua Magnificentiae proficisci. Quid enim ego minus expectare potui, quam abs te litteras? Ac si quae ab humanitate tua venissent, in iis quid minus sperare debui quam excusationem illam tam diligentem tamque exquisitam

---

[27] The original is in Yale University Library MS Osborn fa. 14, fols 36–7.

abitionis tuae? Enimverò cogitavi hic sub alieno nomine tui te Wackere admonet officii: & quando sese tam diligenter excusat: quid tibi faciendum fuisse, scribit.

Planè *enim* si quod res est fateri velim, mei erat muneris, nonmodo discedenti tibi, quod tu scribis, valedicere: verumetiam abeuntem quibuscumq*ue* poteram servitiorum generib*us* prosequi: & quantopere mihi discessus ille insperat*us* dolori esset, non verbis tantum, verum

etiam lachrymis meis testari. Sed sive verè tu scribis: sive quod mihi lubet suspicari *texnikw>j*: utriq*ue* sanè obstitit summa

omnium rerum perturbatio: quae non modo imprudentib*us* & occupatis: sed etiam diligentissimo cuiq*ue* facile negotium potuit facessere. Ante cognovi de discessu tuo, quàm te abiturum à nobis rescirem: ante rescivi; quàm crederem: ante credere coact*us* sum; quam vellem, aut certè q*uam* optarem. Patavium Venetiis reversus, cum ad hospitium vetus tuum, cum ad amicos communes venissem: praeter famam nominis tui, praeterq*ue* suavissimam de te atq*ue* honorificentissimam apud omnes memoriam neminem inveni. Restabat infelici mihi, praeter litteras, nihil quib*us* me tibi excusare: quib*us* vel à negligentia vel à superbia me purgare: quib*us* deniq*ue* valedicere homini amici optimèq*ue* de me merito possem. Sed iis ipsis hacten*us* obstitit, cum pudor quidam meus penè subrustic*us*: tùm negotiorum tuorum multitudo. Hinc *enim* ne plus quàm satis occupato molest*us* nugis meis essem, verebar: illinc ne imprudentiam meam, fateri cogerer metuebam. Ita factum est, ut dum neq*ue* in scribendo audaculus: neq*ue* in me purgando temerarius videri volo; satis multi dies intercurrerint qui non modo nihil è concepto semel dolore levare, verumetiam eundem temporis progressu augere mihi majoremque reddere videbantur. Donec tandem ad vi tid. Sept. exoptatissima illa tua ad me perlata epistola est: quam ego non modo, quod in communib*us* illis fieri consuevit, legi atq*ue* relegi: verum etiam quod in gratiorib*us* facere solem*us*, saepenumero exosculat*us* sum: & inter caetera mea, quae in carissimis habeo, *keimh/lia* diligentissime reposui. Ex illa non modo respirandi facul:

tatem nact*us*: sed etiam tibi respondendi occasionem adeptus: arrepto in man*us* calamo subito has ad te exarandas litteras magna cum opportunitate putavi: partim ut me quoq*ue* tibi, quod hac ratione factum censeo, purgarem: partim ut officii muneriq*ue* meo satisfacerem. Tibi vero mi Colendissime D*o*mine Sydnaee, & singularis huius humanitatis nomine, & caeterorum tuorum in me beneficorum, non quas debeo: sed quas possum gratias habeo plurimas maximasq*ue* ac te oro: ut quod in litteris tuis ultro recipis, in me amando atq*ue* tuendo nemini cedas: quando ego jampridem ita erga te affect*us* sum; ut fideliorem me clientem nec habeas quenq*uam*, nec ullum facile unq*uam* (pace omnium dixerim) sis habiturus. Quod

futurum quo omnem tibi de eo dubitandi occasionem eximam quod ut q*uam* optimum & quam maximo cum utriusq*ue* commodo fiat,ex animo exopto. Vale. D*omin*us Iesvs laudatissim*i*s conatib*us* tuis benedicat: & ab om*ni*b*us* ce malis spiritu suo q*uam* potentissim*e* tueatur. Amen.   Patauio. *die veneris* . iv tid. Sept.

An*n*o ultimi saeculi MDLXXIV
Illust*ri*s et C*e*lsitudinis Servulus
Matthæus Wacker Constantinus

Illustrem & Generosum D*omin*um Comitem Hanovium Illust*ri*s & Gene*ro*sissimae reverenter: ornatissim*os* D*omin*os Veltspergium, C*e*lsitudinis tuae Brusquetum, Delium: imprimis clarissim*um* D*omin*um Languetum, D*omin*um patronum, ac patrem (si patitur)

Servulus meum, amanter atque studiosissime saluto. Resalutant te quam diligentissime Barones Lichtenstenii.

[Greetings in the name of our Lord Jesus Christ.

May God so love me, illustrious and noble Master Sidney, that nothing more welcome and more joyful can befall me than your letter, in which you have spoken to your little servant and have not disdained in your kindness most magnanimously to embrace him. Is Wacker truly so blessed as to receive a letter from Sidney? Am I so fortunate that he, to whose service I long ago utterly dedicated myself, should with his own hand address to me an epistle of uttermost friendship? Indeed (for I will speak the truth) when I examined the letter; and when I recognised both the sign of the ring and the hand itself; and when, what is more, I had already read it through for the second time; I could hardly bring myself to believe that it had come from your Illustrious Magnificence. For what less could I have expected than a letter from you? And even if by your kindness one should come, what less should I hope for in it than that your so scrupulous and so exquisite apology for your departure? For truly, "Here," thought I, "under another name it is you, Wacker, whom he is reminding of your duty: and when he is so scrupulously excusing himself, he is really writing what you should have done."

For clearly, if the truth were told, it was up to me not only to say goodbye to you as you were leaving, as you write (you should have done): but also to accompany your departure with whatever services were in my power; and to witness to the grief that unhoped-for farewell caused me, not so much with words as with my tears. Yet whether you write truly or—as it is my whim to suspect—*pour la forme*, in either case the obstacle was the frightful confusion of affairs, which has effortlessly succeeded in upsetting not only the improvident and the busy, but even the plans of the most diligent. I heard that you had left before I knew that you planned to; I knew that you planned to before I believed it; I was forced to believe it before I wanted to, or certainly earlier than I should have liked. When I returned to Padua from Venice, I went to see your old landlord; I went to see the friends we shared; but apart from the renown of your name, apart from the most delightful and most honourable memory that everyone retains of you, I found no one. So for poor unfortunate me there was no way other than a letter to excuse myself, to clear myself from suspicions of either grave negligence or overweening pride, or—finally—to say farewell to a man who is a friend and deserves nothing but the best from me. But even this was hindered, on the one hand by a certain almost clownish shamefastness on my part; on the other, by the multitude of your engagements. For the latter made me fear that my trifles and I would merely be a bother to you in the press of your affairs; while the former, that I should have to confess my lack of foresight. Thus it is that while I did not want to seem cheeky in writing nor overbold in my penitence, the days went by, quite a few in fact; yet their passing seemed not only in no way to diminish my grief once contracted, but indeed with time only to increase and augment it. Until at last on September 9th that your so cherished epistle was brought to me: which I not only read and reread as one does normally, but rather (as we do with the ones we truly welcome) held it many times to my lips and with utmost care put it away among my most cherished bedside treasures. Not only did it allow me to breathe again, but it gave me the occasion to reply to you: I thought it the perfect opportunity at once to take pen in hand and begin a letter to you, partly to perform my penance to you, which I think I will in this way have done, and partly to do my duty.

Truly, most worshipful Master Sidney, I greatly and heartily thank you, not as much as I should but as well as I can, both for this singular kindness and for your other favours toward me; and I beseech you as you freely promise in your letter, to yield to none in love and care for me: because I already long ago became so devoted to you that you neither have, nor will easily ever have, a client more faithful than myself (I should maintain this against all comers). I heartily wish that you may never have occasion to doubt this, and that it will happen as soon and as much as possible, to our mutual advantage.

Farewell. May the Lord Jesus bless your most praiseworthy projects and protect you to the utmost with His Spirit from all evils. Amen. From Padua, Friday September 11th in this year of the last age 1574.
Your Illustrious and most Noble Highness's
little servant
Matthæus Wacker of Constanz

My reverent greetings to the Illustrious and Noble Count Hanau; friendly and affectionate regards to the most excellent Masters Welsperg, Bryskett, Delius; and especially to the most renowned Master Languet, my Lord, patron and (if I may call him so) a father to me. The Barons Lichtenstein most heartily return your greetings.]

To many, the key word in this letter will be "client." This, they will think, explains the almost ridiculous elaboration of the *sermo*: the whole thing is mere toady-butter to a hoped-for patron. It is, indeed, a letter to one from whom occasional patronage is expected; but Wacker was by no means a nobody or an insignificant figure, and the two had in fact been fellow-students at Padua until quite recently. Had this experience taught Wacker that Sidney could not abide extravagant flattery at any price, he would not have written as he did. On the other hand, Sidney cannot have taken the discourse of such a missive seriously, however benevolent he may have felt toward Wacker's friendship and future clienthood. How, then—and especially in the context of the (discursive) "edge" between private murmur and public oration which is our subject here—are we to take the epistolography? The real key, I suspect, is their recent fellowship at Padua. Sidney may have been a serious youth in many ways, but what we are seeing here is very like a tongue-in-cheek piece of fustian bravura. Its charm, in fact, derives from the fact that, in Erasmian terms, it is *jocans*: both sender and addressee know the *fiorituri* for what they are, and can in friendly irony enjoy the Ciceronian tags (the *pudor subrusticus,* from the letter to Lucceius; *non quas debeo sed quas possum gratias habeo*; not yielding to anyone in your love for me, etc.) for what they are—the edge of form parodied in an amused, *over-the-edge* shared memory of European boyhood learning.

Even this, though, may be too simple a view. One noteworthy feature of Wacker's "epistle" (he significantly uses both *litteræ* and *epistola* for "letter," unlike almost all the other correspondents) is that all the specific personal matter is relegated to a postscript. This is a fairly common practice in certain cases, and it is itself a clue to another aspect of the epistle we are dealing with. "From Petrarch onwards," writes Kathleen Butler, "men who prided themselves on their letters, or knew that others set store by them, tended to relegate all items of a trivial or ephemeral character to the last paragraph, or even to a postscript, either of which could easily be detached without injury to the rest of the letter."[28] Wacker may be writing his flights of rhetoric with his tongue in his cheek; but the thought of publication is perhaps not entirely absent from his naively self-satisfied mind.

A glance at Sidney's epistolary legacy would not be complete without an example from his nine-year correspondence with Hubert Languet. One side of this correspondence—the older man's letters to the younger—was printed as early as 1633, and the French scholar Claude Sarrau wrote to his Burgundian friend Claude Saumaise a few years later, "Habeo prae manibus pusillum volumen Epistolarum Huberti Langueti popularis tui, quod quanti faciam dicere vix ac ne vix quidem possim. Nemo ita familiariter, ita pure scribit" [I have in my hands a little volume of the letters of Hubert Languet your countryman, and I can hardly express— indeed I cannot express at all—how much I prize it. Nobody writes so familiarly, in such pure Latin].[29]

Hubert Languet to Sidney, Frankfurt, 7 October 1577[30]

Literæ quas Illustrissimus Dux Iohannes Casimirus ornatissimo Domino Belo ad te dedit, tibi documento erunt nos non infœliciter apud ipsum perfecisse id quod ad nobis petebas. Meministi cujus injecta sit mentio cum ad ostia Mœni obambularemus. Elector Brandenburgensis eo dicitur respicere, verum alterius constantia ejus dignitate & amplitudine hactenus expugnari non potuit, adeo alte concepta spes animo insederat. Iam igitur gemet ubi se frustra constantem fuisse, ac concepta spe excidisse intelliget. Obsecro ut mihi ignoscas quod in flagitando responso ad ea de quibus inter nos convenerat, modum forte excesserim. Ego testor Deum me id fecisse studio conservandæ tuæ existimationis, quod ita ardeo ut ex nulla re majorem voluptatem capiam quam cum audio te ex aliqua re laudem reportasse. Fiducia etiam mei summi erga te amoris ac tuæ humanitatis facit ut mihi persuadem omnia mihi apud te licere, nec sum valde solicitus quid de me sentias, modo de tua erga me benevolentia nihil remittas. Legi literas Illustrissimi Comitis Leicestriæ ad ducem Ioannem Casimirum, ex quarum lectione summam voluptatem cepi : sunt enim testes ardentissimi ejus erga te amoris, & summæ spei, quam de tua virtute concepit. Vide igitur ne consistas in medio ardui [*p.*

---

[28] Butler, *The "Gentlest Art" in Renaissance Italy*, p. 7.

[29] Hubert Languet, *Huberti Langueti galli Epistolae ad Philippum Sydneium equitem anglum*, ed. David Dalrymple (Edinburgh, 1776), p. 7.

[30] The original is lost; this text is taken from the second printed edition, *Huberti Langueti ... Epistolae Politicae et Historicae ad Philippum Sydnaeum* (Leiden, 1646), no. LVIII, pp. 282–6.

284] illius callis, cui hactenus institisti, sed enitere ad summum quo possis ejus expectationi de te satisfacere, ac voluptatem ei pro benevolentia referre, & patriæ tibi & tuis, plurimum prodesse. Expeditissima autem ad eam rem via est, si te maxime familiarem præbeas iis ex quorum consuetudine non solum voluptatem capias, sed etiam utilitatem referas : nam non dubito (ut solet in aulis accidere) quin multi tuam familiaritatem ambiant, non solum propter tuam virtutem, sed etiam propter tuam fortunam & sua commoda : cujusmodi homines plerunque comparant se ad assentandum & dant operam ut potius jucunda quam honesta aut utilia suggerant iis apud quos aliquid ambiunt. Novi autem tuam facilitatem, quæ quidem est virtus eximia, & præsertim in ista tua fortuna, modo non patiaris alios ea abuti. Vide ad quas ineptias progrediar calore animi, dum scribens mihi persuadeo, me aliqua ex parte tuis suavissimis colloquiis frui. Fuit mihi gratissimum post multos annos frui conspectu & consuetudine ornatissimi Domini Beli, amici veteris & charissimi [*p. 285*], quem quidem video dignitate, prudentia & rerum usu auctum, sed infracto animo erga aulicas vanitates, & erga amicos nihil immutatum. Quid de eo sentiam, dudum tibi aperui. Nullum hominem novi, qui plura sciat quæ ego ignorem & valde cupiam scire. Gaudeo te jam arctiorem amicitiam contraxisse cum D. Plessæo. Nihil ejusmodi amicis preciosius comparare tibi potes. Germania pacata esset, nisi eam sua ambitione & arrogantia turbarent theologi : ab iis enim persuasus, elector Palatinus pleraque acta sanctissimi sui parentis rescindit, & ejus memoriam quantum in se est conculcat. Pellit ex ecclesiis & scholis innumeros viros doctos & pios, quos ejus parens magno studio ad se pellexerat, nec ut id perficeret, quandiu regnavit ulli labori aut pecuniæ pepercit. Audio eos, qui pelluntur, septingentorum numerum excedere. Pelluntur præterea adolenscentuli, quos sua pecunia in literarum studiis alebat pater. Pulsi sunt nuper Heidelberga centum, ex quibus unicus in gratiam Principis a puriore religione defecit. Ea autem severitate (ut nihil durius [*p. 286*] dicam) utitur Princeps, ut miseri pueri rerum omnium inopes, & ignari quo se recipiant, jussi sint statim excedere e scholis in quibus habitabant, & ne quidem obulus est ipsis datus ad viaticum. Publicæ viæ in hac tota vivinia refertæ sunt miseris illis hominibus qui fere omnes confugiunt ad Illustrissimum Principem Johannem Casimirum, qui recipit quotquot potest, eos vero quibus in sua ditione prospicere non potest, prosequitur viatico. Comes Iohannes Nassaviensis se etiam erga plurimos beneficum exhibet. Ego profecto de his rebus sine summo dolore cogitare non possum. Misi nuper ad te libellum de præsidiis Hungaricis, quam peto ut scribas an acceperis. Scripsi etiam de remittenda syngrapha Baronis Slavatæ : nam debitam tibi pecuniam Pragensi Bibliopolæ numeravit. Bene vale. Francofurti non*arum* die Octob. 1577.

[The letter which the most noble Duke John Casimir gave the most excellent Master Beale for you will show you that we have not unsuccessfully achieved with him what you asked us to. You remember who was mentioned when we strolled together at the mouth of the Main. The Elector of Brandenburg is said to nurse hopes in that direction, but so far the other's constancy has not been conquered by his dignity and grandeur, so highly-conceived a hope had settled in his mind. Now he is complaining that he has been constant in vain, and he understands that, just as he had conceived a hope, he has failed.

I beg you to forgive me that in urging a reply to that which we had agreed, I had overstepped the limits. As God is my witness I did it only out of zeal to maintain your reputation, for which I care so strongly that nothing can give me greater pleasure than to hear that something has covered you with glory. Indeed, the confidence bred by my great love for you and your kindness convinces me that with you I can permit myself anything: and I am not much concerned with what you may think of me, as long as you abate nothing of your good will towards me.

I have read the letter of the most noble Earl of Leicester to Duke Casimir. Reading it gave me complete pleasure, for it is a testimony of his most eager affection for you and the supreme hope he has contracted of your virtue. So take care you do not stop in the middle of that hard road which you have so far chosen, but struggle on up to the summit of what you are capable of, in order to satisfy his expectations of you, to give him pleasure in return for his benevolence, and to be of the greatest possible value to your country, to yourself and to your family. The shortest road to achieving that is by showing yourself as friendly as possible to those whose company can give you not only pleasure but use also: for I have no doubt that (as happens in courts) many seek out your company, not only for your quality but also because of your good fortune and its benefits. Most such men are preparing to flatter you and attempt to propose things more pleasurable than useful to those from whom they want something. Still, I know your good nature, which is an excellent virtue, especially in your condition, will not let others abuse it. Notice to what idiocies I am led by my enthusiasm: while I write I am persuaded that I am somehow enjoying the great pleasure of your conversation!

It was a great joy, after all these years, to enjoy (again) the sight and the company of the most excellent Master Beale, my old and very dear friend, and to see him, moreover, matured in dignity, prudence and experience, yet as solid as ever against the vanities of Court and unchanged towards his friends. What I feel about him I told you long ago. I have never known a man who knows so much that I do not but would dearly love to. I am very glad that you have already struck up a deeper friendship with M. Du Plessis. You can acquire nothing more precious than such friends.

Germany would be pacified by now, if the theologians did not disturb it with their ambition and arrogance; for, persuaded by them, the Elector Palatine is rescinding several laws made by his sainted father, whose memory he is trampling underfoot as much as possible. He is expelling from the churches and schools numberless pious and learned men, whom his father had taken great trouble to attract and for whom, in order to do it properly, he had as long as he lived spared neither labour nor money. I hear that those who are being expelled number more than seventy. Also expelled are (a number of) youngsters whom his father supported with scholarships for the study of letters. Recently 100 were expelled from Heidelberg, of whom only one, to please the Prince, renounced the reformed religion. Yet the Prince is using this severity (to use no stronger term) to order poor boys, lacking in everything, and ignorant why this is happening, to move at once out of the schools where they were living, without their getting even a penny's travelling-money. In this whole area the public roads are filled with such miserable men who are almost all fleeing to that most excellent Prince John Casimir. He is taking as many as he can, and is giving travel funds to those he cannot provide for in his jurisdiction. Count John of Nassau is also helping several of them. I cannot even think of these things without the greatest possible pain.

I have just sent off to you the little text on the Hungarian fortifications—please write and let me know when you receive it. I have written also about cancelling the bond of Baron Slavata: for he has paid on your behalf what you owed to the Prague bookseller. Farewell. Frankfurt, the Nones of October 1577.]

At first sight, after the conscious *elegantiæ* of young Wacker and very young Philip, this seems long and chaotic. Subjects follow one another without apparent relation; neither in Latin nor in English is the style very *soigné*; the writer seems to jump, as his fellow Frenchmen might put it, from the rooster to the donkey. Let us, though, not forget "ita familiariter, ita pure," a compliment from an expert. For when we compare this letter—which Languet would have referred to as *literæ*, though his posthumous publisher referred to it as an *epistola*—to those of the greatest of Latin letter-writers, we shall see that in fact of all Sidney's correspondents Languet is the only one to capture almost the exact mood of Cicero. I say "almost," because there is present, in this letter as in several of Languet's to Sidney, a subgenre scarcely found in the Roman: the advice of an older man to a younger setting out in public and noble life.[31] The style, the *genus humile*, is in Languet's letter simpler than Cicero's, but this may be a deliberate kindness to a young Englishman and his still-developing Latinity (about which Languet writes to him on several occasions).

One does see, though, why near-contemporaries a generation or two later found these letters irresistible. In the first place, Languet writes with passion about contemporary politics; and, as a professional political "intelligencer" for the Duke of Saxony for many years and a bachelor wholly dedicated to religion and politics, he knows what he is talking about. There is the gossip aspect: the carefully-discreet reference at the beginning concerns a *sub rosa* project for marrying Sidney to a German princess. There is the emphasis upon the necessity of living in the real world while keeping what we should call moral values (and Languet, the pursuit of virtue) intact—a topic which reappears frequently in the younger man's *Arcadia*. There is the generous outrage about the Elector Palatine's religious turn-around and its effects not only upon Palatine Protestants generally but in particular upon the noble University of Heidelberg and its *Collegium Sapientiæ*, its institution for talented but poor students; and the urge to let a young, noble, Protestant future leader of England know about such things. Such *epistolæ* were thought worth printing, worth reading, worth learning from, and worth emulating.

The next (and penultimate) letter is again from Sidney himself. It is one of the last he was to write; it is from an older Sidney, overworked and frustrated as wartime Governor of Flushing.[32] Characteristically for his last years, it is a letter

---

[31] In Languet's case, this recurring theme has irritated a number of modern critics (for example, Katherine Duncan-Jones, *Sir Philip Sidney, Courtier Poet* [Oxford, 1995], pp. 71–5) and led them to assume that it irritated Philip also. There is no evidence whatsoever for such a view. Even Polonius does not seem to have had this effect upon Laertes, though modern directors almost invariably interpret it that way.

[32] In the autumn of 1585, as Elizabeth finally sent official help to the Netherlands, three strong-points in Zeeland were given to the English as forfeits or cautions for repayment: the Brill, the sea-fort of the Rammekens, and the important deep-water port of Vlissingen, or

trying to do something for both the recipient and a third party; uncharacteristically for this period, it is in Latin, and it is addressed to a humanist. The recipient, in fact, is none other than Lipsius, whom Sidney had met in Leiden on his arrival in the Netherlands,[33] and who was now preparing to leave in a huff in response to what he saw as Leicester's high-handedness in dealing with both the University and a prominent Dutch Anglophile, Pensionary Paul Buys. Like many before and since, Lipsius had given out that he was going to take the waters for his health.

Sidney to Justus Lipsius, Deventer, 14 September 1586 (Feuillerat CXII)[34]

Mi Lipsi . Doleo quod à nobis discedas, et eo magis doleo , quod verear ne istarum rerum tedium tam sit in causa quam ipsa valetudo. Si ita sit , (et nisi etiam de nostra anglia desperes) obtestor te per nostram amicitiam vt velis de te eó transferendo cogitare. Conditionem quam tibi aliquando obtuli ita ratam faciam vt me moriente non deficere potuerit . Noui te gratissimum fore nostræ Reginæ et multis aliis imo omnibus aliis . et meæ fidei te committas tibi non fore iniucundum iter. Si tantum pro valetudine ad illos fontes te confers ipsæ musæ adsint tibi, modo vt redeas nec nos veré tui amantes deseras . Post illum optatum reditum vlterius conferemus . Nunc istorum negotiorum fluctibus pene obruor. Pro Busio egi, et agam, quia tu ita vis et certe miseret me hominis, quamuis de me non optimé meriti. inquietum enim facile iudicarem non infidelem. nos cum multis difficultatibus luctamus, credo deum ita velle, in suis rem mitigare, vt non sint nobis nec currus nec catenæ. Diutius tecum nec calamus potest morari. Tu me ama et vale. Deuentriæ . 14 . septembris . 1586 .

certé tuus.

Ph. Sidneius

[My (dear) Lipsius,

I am sad that you are leaving us, and all the more because I fear that the loathsomeness of that business is as much the reason as your health. If that is so (and if you do not finally despair of our England), I beseech you by our friendship to think about moving there. The position which I once obtained for you I will so settle that even if I should die it will not be able to fail. I know you will be greatly appreciated by our Queen and by many others—indeed by everyone else; and I give you my word that you will not find the journey unpleasant. If, though, you are really going to those springs only for your health, may the Muses themselves be with you, as long as you come back and do not desert us who are your true friends. After that welcome return we will speak further.

Flushing. Of this last, Sidney was appointed governor; and his letters of late 1585 and 1586 are filled with both his determination to do the (militarily crucial) job properly and his frustration at the lack of money and proper organization that left his soldiers indigent and strained relations with the populace.

[33] Cf. van Dorsten, *Poets, Patrons, and Professors*, pp. 117–21.

[34] The original is Leiden University MS Lips 4.

Now I am being virtually drowned under the floods of all that business. I have interceded for Buys and will do so (again) since you want me to; and indeed I pity the man, although he has not deserved the best of me. I would certainly judge him restless, rather than faithless.

We are wrestling with many difficulties: I think God wishes so to temper the matter for His own that we will have neither triumph nor chains. This pen can spend no more time with you. Love me, and farewell. From Deventer, 14 September 1586.

Faithfully yours,
Ph. Sidney]

Clearly, Sidney could not allow himself to neglect the *sermo* of a letter to the famous scholar and stylist. At the same time, he had other things on his mind than the exchange of pleasantries. So here in fact we see what I have called the edge between conversation and oration, between familiarity and self-consciousness, for once completely internalized. It is fascinating to compare this letter with Sidney's first, quoted above. Its Latin is still courteous and far from inelegant; there are conscious figures (the Muses, the divine wishes); but it is emphatically a letter from a busy man, and it is *about* something. Mainly it is about attracting Lipsius to England: it is possible that Sidney had been trying to arrange a Chair in Oxford for him through his contacts at Christ Church and his uncles, and inviting religiously or otherwise harried humanists to England is a constant in Sidney's life and letters.

So a letter such as this introduces a kind of *tertium quid*: neither a leisurely conversation between absent friends such as Languet's, nor an "Orazione in quinta essenzia" like Wacker's, it foreshadows a later kind of letter-writing, still trying (as Lipsius advocated) to put in each letter something that will give æsthetic pleasure, but also the goal-oriented words of a courteous but very busy man.

The final letter is—the final letter. Sidney, consumed by gangrene and fever after his fatal bullet wound at Zutphen, is lying in the house of a judge's widow in Arnhem, dying. He has just enough energy to manage his deathbed like a good and devout Elizabethan: "this," his admirer John Donne would write, meditating on his own future deathbed, "is my playes last scene."[35] Sidney's scene—conceived and directed by the principal actor for the instruction if not the delight of those present—will presently be written down in the proper fashion by one of his entourage, possibly the minister George Giffard.[36] What we do not find there, however, is that the day before his death, barely able to hold a pen, Sidney has a piece of paper brought to him and scrawls a note to an elderly German doctor he knows, Johann Weyer:

---

[35] John Donne, *Divine Poems*, ed. Helen Gardner (Oxford, 1966), p. 7.

[36] *The Manner of Sir Philip Sidney's Death*; most easily available in *Sir Philip Sidney, Selected Works*, ed. Katherine Duncan-Jones (Oxford, 1989), pp. 315–18.

Sidney to Johan Weyer, Arnhem, 16 October 1586 (Feuillerat CXIV)[37]

Mi Weiere veni veni, de vita
periclitor et te cùpio—&
nec viùùs nec mortùùs ero ingrat*us*
plura . non possùm sed obnixe
oro vt festines. uale
Arnemi
    Tuus   Ph. Sidney

[Weyer mine, come, come, I am slipping
away from life and I want you—and
neither alive nor dead will I be ungrateful
I cannot write more but beseech you to hurry. farewell
Arnhem
      yours   Ph. Sidney]

It might seem unfair to include this in a consideration of epistolography. Seeing it in London's National Archives is almost unbearably moving. It is by now nearly illegible, so faded is the ink. The fairly elegant if busy Italic hand one has come to know so well has degenerated into a scrawl; the words—large, widely spaced on a dingy gray scrap of paper—trail off downward. It is attached to a covering letter sent with it to Weyer by the latter's nephew, also a physician and one of those who attended Sidney, Gisbert Enerwitz.

The art of letter-writing, though, still shows a ghostly presence in the control of language. More than any other letter in the correspondence—more, even, than the wonderfully lively and spontaneous exchanges with Languet—this brief note brings us into a *presence*, and joins us to those who were physically there, and to their deep emotion.

What does that say about letters, about epistolography, and about the edge they and it so carefully sought and managed to preserve? We might take this last note as an exception and disregard it. I believe we should be wrong to do so. For since the Greeks the *e)pi-stolh&*, the sent thing, the sent text (whether written down or memorized),[38] could convey deep and condensed emotion, as those who remember Thermopylæ will readily recall. Sidney's last written words were a letter; they

---

[37] The original is in the National Archives, State Papers Domestic, Elizabeth (SP84), vol. 10, fol. 73.

[38] In Fritz Büsser's introduction ("Die Uberlieferung von Heinrich Bullingers Briefwechsel") to Swiss Reformer Heinrich Bullinger's edited correspondence, he rightly points out that for all the self-consciousness of sixteenth-century correspondence, there was still the sense that the written letter was a second-best substitute for an oral communication. See Heinrich Bullinger, *Briefwechsel*, eds Ulrich Gabel and Endre Zsindely (12 vols, Zürich, 1973), vol. 1, p.3.

were composed in Latin; however stressed, they were not formless. And they convey, as they were meant to, a sense of extreme urgency and extreme feeling. Civility, and civilization, shine most under stress. A deathbed is the supreme test of whether, in Marc Fumaroli's words about Erasmus, one's culture has become second nature. From prentice complexity to a dying scrawl, Sidney's had become so; and it is fitting that we can witness it in a letter.

Wolves

There is one further exploration to be made and, using the term I once heard used to describe critical discourses that disconcert (especially those French in origin), I have called it "wolves in the basement." The wolves, in this case, are the outward and visible sign of Barthesian semiology, which (*pace* Barthes himself) is an art and not a science. It might be characterized as the trained understanding of what *else* a text, or a textual phenomenon, means; or (even more accurately) *how* else it means. Such a "trained understanding" has much in common with what Matthew Arnold described as a reader's "tact": they are both essentially undefinable yet clearly present in certain discussions of literature and its works.

Were we to let the wolves loose upon the sixteenth-century familiar letter, what would emerge? In fact, a particularly mangy species of lupine has for some time now had its wicked way with them, with the result that we are told to read them not as conversations between absent friends, but as carefully shaped counters in a power game, as clever and ambitious exercises in self-presentation and self-aggrandizement.[39] To end this essay, I propose a wolf or two much prettier in shape and fur, which can growl as gently as any dove.

We might begin by recalling Fumaroli's description of correspondence as seen by Lipsius: *two thoughtful solitudes which meet in silence and in absence, exchanging affinities in the dark of time.* If we take this as our starting point, and then proceed via the letters themselves to what I have called the "edge," we may approach this from a new angle and acquire a fresh view of it. The humanist familiar letter, because it is so richly worked, allows us to see aspects of *any* letter that might otherwise remain invisible.

The edge is the narrow line, the *arète*, between private and public, between today's Friend and someday's Reader, between the ephemeral and the enduring, between familiar chat and pride in one's mastery. And now we also see that *arète* as the steep and dangerous place where two solitudes meet and (thus) call themselves into question. So it is the *meeting-place in absence*, where people meet without meeting. Jonathan Goldberg has beautifully described it as "a fiction of

---

[39] I am not concerned here to engage in polemic, and will thus omit specific references. The texts to which I refer are numerous, and all around us.

presence that is constituted solely on the basis of absence."[40] Yet fiction it is and is not: the words of the one are *present* in the eye and mind, and sometimes voice, of the other. As Sidney once wrote to Languet, "Robert Beale, Rogers, and your friend Beutterich all arrived at the same time as your most excellent letter, so that I seemed at once to be hearing you and seeing you, with the greatest possible pleasure."[41]

Meeting in absence, then, is always already a paradox. A para-doxa also? Nothing, at first sight, could be more doxical than the Republic of Letters (in every sense). A description like Manfred Fleischer's, indeed, makes it sound like an utterly formal and very Germanic guild:

> The cult of friendship which made Maecenas and protégé partners of the same enterprise involved three highly formalized activities: 1) an exchange of letters, the so-called "literarius cultus amicitiæ," which constituted the "republic of letters"; 2) "amico-poetica," that is, occasional poetry which celebrated weddings, promotions, publications, travels, and leave-takings with "epithalamia," "congratulatoria," "hodoeporica," "propemptica" and "epicedia" as well as the persons who presided over the circles of the "literati"; and 3) the "peregrinatio academica," by which an aspiring academic would visit one scholar after another, offer and receive friendship ("amicitiam offere–in amicitiam accipere"), and present his "Stammbuch," the "album amicorum," in which an academic pilgrim would collect the signature and sage advice of the cultic figures he visited.[42]

Yet there are within the texts of many letters interesting signs of wolves in the basement. In the first place, there is (within the Ciceronian tradition of including pleasantries) the regular and only half-joking complaint about the addressee's laziness and irregularity in writing. The Sidney–Languet correspondence is particularly rich in such remarks, which has led some biographers to conclude that Sidney (to whom most of the letters are addressed) was a particularly bad correspondent. Yet this *topos* (for so it is) goes back as far as Cicero.[43] Such complaining can seem at worst like petulance, at best like harmless teasing; but the effect of its very "topicality" is like the ceaseless plaint of Arnold's islands: "oh,

---

[40] Jonathan Goldberg, *Writing Matter: From the Hands of the English Renaissance* (Stanford, 1990), p. 249. The entire chapter, "Signatures, Letters, Secretaries," is both elegant and illuminating.

[41] Sidney to Hubert Languet, 1 March 1578; Zürich, Zentralbibliothek MS F61, fol. 178.

[42] Manfred Fleischer, "The Success of Ursinus: A Triumph of Intellectual Friendship," in Derk Visser (ed.), *Controversy and Conciliation: The Reformation and the Palatinate 1559–1583* (Allison Park, 1986), pp. 109–10.

[43] Cf. Cicero to Trebatius, VII.12.

might our marges meet again!"[44] In the real affection that underlies these correspondences of *amicitia*, absence, though it may constitute the fiction of presence, is never taken for granted and always somehow intolerable.

A second sign is linked to the Renaissance delivery systems for letters—in itself almost a contradiction, for a true "system" was only very gradually and with great difficulty coming into being—namely, the Imperial postal system, with the De Taxis or De Tassis family as its hereditary Postmasters. Letters—these murmurings of absent friends, touchings of reflective solitudes—are filled with anxiety about their safe transmission. The *intercepted letter* is a topos also, sometimes what we should call an urban legend, a bugbear, which spread fear throughout the Respublica Litterarum. "Do not show my letters to anyone," Languet writes to Sidney on several occasions: it is only to Philip that he shows his feelings and his thoughts about the world with such a lack of circumspection. Another correspondent, Jean Lobbet, is constantly advising Sidney how their letters may not just most efficiently, but most safely, be transmitted: from Strasburg to a doctor in Brussels to a merchant in Antwerp to London, "because why should we trouble Master De Tassis with such unimportant things?"[45] (De Tassis, we should remember, was not only Imperial Postmaster in Antwerp but the nephew of a prominent representative of Philip II and an army commander who fought in the Netherlands with Parma.) And around 1580 a whole pamphlet war was conducted around intercepted letters: first some Spanish ones which really were intercepted, and gleefully published, then some purportedly intercepted ones from the other side, and so forth.[46]

This aspect of correspondence, then, introduces an insecurity—not so much personal as political—that always accompanies the *litteræ familiares* in the sixteenth century, and in England of course has its apotheosis (and its justification) in the episode of the Casket Letters, which sealed the fate of Mary Stuart.

My third and final wolf—a wolfling, really, a mere cub—wears the face of an inextricable pun. The generic familiar letter in the second half of the sixteenth century is still in Latin, where *littera* (singular), is a letter in the sense of a character; *litteræ* (plural) are letters (several characters), *litteræ* (pl.) a letter (epistle); and *Litteræ* (pl.) Letters, as in Literature. Not really puns, nor even homonyms: evolutions of a word. Yet the resulting ambiguities are vast, and their implications startling. We begin with the humble *littera*, scratched in wax,

---

[44] "To Marguerite – Continued," 1.18, in Matthew Arnold, *Selected Poems and Prose*, ed. M. Allott (New York, 1978), p. 29.

[45] Jean Lobbet to Sidney, 22 November 1575, Yale MS Osborn fa. 14, fol. 92.

[46] One example, *Lettre interceptée du Prince d'Orange* (1580), is a vivid forgery showing the Prince offering a docile country to the Duke of Alençon, with vitriolic marginal comments; the whole probably written by Charles d'Assonleville, one of the principal pro-Spanish councillors in the Southern Netherlands.

chiselled in stone, or (quite early on) formed with a sharpened goose-quill dipped in gum and gall or soot. There has been much discussion of the philosophical implications of writing, from Plato to Derrida, the only aspect of which I want to recall here is that thoughts and feelings are best portable over distance through words, and that until the twentieth century the only portable words were written ones, inscribed in *litteræ*.

From there, the original plural remained but denoted a singular object: a folded sheet of paper covered in *litteræ*. It is sometimes hard to know whether a man writing to an assiduous correspondent, "I got your *litteræ* the day before yesterday" is referring to one letter or several. And these "letters" then of course also become that other kind of letters which are Letters: grand, beautiful, and ambitious writing of all kinds—poetry, romances, treatises, sermons. *Litteræ humaniores* are what they become: *more* human? than what? *rather* human? fairly kind? And it is of these Letters that the Respublica is the Commonwealth, though as it turned out the *epistolæ* were a major part of it.

What do the wolves have to do with the edge, with the *arète* between a murmured conversation and *una Orazione*? One might, I think, say that the edge is where the wolves live, as they do on all such edges. The edge is a *pli* or fold, where a text folds back upon itself, where its unwriteable, its unsayable, even its unthinkable, happens. As Derek Attridge wrote many years ago, a text is constituted by its differences, by the difference of its elements not from one central core but from each other.[47] The arète or *Grat* where the wolves live is such a fold, and looking at its fauna can tell us something about its ecosystem. In the case of the humanist familiar letter, the wolves (and others remain to be found there) *show* us the edge in ways that encyclopedic study cannot: we learn that it is not only a fold but an impossible fold, that its two sides cannot yet must, must yet cannot, be read *together*.

Finally

"*Two thoughtful solitudes which meet in silence and in absence, exchanging affinities in the dark* [literally, *the night*] *of time*." The lupine phrase in this characterization is the last: the dark of time. We may suitably end with it. "I have written this *planè dormituriens*"—clearly nodding off—write several correspondents, or words to that effect. Intimate letters were written late at night, often on Fridays.[48] To the French, *la nuit des temps* denotes the prehistoric past or

---

[47] Derek Attridge, *Peculiar Language: Literature as Difference from the Renaissance to James Joyce* (London, 1988), esp. pp. 184–7.

[48] The new "nuit du temps" in which modern friends' and lovers' final, late-night e-mails cross may perhaps be allowed a footnote.

the unimaginably distant cosmic future. *La nuit* du *temps*, says Fumaroli, is the dark where solitudes murmur to each other. A dark of space: the world may have grown smaller with exploration, but it is still mostly crossed at three miles per hour, and the islands of civilization still sometimes feel as small and dark-surrounded as Heorot. A dark of time: for us, these voices have a moving patina of *pastness*, as their thoughtful solitudes communicate with us. A dark of absence, of insecurity, of anxiety, of writing thoughts to be sent and never answered quickly enough to reassure. A dark of the human *animus* that dares, finally, to cross its own borders, its limits of time and space, and find its fellow.

Chapter 9

"Made all of rusty yron, ranckling sore"
The Imprint of Paternity in *The Faerie Queene*

Douglas A. Brooks

> A son is light and fruit; a fruitful flame
> Chasing the father's dimness, carried far
> From the first man in th' East, to fresh and new
> Western discov'ries of posterity.
>
> George Herbert, "The Son"[1]

In this essay, I want to examine how Spenser's great poem, *The Faerie Queene* (*FQ*), imagines a transhistorical discussion of sorts between Ancient Greece and Elizabethan England. Specifically, I hope to show that Spenser facilitates a conversation between these two very different cultural moments by subtly articulating how they are linked by comparably traumatic introductions of new epistemic technologies (alphabet and print, respectively) and how such technological/cultural upheavals affect conceptual constructions of paternity and patriarchal authority.

If, as I will suggest, the introduction of new writing technologies not only generates new cultural constructions of parenting, but also necessitates the production of narratives to account for such constructions, then *FQ* can be read as the tale of the victory of the Gutenberg father over the biological mother. Furthermore, because such narratives frequently present the emergence of newly technologized notions of paternity within the context of kingship and dynastic anxiety, I point to some of the ways in which Spenser's poem is necessarily complicated by the bodily politics of its putative subject, Elizabeth I.

Spenser's commentators have frequently noted the poet's canny typographical self-consciousness, especially as it manifests itself in the textual apparatus of *The Shepheardes Calender*. What has received considerably less attention, however, is Spenser's preoccupation in *FQ* with the effects of an emergent print culture. Even an otherwise careful reader of *FQ* such as James Nohrnberg only briefly notes that

---

[1] George Herbert, *The Complete English Poems*, ed. John Tobin (New York, 1991), p. 158.

there are "minor evidences of the transformation of the subject of the book into the book-as-subject" in Book VI, which features character names such as Calepine, a standard Latin Dictionary, and Aldus, the great printer of classical texts.[2] Such critical neglect is surprising because Spenser's poem is keenly responsive to the ways in which the material processes of textual reproduction reconfigured important patriarchal aspects of the metaphorical field of parenting in early modern England.

Dynasty is Destiny

In an essay that considers the efforts made by Renaissance poets to sort out the languages of myth and Realpolitik, Clark Hulse finds that *FQ* raises a number of questions about inheritance and other elements of dynastic rule. With regard to the complex interlacing of mythic and dynastic storytelling in the period, Hulse rightly notes Spenser's peculiarly Elizabethan version of things: "Artegall's rights are established purely by deeds, and [his] legendary predecessors … are offered as analogies, not as progenitors."[3] The word, not the flesh, gets invoked.

Compelled to chronicle one of the synaptic leaps in the spinal cord of patriarchy, Spenser's task was an enormously complicated one. No doubt, the myth of the giants' rebellion—and its appropriation by Charles V—underscored the anomaly of Elizabeth's position as a monarch within the dynastic narratives of her day. However, I would suggest that a rather different story, the myth of Oedipus, not only depicts a comparably anomalous monarchy, but also prefigures the Christian version of maternal and paternal inheritance the queen would appropriate by ruling as a virgin married to her realm.

Spenser only makes one unnamed reference to Oedipus as the "Theban Knight."[4] Yet even this one reference resonates greatly when we consider the extent to which Oedipus haunted the literary boundaries of the Elizabethan succession controversy. A translation of Seneca's *Oedipus* by Alexander Neville was first performed in 1563 (one year after *Gorboduc* was first performed);[5] and, as Freud famously observed, "Another of the great creations of tragic poetry, Shakespeare's *Hamlet*, has its roots in the same soil as *Oedipus Rex* …."[6] Two

---

² James Nohrnberg, *The Analogy of "The Faerie Queene"* (Princeton, 1976), p. 683.

³ Clark Hulse, "Spenser, Bacon, and the Myth of Power," in Heather Dubrow and Richard Strier (eds), *The Historical Renaissance: New Essays on Tudor and Stuart Literature and Culture* (Chicago, 1988), p. 324.

⁴ Thomas P. Roche, Jr. (ed.), *The Faerie Queene* (New York, 1978), V.xi.25; references are to this edition.

⁵ *Annals of English Drama: 975–1700*, ed. Sylvia Stoler Wagonheim based on the original texts by Alfred Harbage and S. Schoenbaum (3rd edn, London, 1989), p. 38.

⁶ Sigmund Freud, *The Interpretation of Dreams*, trans. James Strachey (New York, 1965), p. 298.

plays from the early years of Elizabeth's reign—*Gorboduc*, a Seneca-like portrait of the Tudor kingdom in crisis, the other a translation of Seneca's portrait of the Cadmean kingdom in crisis—appear one after the other and merge by the end of that reign, in *Hamlet*, into a vivid representation of a monarchy that has collapsed and taken a dynasty down with it. If we follow Freud and move directly from Sophocles to Shakespeare, we skip over the Senecan link in the intertextual chain. To do so, I would suggest, is to risk missing Spenser's position on the Tudor dynasty and Elizabeth's maternity.

What makes the story of Oedipus so compelling in the context of Elizabethan England is its status as the tale of an anomalous monarchy—anomalous, that is, in light of what Jean-Joseph Goux identifies as the "monomyth of royal investiture."[7] Matricide, not patricide, is at the heart of other Greek kingship tales (Jason, Bellerophon, Perseus) because, according to Goux, each monster the hero confronts is feminine. Additionally, each monster is killed in bloody battle and each victory over the murdered female monster enables the hero to marry a king's daughter and ultimately become king.[8] Oedipus, of course, goes about things quite differently. Arriving at Thebes, the young man who unwittingly killed his father finds that a female monster stands between him and a former king's wife and a future king's mother. But what is truly anomalous about the young man's accession to the Theban throne is that, as Goux notes, "Oedipus alone triumphs through sheer intelligence, with his explanation of the famous riddle that is itself a trial by language. His is not a martial victory."[9]

Renaissance man and proto-Cartesian subject, Oedipus thinks himself into the kingship even though, as the legend's notorious final irony makes clear, he had begun his life as the legitimate blood heir to the throne. Responding to the dynastic anxiety inherent in this story, Spenser introduces the "Theban Knight" into a context that is heavily charged with intimations of fatherhood. Indeed, Oedipus is suggestively linked here to Prince Arthur, the elder brother of the future Henry VIII and the first husband of Catherine of Aragon. The sharing of a queen between these two brothers (later recalled by Shakespeare in his version of Oedipus) provided Henry VIII with the grounds to declare his marriage to Catherine invalid because incestuous and to begin a lengthy legislative battle in 1534 to bring blood under the control of statute.[10] When Elizabeth wedded her self "to an husband, which is the kingdom of England" and famously proclaimed that "every one of

---

[7] Jean-Joseph Goux, *Oedipus, Philosopher* (Stanford, 1993), p. 7.

[8] Goux, pp. 2–16.

[9] Goux, p. 16.

[10] As Bruce Thomas Boehrer observes, "Henry VIII's Reformation Parliament ratified a bill called an Act concerning the King's Succession, and it became law that year. It was a landmark piece of legislation, being the first (and by no means the last) of Henry's attempts to sequence his heirs by statute" (*Monarchy and Incest in Renaissance England: Literature, Culture, Kinship, and Kingship* [Philadelphia, 1992], p. 1).

you, and as many as are English, are my children and kinsfolks,"[11] she left nothing to fleshly chance. Having reduced her reproductive activities to words, she gained the kind of control over the *issue* of succession of which her father could only dream. To do so, however, she was compelled to put herself into a symbolic parental position that was identical to Jocasta's: she reigned as both wife and mother to the same brood.[12]

Spenser emphasizes the dynastic element of this mythic counterpart to Elizabeth's reign when he clarifies exactly which version of the "Theban Knight" he intends: he doesn't remind them of those notorious crimes for which Oedipus is famous; rather, he identifies the knight as "The father of that fatall progeny" (V.xi.25). Dynasty is also foregrounded in Spenser's anachronistic use of the title "Knight" for Oedipus. By the beginning of the twelfth century, knighthood was principally a society of heirs. As George Duby observes, "the language of legal documents treats knighthood as a coherent body, compact, closely defined by family and hereditary characteristics."[13] Though only a brief allusion in a large work that is rich with references to classical mythology, Spenser's recourse to the figure of Oedipus near the end of Book V nevertheless represents an important moment in an underlying or "shadowed" dynastic narrative he has been piecing together from the outset of *FQ*. Bringing that narrative into the light is the principal task of this essay.

The Error of Her Ways

The slaying of the monster on the altar in the Theban Knight episode may well be more than just a brief allusion to a troubled father-figure in ancient Greece, because, like England's queen—and kings before her—it appears to have two bodies. One of these bodies, sacred, representing the Spanish Catholic Church and the Inquisition, is subtly alluded to when Arthur strikes the "image with his naked blade" (V.xi.22) before striking the dragon. In this sense, then, the sphinx killed on the altar by Prince Arthur's Theban Knight retains the contextual traces of that divine or sacred body that initially informed the ecclesiastical formulation of the King's two bodies. The other body of the sphinx, its natural body, is maternal, as Spenser makes clear when he explains that "Vnder her wombe [Arthur's] fatall sword he thrust" (V.xi.31). The sphinx thus brings into focus a royal maternal body that, by the time the second installment of *FQ* was published, had become an overwhelming source of anxiety. To better grasp the nature of that anxiety and

---

[11] "1559. Her answer to [the Commons'] petition that she marry," in Leah S. Marcus, Janel Mueller, and Mary Beth Rose (eds), *Elizabeth 1: Collected Works* (Chicago, 2000), p. 59.

[12] George Gascoigne translated Dolce's *Giocasta* with Francis Kinwelmershe in 1566.

[13] George Duby, *The Chivalrous Society*, trans. Cynthia Postan (Berkeley, 1977), p. 160.

Spenser's response, we need to move back from the sphinx at the gates of Thebes to the threshold of Spenser's poem and to the notion of the allegorical threshold itself.[14] There we find the Redcrosse Knight, a rustic outsider whose path to success is as short and unexpected as that of the Theban Knight. For the first stage of this rapid rise to power, which also entails an encounter with the sphinx,[15] Spenser wastes no time casting the Knight of Holiness in the role of initiate working through the ritualized stages of royal investiture. Redcrosse, as Spenser explains to Raleigh in "A letter of the authors," is the "tall clownishe younge man" (p. 17) who wanders into *"Errours Den"* (I.i.13), murders the monstrous mother, and then returns to Una, the daughter of "an ancient King and Queene" (p. 17).

With considerable audacity, Spenser begins the great epic poem he has ostensibly written to celebrate Queen Elizabeth by introducing the basic elements of a mythic fantasy scenario in reserve, a scenario in which the bloodless anomaly of a monarchy like that of Oedipus is violently exposed and sidestepped so that the patriarchal narrative of royal investiture can get on with its business. A novice knight savagely kills a monstrous mother, wins the daughter of a king and queen who have no male heir—"The fairest Vn' his onely daughter deare, / His onely daughter, and his onely heyre" (I.xii.21)—and marries her to become king. Indeed, the process of royal investiture is put in motion before the action of the poem begins, when Virgin princess Una takes the "clownishe younge man" away from the matriarchal figure of the Queene of Faeries. From the moment Spenser begins his plot summary, he chronicles the procedure by which a king is fashioned.

The confrontation between Error and Redcrosse has posed few difficulties for interpreters. Anthea Hume, for example, argues that Book I depends "not only on a Protestant reading of Revelation, but also on a Protestant recreation—effected by Spenser himself—of the St. George legend .... [T]he familiar story of knight, lady and dragon has been shaped by a Protestant vision."[16] Relying in part on Hume's reading, Humphrey Tonkin notes that Redcrosse's victory over Error suggests that "the patron of England is successful in overcoming religious error ...."[17] Tonkin also suggestively remarks that Spenser had two audiences in mind: the "popular audience" that recognized and appreciated the familiar story of knight, lady and dragon; the "learned audience" that recognized that Redcrosse was a type for the St

---

[14] Nohrnberg suggests *Cebes' Tabula*, a textbook allegory about education, as a possible source for the Error episode and observes, "The association of *Cebes' Tabula* and the thresholds of a text is reinforced by the use of the table as a border design for the frontispiece of several Renaissance books" (p. 124n86).

[15] According to Nohrnberg, the sphinx appears twice in Spenser's poem: once as Error and once as the monster that Arthur slays in the Theban Knight episode (p. 124).

[16] Anthea Hume, *Edmund Spenser: Protestant Poet* (Cambridge, 1984), p. 72.

[17] Humphrey Tonkin, *The Faerie Queene* (London, 1989), p. 61.

George who "wears the armor of a Christian man that he has *in effect inherited* directly from the apostle Paul."[18]

In other words, St Paul's armor is to Redcrosse what Jove's sword Chrysaor is to Artegall: a virgin (Una and Astraea, respectively) steps in to close "maternally" a tremendous historical gap between a patriarchal figure and a youthful initiate. The dynastic link that has been established in both cases is merely analogous or "in effect inherited," as Tonkin puts it, not consanguinal. Furthermore, Tonkin and Hulse locate the respective episodes within Spenser's ostensible effort to glamorize Elizabeth's role as the monarch who revived and restored imperial rule to England after many centuries of "weak or corrupt rulers who did not keep the faith and brought confusion and misery on their subjects."[19]

Having passed from St Paul to St George and *via* Spenser to the not-yet-saintly Redcrosse, the "armour of a Christian man" (p. 17) brought to the Faerie court by Una suggests a troubled lineage that Spenser's learned audience may have associated with the fate of the Church in England after its founding by King Lucius around 180. The semi-historical accounts of the Church that Spenser was working from and the popular mythical narrative of St George both point to a simple and disturbing story: by establishing the church, Lucius had put Britain in a position to play an important role in the Roman Empire, an imperial role that in reality remained beyond the reach of England's monarchy presumably until the Tudors— especially Elizabeth—came to the throne. As for what happened between 180 and the Henrician era, Tonkin notes that "Spenser knew his Foxe" and quotes from the *Book of Martyrs:*

> [S]uch trouble and variance fell among the Britons (as it happeneth in all other realms, and namely in this realm of England, whensoever succession lacketh) that not only they brought upon them the idolatrous Romans and at length the Saxons but also enwrapped themselves in such misery and desolation as yet to this day remaineth.[20]

In Foxe's vision of what transpired between the glorious establishment of the church in England and the subsequent supplication to Rome, the lack of royal succession is the principal culprit responsible for the realm's catastrophic history and its current malaise. Lucius died without resolving the issue of succession because he died childless. Therefore, the lack of royal children was to blame for the difficulties England suffered, especially at the hands of the Roman Church. In short, church, state, and empire require that orderly royal succession be woven into the fabric of English nationhood.

There was certainly a great deal at stake by the time Henry's "onely daughter" found herself on the throne, and this in part explains why Henry had worked so

---

[18] Tonkin, p. 62, emphasis added.
[19] Tonkin, p. 60.
[20] Tonkin, p. 60.

hard to bring succession under statutory control. It must have been difficult for Spenser to subscribe to interpretations of history espoused by apologists for the Church of England without fretting that whatever the Tudors had done to promote England and its church to a position of imperial importance would quickly be undone upon the death of a childless Queen Elizabeth. Perhaps this anxiety is addressed—at least, inversely—by Una's extraordinary concern to rescue her parents' troubled dynasty; and the meeting between Una and the Faerie Queene is the set-up for commissioning Redcrosse to be that dynasty's salvation. By contrast, the image of a "Queene much wondering" (p. 17) upon learning of Una's predicament, suggests some rather troubling images of a ruler who, when confronted with a dynastic crisis, is incapable of acting. Indeed, the aural resemblance of "wondering" and "wandering," the latter linked by Una to the naive knight's confrontation with Error—"This is the wandring wood, this Errours den / A monster vile, whom God and man does hate" (I.i.13)—intimates that not all is well. Spenser's learned reader familiar with either the Latin original or Richard Hyrde's English translation of Juan Luis Vives' well-known handbook, *The Instruction of a Christian Woman*, might have been concerned. According to Vives, "Womans thought is swifte and for the most parte unstable, walking and wandring out from hoame, and soone will slyde by the reason of it owne slippryness, I wot not howe farre."[21] In this sense, the "much wondering" queen was by nature much "wandrynge," according to at least one influential humanist. Subsequently flattered by seeing his first major poem mentioned by Sidney in the same breath as *Gorboduc*, Spenser may have appreciated that play's critical lines on succession: "We remain with out a certain prince / To wield the realm, or guide the wand'ring rule."[22] Because the Faerie Queene can't decide whether Redcrosse is ready to rescue a dynasty, Una is compelled to set the knight on the path to her royal parents. In doing so, she is the one who passes on the legacy of the Church.

Gestation and its Discontents

Shakespeare waited till the early years of James I's reign to have an aging monarch say, "O, how this mother swells up toward my heart! / Hysterica passio, down, thou climbing sorrow" (*King Lear*, II, iv, 55–6).[23] Edward Jorden, however, was slightly more brazen when, as Helen King notes, he published in England "the key hysteria text of the early seventeenth century," *A Briefe Discourse of a Disease*

---

[21] Juan Luis Vives, *A very fruitfull and pleasant booke, called the Instruction of a Christian Woman* (1585), p. 10.

[22] *Gorboduc*, ed. Irby B. Cauthen, Jr. (Lincoln, 1970), V, ii, 259–60.

[23] All references to Shakespeare are from *The Norton Shakespeare: Based on the Oxford Edition*, Stephen Greenblatt et al. (eds) (New York, 1997).

Called the Suffocation of the Mother, shortly before Elizabeth's death in 1603.[24] The first important post-inquisition study to attribute hysteria to natural, rather than demonical causes, Jorden's book put into print what had become more or less received wisdom in the final two decades of the sixteenth century: "delayed virginity" was the primary natural cause of hysteria. G.S. Rousseau observes, "[t]he transition from demonic profile to medical malady was indeed in the thick process of transition during the Elizabethan period."[25] Plato, of course, had already positioned hysteria securely within the symptomology of suffocation when he wrote in the *Timaeus* that, "The animal within them is desirous of procreating children, and when remaining unfruitful long beyond its proper time, gets discontented and angry, and *wandering in every direction* through the body, closes up the passages of the breath, and, by obstructing respiration, drives them to extremity, causing all varieties of disease ...."[26]

While the discourse on hysteria most readily available in Spenser's day would have been a strange mixture of Plato, Galen, and superstition, what matters here is that the brief expanse of "plain" (I.i.1) between the wondering Faerie Queene and the wandering monstrous mother figure of Error is extraordinarily over-determined in terms of what might be called—with a nod to Greenblatt's *Marvelous Possessions*—the "discourse of wander." Any number of common associations in Spenser's time come into play: woman's thought, according to Vives, is a "wandring out from hoame"; Gorboduc worries about "the wand'ring rule"; and an elderly virgin queen suffers from a "wandering womb."

According to G.S. Rousseau, "Historically speaking, hysteria has been the condition beyond others that wedded the body to body language ... that captured the chronic numbness and ineffable despair usually incapable of being grasped in the subtleties of written language."[27] Spenser seems to literalize this hysterical history by having Mother Error vomit up books, papers, and embryonic creatures "blacke as inke" (I.i.22). Fashioned by Spenser to reflect the exigencies of Renaissance epistemology and Elizabethan Realpolitik, Mother Error

> ... spewed out of her filthy maw
> A floud of poyson horrible and blacke,
> Full of great lumpes of flesh and gobbets raw,
> Which stunck so vildly, that it forst [Redcrosse] slacke

> His grasping hold, and from her turne him backe:

---

[24] Helen King, "Once Upon a Text: Hysteria from Hippocrates." in Sander L. Gilman et al. (eds), *Hysteria Beyond Freud* (Berkeley, 1993), p. 29.

[25] G.S. Rousseau, "'A Strange Pathology': Hysteria in the Early Modern World, 1500–1800," in Gilman et al. (eds), pp.114, 128.

[26] *The Collected Dialogues of Plato*, eds Elizabeth Hamilton and Huntington Cairns (Princeton, 1961), p. 1210, emphasis added.

[27] Rousseau, p. 95.

Her vomit full of bookes and papers was,
With loathly frogs and toades, which eyes did lacke .... (I.i.20)

Thomas P. Roche, Jr. glosses these "bookes and papers" as "theological books, tracts, and pamphlets, debating often violently the nature of the one, true Church, that is, theological controversy which involves men in Error's den."[28] Tonkin alternatively suggests that they are "the filthy romances so roundly denounced by many of Spenser's contemporaries, the 'bawdrye' identified by Ascham."[29] The critical divide glimpsed here between the theological and the bawdy, between the learned and the popular, between the narrative of the church and the typical "filthy" romance narrative of a lineage restored, was easily straddled by Spenser who recognized that in England story lines and storied lines were often inseparable. But the mess in Error's stomach is peculiarly English in another way: the odd stew of "great lumpes of flesh" and "books and papers" vomited up here can still be recognized as the favorite family recipe for the Henrician statutory legacy. No one mixed words with wombs better than Elizabeth's father, who desperately struggled to have the final edit on the Tudor dynasty—no one, that is, except his "onely daughter," who had the "stomach of a King" and began her reign where her father had attempted to leave his: with total verbal control over the "yssew" of succession.

Roche traces the phrase "loathly frogs and toades" to Revelation 16: 13: "And I saw three unclean spirits like frogs come out of the mouth of the dragon ...." But when Spenser follows the Johanine frogs back to their source in the next stanza— "As when old father *Nilus* gins to swell / With timely pride above the *Aegyptian* vale" (I.i.21)—he returns to the birthplace of the sphinx and the biblical story of the plagues: "And Aaron stretched his hand over the water of Egypt, and the frogs came up and covered the land of Egypt" (Exodus 8: 6). Coupling Error with Nilus, monstrous mother with "old father," the poet not only provides the reader with an alternative to the pairing of Redcrosse and Una, but also muddles gender divisions along lines that seem to acknowledge Elizabeth's body politics. Mother Error may be a ferocious fighter, but Father Nilus appears to be pregnant. Referring to Renaissance traditions that link time, pregnancy, and rhetorical swelling, Patricia Parker offers the following notions of *dilatio*:

> A second, related meaning [of *dilatio*] is as a synonym for temporality .... [A] third is the sense of dilation as the puffing up of pride .... [S]till another use of "dilation" occurs in the context of propagation or generation .... [O]bstetrical descriptions in the Renaissance frequently start with a reminder of the divine command to "increase and

---

[28] Roche (ed.), p. 1077n.
[29] Tonkin, p. 63.

multiply" and see the "mouth" of the matrix or womb as "an orifice at the entrance into the body which may be dilated and shut."[30]

All of these meanings converge in the paternal Egyptian river. Writing forward from Error to Nilus, Spenser moves backward from the New Testament to the Old and from the statutorily wordy "mouth" of a daughter's womb to the statutorily womby words of her father's mouth. Here at the entrance to the allegory where Error spews and Nilus swells, the text itself threatens to flood its margins. In this already over-determined moment, the story of royal investiture Seneca retells in English during the first years of Elizabeth's reign can also be heard.

Faced, as Spenser often was, with competing traditions, Seneca, like Spenser, collapsed or fused them. The first line uttered by the chorus in *Oedipus*, "O more then thrise renowned stock / of auncient Cadmus race. / O Mighty Thebes Citie great," brings dynasty and state together in a way that neither of Seneca's chief dramatic predecessors had attempted.[31] From there, the chorus catalogues "a thousand yls, / whiche wretched eyes have seen" (sig. A6^r). And although Oedipus has just appealed to "Phoebus heavenly might" for "any meanes" or "way of mercye" (sig.A7^v), the morning sun rising over the chorus reveals that "all his stock dispersed quight, / the soly Shephard dyes" (sig.A6^r). Spenser compares Redcrosse to a "gentle Shepheard in sweete even-tide / When ruddy Phoebus gins to welke in west. / High on an hill, his flocke to vewen wide" (I.i.23). Where Error's venomous miscarried foetuses are the "cursed spawne of serpents small / Deformed monsters, fowle, and blacke as inke" (I.i.22), in Seneca we find "The ugly Serpent that was want, / the rocky Dennes to kepe. / Oft quaffyng poisoned venom soups / in inwarde heate she boyles" (sig.A6^r). Seneca writes, "And whyther long of Acheron, that lothsom flud that flowes / All stynkyng streames: or of ye earth, that out her Bowels throwes / Dead corpses to recyue" (sig. D^r), and Spenser's Error "spewed out of her filthy maw / A floud of poyson horrible and blacke / Full of great lumpes of flesh and gobbets raw / Which stunck so vildly." Seneca's Theban Knight and Spenser's Knight of Holinesse wade through strikingly similar floods of filth and gore.

As Egyptian plague tales merge with Theban plague tales, the subtextual waters continue to rise. I will discuss the significance of Spenser's reliance on Seneca in greater detail below. For now, I merely want to suggest that Spenser is borrowing from Seneca's plague-ridden landscape when he dispatches Redcrosse to the primordial womb for the sake of committing what amounts to ritual matricide. The womb he confronts (some thirty years into Elizabeth's reign) is a hysterical, suffocating, wandering animal. This makes the task more difficult, and Redcrosse's

---

[30] Patricia Parker, *Literary Fat Ladies: Rhetoric, Gender, Property* (London, 1987), p. 15.

[31] All citations of Seneca's *Oedipus* are from *The lamentable tragedie of Oedipus the sonne of Laius Kyng of Thebes out of Seneca. By Alexander Neuyle* (1563).

encounter with Error is among the poem's longest and most furious.[32] As the princess waits outside to bring him home and make him her king, the youthful knight is inside groping and slashing his way through a peculiarly Elizabethan brand of Tudor allegoresis in which words and wombs, chunks of books and hunks of flesh, blood and ink, threaten to drown him. When Redcrosse comes up for breath, the air is a heady mix of Bible and Seneca first trapped by clouds over England in the late 1550s.

Tongue Ties, or The Matrix Unloaded

Unlike the legendary sphinx, Arthur's sphinx, Una's dragon, Seneca's Black Death, and the other dragons in *FQ*, Error has no wings. Instead, Redcrosse is covered with the murmuring "tender wings" of gnats (I.i.23).[33] In juxtaposing the gnats' murmuring wings with the swarming, ink-black serpents' stings, Spenser seems to be staging an encounter between *logos* and *graphos*, between winged orality and poisonous writing.[34] This encounter, in turn, may be seen as a synecdoche for a larger, more complex project in which Spenser offers up the figure of an extraordinarily fertile hysterical mother at an abruptly fertile period in the historical matrix of literacy—an offering that is itself reducible to an etymology. Christie V. McDonald succinctly elaborates what may well be at stake in the allegorical figure of Error:

> The word matrix in English like *matrice* in French comes from the Latin *Matrix* meaning womb. In both languages it has taken on, among others, the following two meanings: 1) a situation or surrounding substance within which something originates, develops, or is contained; 2) in printing it means a metal plate used for casting typefaces.[35]

If parenting and printing converge in *FQ*'s first episode *via* the matrix, it's because Spenser relies on a metonymic economy in which motherhood, words, and print

---

[32] Redcrosse's subsequent battle with the dragon that stands between him and Una's Kingdom is the poem's longest, lasting three days.

[33] Dorothy Stephens argues, "because the imps spew from Errour's mouth in a 'filthy parbreake' of 'bookes and papers,' the 'murmurings' of stanza 23 serve to make her text audible" ("'Newes of devils': Feminine Sprights in Masculine Minds in *The Faerie Queene*," *ELR* 23 [1993]: 380).

[34] The long tradition linking writing and poison is explored by Jacques Derrida in *Dissemination*, trans. Barbara Johnson (Chicago, 1981), pp. 63–173.

[35] Christie V. McDonald, "Choreographies: An Interview between Jacques Derrida and Christie V. McDonald," *Diacritics* 12 (1982): 67.

circulate as readily exchangeable currency.[36] And as Spenser turns to Seneca in relating the confrontation between Redcrosse and Error, he may well be gesturing toward a larger project, the scope of which he hints at in a letter to Gabriel Harvey: "Why a God's name may not we, as else the Greeks have the kingdom of our own language and measure our accents by the sound, reserving the quantity to the verse?"[37] Commenting on these lines, Richard Helgerson succinctly brings together the issues of language and dynasty: "A kingdom whose boundaries are determined by the language of its inhabitants is no longer a kingdom in the purely dynastic sense, but neither, so long as it goes on identifying itself with the person of a hereditary monarch, is it quite a nation."[38] In the end, England was compelled to go outside its geophysical "boundaries" for another dynasty—one that was intently eavesdropping all the time. But Spenser's poem remains committed to promoting both the queen mother and "our mother tongue," a concept that is closely linked in the letter to "the kingdom of our own language."

Arguably, the non-inked white space between the two words of the phrase "mother tongue" constitutes the monstrous space of *The Faerie Queene* itself, situated as it is between Mother Error in the first episode and the Blatant Beast in the last. There the mouth is no longer an opening into the monstrous womb, it is merely a monstrous mouth:

> And therein were a thousand tongs empight,
>   Of sundry kindes, and sundry quality,
>   Some were of dogs, that barked day and night,
>   And some of cats, that wrawling still did cry:
>   And some of Beares, that groynd continually,
>   And some of Tygres, that did seeme to gren,
>   And snar at all, that ever passed by:
>   But most of them were tongues of mortall men. (VI.xii.27)

From "a thousand yong ones" (I.i.15) to a "thousand tongs empight," the Blatant Beast, like Error, is wandering and monstrous.

Having written an epic that begins and ends with the mouth,[39] Spenser appears to rely on an oral epic strategy of returning at the end of an episode to elements from the episode's beginning. This strategy is punningly announced in the first two lines of the Book VI's last stanza: "Ne may this homely verse, of many meanest / Hope to escape his venemous despite" (VI.xii.41). Returning home lands us in

---

[36] For a range of perspectives on this metonymic economy, see the essays in Douglas A. Brooks (ed.), *Printing and Parenting in Early Modern England* (Burlington, 2005).

[37] Quoted in Richard Helgerson, "Barbarous Tongues: The Ideology of Poetic Form in Renaissance England," in Dubrow and Strier (eds), p. 273.

[38] Helgerson, p. 273.

[39] *FQ* is in some respects an epic of the mouth. The reader enters the mouth of Error's cave at one end of the poem, and they leave the Blatant Beast's mouth at the other.

Error's venomous mouth, but it may also place us again at the first Senecan chorus and at another incarnation of the plague. According to the Chorus, "That hellishe dogges with Bawling sound / were herd to howle and cry, / And that the ground with trembling shooke, / and under fete dyd move" (sig. B1ʳ).[40] When Calidore captures the Blatant Beast, Spenser writes:

> Like as whylome that strong Tirynthian swaine,
> > Brought forth with him the dreadfull dog of hell
> > Against his will fast bound in yron chaine,
> > And roring horribly, did him compell
> > To see the hatefull sunne, that he might tell
> > To griesly Pluto, what on earth was donne,
> > And to the other damned ghosts, which dwell
> > For aye in darkenesse, which day light doth shonne,
> > So led this Knight his captyve with like conquest wonne. (VI.xii.35)

When Roche glosses the stanza, however, he points us to Ovid "*Met.* 7.408–15"[41] and, presumably, the following lines in Arthur Golding's popular 1567 English translation:

> [W]ith triple cheyne made new
> Of Strong and sturdie Adamant the valiant Hercle drew
> The Currish Helhounde Cerberus: who dragging arsward still
> And writing backe his scowling eyes bicause he had no skill
> To see the Sunne and open day, for verie moodie wroth
> Three barkings yelled out at once, and spit his slavering froth
> Upon the greenish grasse.[42]

Keeping in mind that Seneca was indebted to Ovid, it seems reasonable to suspect that rather than putting down *Oedipus* to pick up the *Metamorphoses*, Spenser was either merely flipping through a few pages of the former, reading the two at the same time, or conflating the two works in his memory.

Roger Ascham used to counsel his teachers to "set side-by-side before students several classical authors' treatments of the same theme, myth, or story, to facilitate stylistic comparisons."[43] In one such lesson, a teacher might have directed his students to look ahead some four hundred lines after the Hound of Hell reference to where Cerberus makes an appearance in Seneca's *Oedipus*:

---

[40] This identification is the sole reference to Seneca's *Oedipus* in Nohrnberg's *Analogy* (p. 693)

[41] Roche (ed.), p. 1230. Roche does not indicate to which edition of Ovid he is referring.

[42] *Ovid's Metamorphosis: The Arthur Golding Translation, 1567*, ed. John Frederick Nims (Philadelphia, 2000), p. 175 (7.522–8). All references to Ovid are to this edition.

[43] Linda Woodbridge, "Patchwork: Piecing the Early Modern Mind In England's First Century of Print Culture," *ELR* 23 (1993): 18.

                    Or of
that fyerce infernall Hownd
That at suche tymes doth bustlyng make
with chayns, and ratlyng sownd.
The Earth all wide it open gapes.
And I did se on grownd,
The Gods with colour pale and wan,
that those darke kingdoms keepe.
And very night I saw in dede. (sig. C5^r)

As was the case with the Theban Knight reference, Spenser once again substitutes the locative for the nominative when—according to the logic of Roche's gloss—he alters Ovid's "Hercules" to his own "Tirynthian swaine." But the real dilemma presented by Roche's attribution is what to do about those "damned ghosts," especially since they appear nowhere in the vicinity of the Ovidian passage under consideration here.[44] When Spenser introduces his version—an introduction that is typically unnamed—the two poets show themselves to be kindred spirits. Neville's translation of Seneca reads, "The Gods with colour pale and wan / that those darke kingdoms keepe," and Spenser follows with, "And to the other damned ghosts, which dwell / For aye in darkenesse." In this case, Spenser would seem to be the more faithful translator, because Seneca uses the word "umbras," which can mean "shades" or "ghosts."[45] Neville does, however, provide the equivalent of Spenser's "damned ghosts" fifteen lines later when he writes, "And all the fowlest feends of Hell, / and furies all were there. / And all transformed Ghosts and sprights, / that ever Hell did beare" (sig. C5^r). Moreover he links "Dogs" to "Ghosts" in an earlier passage that Spenser, as I suggested above, may have pillaged for the figure of spewing Mother Error:

                Dogs do bawl
And Ghosts are herd to cry.
And whyther long of *Acheron*,
that lothsom flud that flowes.
All stynkyng streames: or of that earth,
that out her Bowels throwes,
Dead Corpses to receive. Or of
that fyerce infernall Hownd
That at suche tymes doth bustling make
with chayns, and ratling sownd. (sigs. C4^v–C5^r)

---

[44] That Spenser's ghosts are "damned" may be a reflection of his protestant politics. As Keith Thomas observes, "[w]hile it may be a relatively frivolous question today to ask whether or not one believes in ghosts, it was in the sixteenth century a shibboleth which distinguished Protestant from Catholic almost as effectively as belief in the Mass or the Papal Supremacy" (*Religion and the Decline of Magic* [New York, 1971], pp. 588–9).

[45] Seneca, *Tragedies*, ed. and trans. John G. Fitch (2 vols, Cambridge, 2004), l. 584.

What risks getting lost in the shuffle of so many similar texts, lines, and images, however, is the fact that Ovid and Seneca turn to the Greek myth of Cerberus and Hercules for remarkably different reasons. Ovid's reference is an aside to identify the deadly poison Medea has prepared for Theseus out of the "juice of Flintwoort venemous" extracted from the "teeth of Cerberus" (7.518, 520). Seneca, on the other hand, turns to the "infernal Hound" in order to set the scene for the grand moment of his contribution to the history of Oedipus: the ghostly return of the dead father. Cerberus has abandoned his post, the gates of hell have swung open, and out comes the founding male line so integral to mythic accounts of royal investiture. In this case, it's the House of Cadmus, so the "children of the dragon's teeth" (Watling 589) / "Whole armies of kyng *Ditis* men" (Neville, sig. C5ᵛ) are the first to climb out of the "dark womb" (Watling 593) / "clustryng in a Rowt" (Neville, sig. C5ᵛ), followed by other "insubstantial shapes" (Watling 603) / "dyvers formes" (Neville, sig. C5ᵛ), "floating like clouds" (Watling 604) / "al flittring thin like Clowds" (Neville, sig. C5ᵛ). At the end of this infernal royal procession of a fallen dynasty, Creon exclaims: "And there stood Laius!" (Watling 618) / "Tyll out at length coms *Laius*" (Neville, sig. C6ʳ).[46]

While Seneca follows the mythic line on Oedipus's anomalously patricidal accession to the Theban throne through the power of the word, he also does everything in his power to re-embody the myth, even going so far as to drag the corpse of the murdered king out of hell. Yet in the new kingdom of language to which Laius returns, all the angry king can do is curse his grandfather, "O *Cadmus* cruell Cytie vile, / that styll delightst in blood, / O *Cadmus* thou, which kinsmens deth, / acowntst as chiefest good" (Neville, sig. C6ʳ), and women: "Loe Mothers love, (Alas) / Is now, the ryfest fault outryght / that ere in *Theba* was" (Neville, C6ᵛ). In short, all he can do is hope to have the last word. When Spenser sets the scene to have the last word of his poem some six stanzas from its end, he returns to this Senecan scene of hell unbound and the returning rageful father because he knows that an angry father in his kingdom of language waits to have the last word on his words. Preparing to send his "homely verse" homeward for publication, Spenser devotes the final stanza of the 1596 edition of *FQ* to recalling "a mighty Peres displeasure" with "my former writs" (VI.xii.41).[47] And the subsequent reference in the penultimate line to prosody ("my rimes keep better measure") suggests that the Greek fantasy realm of the letter to Harvey has never been far from the poet's mind.

---

[46] For the sake of comparison, I include a modern translation of Seneca's play beside Neville's: *Four Tragedies and Octavia,* trans. E.F. Watling (New York, 1966).

[47] A reference to Lord Burleigh, who had been displeased by *The Shepheards Calender*. Spenser first uses "Pere" to refer to Una's father as he prepares to make Redcrosse his successor: "Then said the royall Pere in sober wise" (I.xii.17.1).

Spelling the Name of the Father

Standing guard on either side of Spenser's "moniment" of words written in and between the mother tongue is a Senecan mouth. One spews up the printed contents of a monstrous mother's womb, the other is linked via the dark dynastic womb of hell to an angry father's displeasure over writing. These two mouths, forced by Elizabeth's oral maternity to synecdochally carry the burden of her body natural and her body politic, will ultimately give way to a Senecan ghost king's two ears some four years later in *Hamlet*. If Seneca appears to have haunted the beginning and end of Elizabeth's reign, especially as a source for literary interrogations of her decision to leave the issue of royal succession to words, his presence interfaces with concurrent transformations under the reign of the printing press. Elizabeth Eisenstein observes that "one must wait until a full century after Gutenberg before the outlines of a new world picture begin to emerge into view."[48] When this new world picture emerges, the beginning of Elizabeth's reign and the first English translations of Seneca's plays come into view at the same moment.

In Marshal McLuhan's early study of the advent of print culture, Seneca plays the role of the ghost. Asserting that the acceptance of print in a given time and place can be gauged "by its effect in eliminating pun, point, alliteration, and aphorism from literature," McLuhan identifies Seneca as the figure "for whom auditory modes were of great authority" and concludes:

> the oral tradition in Western literature is transmitted by the Senecan vogue, and was gradually obliterated by the printed page .... The paradox that Senecanism is both highbrow in medieval scholasticism and lowbrow in the Elizabethan popular drama will be found to be resolved by this oral factor .... When only the eye is engaged, the multi-levelled gestures and resonances of Senecan oral action are quite impertinent.[49]

In the early hours of print culture's great day, Senecan orality shakes its muffled chains in English one last time before the printing press puts it to bed for a long rest.

The first decade of Elizabeth's reign saw the appearance of a number of Senecan ghosts or "portentous Senecan stalkers from the revenge tradition," as Marjorie Garber depicts them.[50] Julia Reinhard Lupton and Kenneth Reinhard suggest that the return of Seneca's *Oedipus* marks the return in English of the rageful father.[51] Benedict Anderson, however, offers us a way of viewing that

---

[48] Elizabeth Eisenstein, *The Printing Press as an Agent of Change: Communications and Cultural Transformations in Early-Modern Europe* (2 vols, Cambridge, 1979), vol. 1, p. 33.

[49] Marshall McLuhan, *The Gutenberg Galaxy* (Toronto, 1962), p. 128.

[50] Marjorie Garber, *Shakespeare's Ghost Writers: Literature as Uncanny Causality* (New York, 1987), p. 25.

[51] Julia Reinhard Lupton and Kenneth Reinhard, *After Oedipus: Shakespeare in*

return in the context of the "dethronement of Latin," an event that was brought on by the "half-fortuitous, but explosive, interaction between a system of production and productive relations (capitalism), a technology of communications (print), and the fatality of human linguistic diversity."[52] Seneca's *Oedipus* is the story of just such a dethronement, one that gets staged at the play's center when Seneca opens the gates of Hell and the entire founding male line of the House of Cadmus climbs out of the darkness. Significantly, Seneca's is the only classical drama of Oedipus that attempts to present the dynastic history of the Cadmean line, and it does so for more than fifty lines.

In his study of the materiality of space, Henri Lefebvre provides some clues as to why the task of dragging Cadmus' family out of Hell might have befallen Seneca:

> Rome was itself the exorcist of the forces of the underworld, challenging those forces by representing them in a graspable manner …. The Father predominated; he became what he was: chief, political soldier, and hence Law or Right …. Patriarchal power was inevitably accompanied by the imposition of a law of signs upon nature through writing, through inscriptions—through stone.[53]

There is little in this brief sketch of Rome that resembles mythic accounts of Thebes in which, according to Robert Graves, the city-state initially made do without a notion of paternity or the capacity to impose inscriptions.[54] The close links between the father, the law, property, paternity, and writing not only offer a powerful explanation for Latin's longevity as England and Western Europe's father tongue, but also intimate why it might have taken the printing press—a new technology for imposing the "law of signs upon nature"—to ultimately dethrone Latin from its position as the inherited chirographic language of what Lefebvre terms the "Pater-Rex."

To bring back the murdered father king of the Homeric/Sophoclean tradition for a Roman audience, as Seneca first did, may be seen as an effort to culturally transform a passive monarch who previously held onto the reigns of Greek patriarchy with a weak and inexperienced grip. Once Laius speaks—and writes—Latin, he returns to blame his troubles on "Cadmus" and "Mothers Love." Translating the story of Oedipus for the crowd at London's Inns of Court was likely linked to an equally vulnerable moment in the patriarchy. Susan Dwyer Amussen maintains that "central to one of the major strands of political thought in the period, patriarchalism … [was] the analogy between family and state," and that

---

Psychoanalysis (Ithaca, 1993), pp. 89–91.

[52] Benedict Anderson, *Imagined Communities: Reflections on the Origin and Spread of Nationalism* (London, 1991), p. 42.

[53] Henri Lefebvre, *The Production of Space,* trans. Donald Nicholson-Smith (Oxford, 1991), p. 243.

[54] Robert Graves, *The Greek Myths: Volume I* (New York, 1957), p. 11.

"the authority of the father was clear to all."[55] With an unwed virgin mother on the throne in 1558, the time of the Pater-Rex perhaps had come again. But Seneca's dramatization of the phantasmatic return of the Cadmus dynasty in 1563 might have had some other implications for a London audience. According to a number of traditions, the House of Cadmus, like the House of Tudor, also ruled over a kingdom recently exposed to a new technology of inscription that was only later fully domesticated in the house of the Father-King.[56] Less than a decade before Henry VII's 1485 declaration to parliament that "he had come to the crown by inheritance,"[57] William Caxton set up England's first printing press. In 1504, William Faques was appointed as the first King's Printer. Six years later, Richard Pynson became the first printer commissioned to print statutes legitimating a king's (Henry VIII) succession.

McLuhan succinctly explicates what the Cadmus myth attempts to report about the transition from pictographic to alphabetic culture:

> The Greek myth about the alphabet was that Cadmus, reputedly the king who introduced the phonetic letters into Greece, sowed the dragon's teeth, and they sprang up armed men. Like any other myth, this one capsulates a prolonged process into a flashing insight. Unlike pre-alphabetic writing, which with its innumerable signs was difficult to master, the alphabet could be learned in a few hours.[58]

The shared Cadmean morpheme of orthography and orthodontics continues to bear witness to the link between teeth and writing. But McLuhan is not the first to associate the myth of Cadmus with technologies of writing. Reviewing the dynastic beginnings of the house that Oedipus would pull down, Thomas Bulfinch concludes, "There is a tradition that Cadmus introduced into Greece the letters of the alphabet which were invented by the Phoenicians."[59] A.C. Moorhouse observes, "In Herodotus, letters are called Cadmean or Phoenician: and Cadmus was a mythical Greek who was said to have lived in Phoenicia and to have brought the alphabet back to Greece. Other ancient Greek authorities also spoke of Phoenician letters."[60] More recently, Martin Bernal has argued, "it is virtually certain that [the western alphabets] came from the Phoenician coast .... Tyre seems much more likely as the source. It was commonly supposed to have been the home

---

[55] Susan Dwyer Amussen, *An Ordered Society: Gender and Class in Early Modern England* (New York, 1988), pp. 54–7.

[56] George Chapman linked Cadmus to print and writing in Act IV of *Bussy D'Ambois* (1595).

[57] G.R. Elton, *England Under the Tudors* (London, 1992), p. 19.

[58] Marshall McLuhan, *Understanding Media: The Extensions of Man* (London, 1973), p. 92.

[59] Thomas Bulfinch, *Bulfinch's Mythology: The Age of Fable* (New York, 1968), p. 79.

[60] A.C. Moorhouse, *The Triumph of the Alphabet* (New York, 1953), p. 127.

of Cadmus, the legendary introducer of letters."[61] This mainstream mythic tradition regarding the origin of the alphabet is remarkable because it suggests that the initial transition from ideogramic to phonogramic writing transpired during the reign of a single ruler.

Noting that Phoenicians and other Semites modeled the alphabet after Egyptian signs, Moorhouse concludes, "If the original idea of alphabetic writing came from Egypt, as seems likely, then the borrowing of it was an act of genius of the first order."[62] As for the identity of this genius, here myth and archeology seem to converge:

> The Greek tradition about Cadmus assigns his life to the fourteenth century; and it is a curious fact that the island of Thera, according to tradition, was originally settled by Phoenicians and was also the place where Cadmus first landed on his return to Greece. It is strange that Thera should be the home of some of the oldest inscriptions. Possibly this is coincidence, but could be regarded as support for the truth of the tradition.[63]

The mythic story of Cadmus—and the subsequent drama that brings his dynasty to an untimely end—points beyond its fanciful narrative to some event in the *episteme* of ancient Greece that was linked to the introduction of alphabetic writing. It is tempting, therefore, to read the ominous presence of the sphinx at the city gates during Laius' absence as the monstrous return of the repressed—a kind of string around the Theban finger to remind the city of its Egyptian hieroglyphic legacy while a descendant of Cadmus is absent from the throne. Upon Oedipus's arrival at Thebes, the alphabetic dynasty of his great grandfather is restored. The sphinx, who embodies an earlier writing technology, commits suicide.

When the sphinx reappears in the Renaissance, this time on the thresholds of printed dictionaries and other books, it does so at a point in the history of writing when the Western European imagination is suddenly quite captivated by Egyptian hieroglyphics.[64] Rabelais, for example, nostalgically turns to Egyptian signs as an alternative to the abruptly expanded world of literacy around him, and he longs for the sacred inner sanctum of a priestly language to which not everyone has access: "The sages of ancient Egypt followed a very different course, when they wrote in letters that they called hieroglyphs—which none understood who did not understand, and which everyone understood who did understand, the virtue, property, and nature of the thing thereby described."[65]

---

[61] Martin Bernal, *Cadmean Letters: The Transmission of the Alphabet to the Aegean and Further West before 1400 BC* (Winona Lake, 1990), p. 29.

[62] Moorhouse, p. 124.

[63] Moorhouse, p. 127.

[64] For a discussion of George Herbert's interest in hieroglyphics, see Martin Elsky, *Authorizing Words: Speech, Writing, and Print in the English Renaissance* (Ithaca, 1989).

[65] François Rabelais, *Gargantua and Pantagruel,* trans. J.M. Cohen (New York, 1955), p. 58.

No doubt the fascination with Egyptian letters nourished itself on the robust health of an emergent print culture. Yet, there is another closely related context for the return of the house of Cadmus, especially during the first years of Elizabeth's reign. Noting that the "Oedipus myth or legend derives its narrative force from generational impiety," Jane Silverman Van Buren concludes,

> Cadmus's act of slaying the dragon signifies lack of respect for the maternal goddesses. As the narrative is structured on or emphasizes the sins of the male line, descended on a male child separated from his mother's care, it conveys the splitting off and disavowal of maternal presence and potency.[66]

Jean-François Lyotard contends that the Cadmus myth is organized around a fantasy of self-fashioning or autogenesis: "The warrior race sprang from the earth armed and armoured, but without parents; they were not born. This is the myth of autochthony .... [T]he important point about the myth of autochthony is that it excludes the parental dialectic."[67] Similarly, Jean-Pierre Vernant and Pierre Vidal-Niquet write of the Cadmus myth, "These warriors are autochthonous, and autochthony is a mythical procedure that eliminates the role played by women in originating the human species and that makes it possible for men to establish themselves as warrior fraternities. There is no such thing as autochthony for women."[68] And finally, Lyotard usefully speculates on the consequences of this patriarchal self-fashioning: "What the invaders are expressing by means of this myth is the fact that, unlike the people they dominate, they do not belong to any Mother Earth who can be impregnated, that they are born of themselves. We can see in this configuration an erasure of the female element, in other words foreclosure."[69] Together, these readings of the Cadmus myth suggest that the advent of patriarchy was concurrent with the advent of alphabetic writing and a related desire for autogenesis. And because the alphabet initially subsidizes a system of patrilineal rule, very little of the pre-scriptive past is preserved. As Paul Ricoeur notes, "The father is an unreality set apart, who, from the start, is a being of language .... Thus the father figure was bound to have a richer and more articulated destiny than the mother figure."[70]

---

[66] Jane Silverman Van Buren, *Modernist Madonna: Semiotics of the Maternal Metaphor* (Bloomington, 1989), p. 30.

[67] Jean-François Lyotard, *The Lyotard Reader,* ed. Andrew Benjamin (Oxford, 1989), p. 76.

[68] Jean-Pierre Venant and Pierre Vidal-Niquet, *Myth and Tragedy in Ancient Greece,* trans. Janet Loyd (New York, 1990), p. 298.

[69] Lyotard, p. 76.

[70] Paul Ricoeur, *Freud and Philosophy: An Essay on Interpretation,* trans. Denis Savage (New Haven, 1970), p. 543.

Daddy Dearest, or The Rise of the Gutenberg Father

Alphabetic Thebes returned to printerly London, appropriately enough, during the inaugural spectacle of a dynasty that attempted to use statutes to strengthen its patriarchal hold on power. But where once the latest innovation in writing had to be sown into the womb of the earth, the new technology had merely appropriated the womb.

Spenser, as was noted earlier, introduces the Theban Knight as a doomed father figure in Book V. Although there is no named reference to Cadmus in *FQ*, Spenser does conflate elements of the Oedipal infant prince tradition with a dynastic twist from the House of Cadmus in Book III. Cadmus plants the serpent's teeth and founds a purely patrilineal dynasty of warrior brothers that, in its initial stage, elides the maternal. Similarly, Artegall—"for his warlike feates renowmed" (III.iii. 27)—"sonne of *Gorlois*," "brother unto *Cador* Cornish king," and "firmely bound" to "his native soyle" doesn't seem to have a mother until Astraea adopts him (III.iii.27). Like the Virgin Mary and Elizabeth, Astraea gets children without actually begetting them.

Suggestive as Artegall's intertextual past might be, it seems strange that a poem that begins with a monstrous mother doubling as a printing press, and proceeds to fret about dynasty and lineage, never makes a direct reference to such a prominent tradition about fatherhood and writing. This conspicuous absence, I would argue, suggests that Spenser sidestepped the Cadmus myth in order to offer a new story of dynasty and paternal inscription, one that coheres closely with the transformed status of paternity in the age of mechanical reproduction and Elizabeth's disembodied maternity. This new story of parenting and printing, of kin and ink, of prince and prints, plays a prominent role in Book VI of *FQ*. Indeed, Spenser's engagement in Book VI with issues of patrilineal succession, especially as they intersect with contemporary uneasiness over being "a man in print," deserves more attention than it has received.

As noted earlier, Nohrnberg observes that there are "minor evidences of the transformation of the subject of the book into the book-as-subject" in Book VI. One such minor evidence is the character Calepine, named for a standard Latin Dictionary in Spenser's day. Yet another indication that parenting and printing is a thematic concern in Book VI is Spenser's decision to borrow from Seneca's dramatization of Cerberus and the alphabetic dynasty of Cadmus for his depiction of the Blatant Beast in the poem's final canto. When Spenser introduces the dynastic credentials of the monster—who stands between Calidore and a dynasty with close ties to early modern printing—in the gestationally numbered 9th stanza of Canto vi, he begins, appropriately enough, where the House of Cadmus begins, with the teeth:

> For that beastes teeth, which wounded you tofore,
> Are so exceeding venemous and keene,

Made all of rusty yron, ranckling sore ....
For that same beast was bred of hellish strene,
And long in darksome Stygian den vpbrought,
Begot of foule Echidna, as in bookes is taught. (VI.vi.9) [71]

No longer the pearly white dragon fangs that alphabetically generated Thebe's first patrilineal dynasty, the "rusty yron" teeth of the Blatant Beast indicate that the monster in Spenser's tale of paternal inscription belongs to an age when molten "yron" was poured into the mouth of a mold or matrix that, etymologically, was also a womb. In this sense, *FQ* ends where it began—with a story of monstrous printing in which the hysterical womb of Elizabeth's oral maternity has rusted from lack of use. Fittingly, the lineage of this monster is taught in "bookes."

Like a printing press, the Blatant Beast is one of the poem's noisiest figures, and its trail leads us directly into the heart of Spenser's Gutenberg myth. The monster is first named during a brief "succession" meeting between Artegall, whose knightly reign has come to an end, and Calidore (VI.i.4), whose knighthood has just begun. Not surprisingly, Artegall, whose Cadmean lineage has already been noted, is the only person in all of Calidore's "weary travell" (VI.i.10) who has encountered the monster. When the Blatant Beast finally appears, it has a woman in its mouth: "forth rushing unaware / Caught her thus loosely wandring here and there / And in his wide great mouth away her bare" (VI.iii.24). Here Spenser seems to literalize the Blatant Beast's etymological/mythical heritage ("her bare") and to link it back to Error, the poem's other monstrous matrix who resides in "the wandring wood." The woman is Serena, and she has attracted the attention of a young man named Aldine (or Aladine), whose name links him to a dynasty of printers. But if being rescued from the toothy mouth of a monstrous printing press frees Serena's matrix to imprint Aldine's progeny, Spenser seems pessimistic about her future maternity. The Blatant Beast finds her "loosely wandring here and there," and when we first learn her name, she has just "Wandered about the fields, as liking led / Her wavering lust after her wandring sight" (VI.iii.23). Like Elizabeth and other early modern women who remain virgins too long, her body language belongs to the discourse of hysteria. Indeed, subsequently cared for by a bookish Calepine, her "ranckling wound" (VI.iv.9)—note the gestational significance of the ninth line of a ninth stanza—proves to be so severe that not even the salvage man can save her: "But that same Ladies hurts no herbe be found, / Which could redresse, for it was inwardly unsound" (VI.iv.16). An "unsound" "wound" (both words appearing in the ninth line of their respective stanzas) suggests an injured womb, damaged perhaps, as writers from Plato to Jorden would have surmised, by lack of use. Serena will eventually recover, only to be captured in Canto VIII by cannibals who also want to sink their teeth into her flesh.

---

[71] The Blatant Beast is therefore akin to Arthur's Sphinx, who is "Horrible, hideous, and of hellish race / Borne of the brooding of Echidna base" (V.ii.23).

The link between cannibalism and paternal anxiety, of course, has a long history; an important early phase constituted by the episode of Hesiod's *Theogony* in which Kronos kills his father then devours his own children.[72]

The Blatant Beast makes its toothy mark on Aldine's plans for paternity, and the very next stanza literalizes the peculiarly Elizabethan form of oral maternity Calepine is offered once he recovers from wounds he suffered at the hands of Turpine. Playing on the double meaning of "bear" within the same line, Spenser introduces a "A cruell Beare, the which an infant bore / Betwixt his bloodie jawes, besprinkled all with gore" (VI.iv.17). Consistent with the Elizabethan version of the romance tradition of the infant prince, a baby has been passed—via a bloody mouth—from his biological mother to the care of a foster parent; and as was the case with Artegall and Redcrosse, analogy displaces bloodlines in the promotion of dynastic continuity. Even the blood that "besprinkled" this birth of sorts plays no role, because Spenser assures us six stanzas later, "And every litle limbe [Calepine] searcht around, / And every part, that vnder sweathbands lay, / Least that the beasts sharpe teeth had any wound / Made in his tender flesh, but whole them all he found" (VI.iv.23). A would-be mother is left for dead from an "inwardly unsound" wound, a male child is saved, and Calepine, whose name is derived from the Greek for "beautiful speech,"[73] is thrust, Cadmus-like, into fatherhood without having to rely on a woman. The site of this immaculate conception is a dynastic kingdom headed by a patriarch named Aldus —the first character in Book VI to be explicitly identified as a father. It is the closest Spenser will get to having "the kingdom of our own language" that he envies of the Greeks in his letter to Harvey.

To read on in *FQ* from here is to encounter other key elements in Spenser's tale of parenting and printing, culminating in canto xii with the romance genre's raison d'etre: Pastorella, named for a type of short medieval narrative poem, comes to learn the identity of her parents even as Calidore subdues, binds, and gains control of the monstrous printing press that is the bane of maternity in Book VI. If, however, we retrace the steps that lead up to Calepine's disembodied brush with paternity, we find, as with most dynastic myths, the most important information at the beginning of the story.

Early in canto iii, Calidore brings the injured Aldine home to his father's castle, and when he wakes up the next day to continue his pursuit of the monstrous mouth, Spenser paints the morning scene in some detail for us: "Earely so soone as Titans beames forth brust / Through the thicke clouds, in which they steeped lay / All night in darkenesse, duld with yron rust" (VI.iii.13). The sun is no longer named Phoebus, as it was in the evening of the gentle shepherd analogy of the Error

---

[72] See Marina Warner, "Why do Ogres Eat Babies? Monstrous Paternity in Myth and Fairy Tales," in Lieve Spaas and Trista Selous (eds), *Paternity and Fatherhood: Myths and Realities* (London, 1998), pp. 195–203.

[73] Nohrnberg, p. 682.

episode and the morning of the Senecan plague chorus. The switch to Titan here in Calidore's first day as Aldine's guest suggests that Spenser has Oedipus' first Senecan morning in mind. Here is how that first morning begins in English: "The night is at an end; but dimly yet / The Lord sun shows his face—a dull glow rising / Out of a dusky cloud" (Watling 1–3). And here is Oedipus speaking Seneca's father tongue: "Iam nocte Titan dubius expulsa redit / et nube maestus squalida exoritur iubar" (Fitch 1–2). The sun rising over the land of Aldus merges two closely related mythic traditions of paternal inscription. In one, the myth of Ra and Thoth, the sun god parthenogenetically gives birth to a son and hieroglyphics; in the other, a slain dragon's alphabetic teeth generate a line of sons. Spenser writes that "Titans beames" are "duld with yron rust," and when we subsequently read the lineage of the Blatant Beast "taught in bookes," we learn that the "beastes teeth" are "Made all rusty yron." The story of the paternal sun and the story of paternal teeth converge in *FQ*, because Gutenberg succeeds Cadmus as heir to the legacy of writing technology and fatherhood first founded in Egypt.

Certainly, Spenser could have chosen no more appropriate site for this succession then the castle of Aldus, "a worthy auncient Knight" (VI.ii.48), and his son Aldine. According to Phillip Gaskell, "The cursive style of Greek type was an immediate success: introduced by Aldus in the 1490s and perfected by Garamont and Granjon in the mid-sixteenth century, it dominated Greek typography for nearly 300 years."[74] Indeed, there was even some self-conscious material acknowledgement of the dynastic nature of this typographic enterprise. As H. George Fletcher notes, on books issued from the Aldine press after Aldus' death "the generic imprint was 'The Sons of Aldus.'"[75]

A century after an Italian printer upgraded Greek letters from teeth sewn into the earth's womb to iron type fonts formed in a type caster's matrix, Spenser erected the House of Aldus on the mythic terrain where the House of Cadmus once stood. Like the sphinx who haunted the gates of Thebes as a reminder of the alphabet's treacherous patriarchal past, the Blatant Beast prowls the grounds of the Aldine estate with a woman in his mouth to remind us of the new dynasty's Cadmean past. Yet, when Spenser began to dig the foundation for this new house in Book VI sometime during the last decade of Elizabeth's reign, I would suggest that he found another dynasty buried there—one that was equally committed to mixing words and wombs. Not only was the House of Aldine type the same age as the House of Tudor, but also the two dynasties had some major points of succession in common. Henry VII cleared the way to the throne in August of 1485 with his victory near the Leicestershire township of Market Bosworth. But his reign and the Tudor dynasty were first secured oppositionally against

---

[74] Philip Gaskell, *A New Introduction to Bibliography* (New York, 1972), p. 30.

[75] H. George Fletcher, *In Praise of Aldus Manutius: A Quincentenary Exhibition* (New York, 1995), p. 7.

parliamentary actions in the first half of the next decade.[76] Thus, the two patriarchs were busy securing their respective kingdoms in the same moment. As Fletcher notes, "between the summer of 1490 and the spring of 1495" Aldus was "working up, if not yet perfecting, the tremendously (and probably excessively) complicated system of Greek typefounding that he invented."[77] Aldus' son, Paulus Manutius (1512–74), took over the Aldine press within a year of the birth of Henry VIII's son. Finally, Aldus Manutius the Younger (1547–97), the last of the Aldine clan, entered the family business when his father, Paulus, left Venice to work in Rome sometime in 1559 or 1560. The House of Aldus entered its last phase just as Elizabeth was announcing the marital and childbearing arrangements that would spell the end of the Tudor line. Six years before the crown was passed from Tudor to Stuart, the Aldine press reverted back to the sole ownership of the Torresani family.

It is difficult to judge which of the two houses mixed words with wombs more successfully. Having ruled concurrently for a little more than a century, the two dynasties were united by a common dream of attaining mastery over their respective means of reproduction. It was a dream that Euripides' Jason had once succinctly expressed in Greek to Medea, the most monstrous of mythic mothers. Taught to speak Latin by George Buchanan between 1539 and 1542, when Henry VIII was frantically supplementing kinship with inkship, Jason tells the wife he's recently abandoned:

> What we poor males really need is a way of having babies
> on our own—no females please.
> Then the world would be completely trouble free.[78]

---

[76] Elton, p. 35.

[77] Fletcher, p. 2.

[78] Euripides, *Medea*, trans. Paul Roche (New York, 1974), lines 573–5. Buchanan's translation is lost.

Bibliography

Manuscript Sources

British Library MS Add. 22285.
British Library MS Lansdowne 777, f 43^v.
De L'Isle and Dudley MS 1475, C7/15.
Leiden University MS Lips 4.
National Archives, State Papers Domestic, Elizabeth (SP12), vol. 49, no. 63, fols 135–6.
National Archives, State Papers Domestic, Elizabeth (SP84), vol. 10, fol. 73.
Valladolid Ser. II, L. 5, no. 13.
Yale University Library MS Osborn fa. 14, fols 36–7.
Yale University Library MS Osborn fa. 14, fol. 92.
Zürich Zentralbibliothek MS F61, fol. 178.

Printed Sources

Allison, A.F., "New Light on the Early History of the *Breve Compendio:* The Background to the English Translation of 1612," *Recusant History*, 4 (1957): 4–17.
—— and Rogers, D.M., *The Contemporary Printed Literature of the English Counter-Reformation between 1558–1640* (2 vols, Aldershot: Scolar, 1989–94).
Altman, Joel B., *The Tudor Play of Mind: Rhetorical Inquiry and the Development of Elizabethan Drama* (Berkeley: University of California Press, 1978).
Amussen, Susan Dwyer, *An Ordered Society: Gender and Class in Early Modern England* (New York: Columbia University Press, 1988).
Anderson, Benedict, *Imagined Communities: Reflections on the Origin and Spread of Nationalism* (London: Verso, 1991).
Anderson, Judith H., "Redcrosse and the Descent into Hell," *ELH*, 36 (1969): 481–5.
——, "The 'couert vele': Spenser, Chaucer, and Venus," *English Literary Renaissance*, 24 (1994): 638–59.
——, *The Growth of a Personal Voice: "Piers Plowman" and "The Faerie Queene"* (New Haven: Yale University Press, 1976).

Annals of English Drama: 975–1700, eds Sylvia Stoler Wagonheim, Alfred Harbage and S. Schoenbaum (3rd edn, London: Routledge, 1989).

Ariani, Marco, *Petrarca* (Rome: Salerno, 1999).

Aristotle, *The Complete Works of Aristotle*, ed. Jonathan Barnes (2 vols, 1984; Princeton: Princeton University Press, 1985).

Armitage, David, "Empire and Liberty: A Republican Dilemma," in Martin van Gelderen and Quentin Skinner (eds), *Republicanism: A Shared European Heritage* (2 vols, Cambridge: Cambridge University Press, 2002), vol. 2, pp. 29–46.

Arnold, Matthew, *Selected Poems and Prose*, ed. M. Allott (New York: Dutton, 1978).

Ascham, Roger, *The Scholemaster* (1570).

Askew, Anne, *The first examinacyon* ... (Wesel, 1546).

Attridge, Derek, *Peculiar Language: Literature as Difference from the Renaissance to James Joyce* (London: Methuen, 1988).

Austin, J.L., *How to Do Things with Words* (2nd edn, London: Oxford University Press, 1978)

Babb, Howard S., "Policy in Marlowe's *The Jew of Malta*," *ELH*, 24 (1957): 85–94.

Bacon, Francis, *Novum Organum, With Other Parts of The Great Instauration*, trans and eds Peter Urbach and John Gibson (Chicago: Open Court, 1994).

Baker, J.H., *An Introduction to English Legal History* (3rd edn, London: Butterworths, 1990).

Bakhtin, M.M., *The Dialogic Imagination: Four Essays*, trans. Michael Holquist (Austin: University of Texas Press, 1981).

Baldensperger, Fernand, *Les Sonnets de Shakespeare traduits en vers français et accompagnés d'un commentaire continu* (Berkeley: University of California Press, 1943).

Baldwin, T.W., *William Shakspere's small Latine and lesse Greeke* (2 vols, Urbana: University of Illinois Press, 1944).

Barney, Stephen A., *Allegories of History, Allegories of Love* (Hamden: Archon, 1979).

Bate, Jonathan, *The Genius of Shakespeare* (London: Picador, 1997).

Battenhouse, Roy, "*Measure for Measure* and the Christian Doctrine of Atonement," *PMLA*, 61 (1946): 1029–59.

Bawcutt, N.W., "Machiavelli and Marlowe's *The Jew of Malta*," *Renaissance Drama*, 3 (1970): 3–49.

Bednarz, James P., *Shakespeare and the Poets' War* (New York: Columbia University Press, 2001).

Bell, Maureen, Parfitt, George and Shepherd, Simon (eds), *A Biographical Dictionary of English Women Writers, 1580–1720* (Boston: G.K. Hall, 1990).

Bellot, Jacques, *French Methode* (1588), ed. R.C. Alston (Menston: Scolar, 1970).

——, *Le Maistre d'Ecole Anglois* (1580), ed. R.C. Alston (Menston: Scolar, 1967).

Ben Jonson's Conversations with William Drummond of Hawthornden, ed. R.F. Patterson (London: Blackie, 1923).

Benjamin, Jessica, *The Bonds of Love: Psychoanalysis, Feminism, and the Problem of Domination* (New York: Pantheon, 1988).

Bennett, Lyn, *Women Writing of Divinest Things: Rhetoric and the Poetry of Pembroke, Wroth and Lanyer* (Pittsburgh: Duquesne University Press, 2004).

Bernal, Martin, *Cadmean Letters: The Transmission of the Alphabet to the Aegean and Further West before 1400 BC* (Winona Lake: Eisenbrauns, 1990).

Bernthal, Craig, "Staging Justice: James I and the Trial Scenes in *Measure for Measure*," *Studies in English Literature*, 32 (1992): 247–69.

Bindoff, S.T., *Tudor England* (Middlesex: Penguin, 1980).

Blissett, William, "Lucan's Caesar and the Elizabethan Villain," *Studies in Philology*, 53 (1956): 553–75.

Bodin, Jean, *Colloquium of the Seven about Secrets of the Sublime: Colloquium Heptaplomeres de Rerum Sublimium Arcanis Abditis*, trans. Marion Leathers Daniels Kuntz (Princeton: Princeton University Press, 1975).

Boehrer, Bruce Thomas, *Monarchy and Incest in Renaissance England: Literature, Culture, Kinship, and Kingship* (Philadelphia: University of Pennsylvania Press, 1992).

Boulton, Jeremy, *Neighborhood and Society: A London Suburb in the Seventeenth Century* (Cambridge: Cambridge University Press, 1987).

Bourdieu, Pierre, "The Economics of Linguistic Exchanges," *Social Science Information*, 16 (1977): 645–68.

——, *Outline of a Theory of Practice*, trans. Richard Nice (Cambridge: Cambridge University Press, 1977).

Bradshaw, Graham, *Shakespeare's Scepticism* (Ithaca: Cornell University Press, 1987).

Brandolini, Lippi, *De ratione scribendi tres ... adiecti sunt Io. Ludovici Vivis ... de conscribendis epistolis libelli* (Frankfurt, 1568).

Braudy, Leo, *The Frenzy of Renown: Fame and Its History* (New York: Oxford University Press, 1986).

Brennan, Michael G., "The Queen's Proposed Visit to Wilton House in 1599 and the 'Sidney Psalms'," *Sidney Journal*, 20 (2002): 27–54.

Brooks, Douglas A. (ed.), *Printing and Parenting in Early Modern England* (Burlington: Ashgate, 2005).

Brown, Georgia, "Marlowe's Poems and Classicism," in Patrick Cheney (ed.), *The Cambridge Companion to Christopher Marlowe* (Cambridge: Cambridge University Press, 2004), pp. 120–24.

Brown, Penelope and Levinson, Stephen, *Politeness: Some Universals in Language Usage* (Cambridge: Cambridge University Press, 1987).

Bruns, Gerald, *Inventions: Writing, Textuality, and Understanding in Literary History* (New Haven: Yale University Press, 1982).

Bulfinch, Thomas, *Bulfinch's Mythology: The Age of Fable* (New York: Doubleday, 1968).

Bullinger, Heinrich, *Briefwechsel*, eds Ulrich Gabel and Endre Zsindely (12 vols, Zürich: Theologisches Verlag Zürich, 1973).

Burlin, Robert, *Chaucerian Fiction* (Princeton: Princeton University Press, 1977).

Burrow, Colin, *Epic Romance: Homer to Milton* (Oxford: Clarendon Press, 1993).

Butler, Kathleen T., *The "Gentlest Art" in Renaissance Italy* (Cambridge: Cambridge University Press, 1954).

Calendar of state papers, domestic series, of the reigns of Edward VI, Mary, Elizabeth [and James I] 1547–1625: preserved in the State Paper Department of Her Majesty's Public Record Office, ed. Robert Lemon (12 vols, London: HMSO, 1856).

Calvin, John, *Institutes of the Christian Religion*, trans. John Allen (2 vols, Philadelphia: Presbyterian Board of Christian Education, 1936).

——, *The Psalmes of David and others. With M. John Calvins Commentaries*, trans. Arthur Golding (London, 1571).

Carrington, Laurel, "Women, Rhetoric, and Letter Writing: Marguerite d'Alençon's Correspondence with Bishop Briçonnet of Meaux," in Molly Meijer Wertheimer (ed.), *Listening to Their Voices: The Rhetorical Activities of Historical Women* (Columbia: University of South Carolina Press, 1997), pp. 215–32.

Cary, Elizabeth, *The Tragedy of Mariam The Fair Queen of Jewry with The Lady Falkland Her Life by One of Her Daughters*, eds Barry Weller and Margaret W. Ferguson (Berkeley: University of California Press, 1994).

Castiglione, Baldesar, *The Book of the Courtier*, trans. George Bull (Harmondsworth: Penguin, 1967).

Cavendish, Margaret, *A True Relation of My Birth, Breeding, and Life* (London, 1656).

Chambers, E.K., *William Shakespeare: A Study of Facts and Problems* (2 vols, Oxford: Clarendon Press, 1930).

Chambers, R.W., *Man's Unconquerable Mind: Studies of English Writers, from Bede to A.E. Houseman and W.P. Ker* (London: Jonathan Cape, 1939).

Chaucer, Geoffrey, *The Riverside Chaucer*, ed. Larry D. Benson (3rd edn, Boston: Houghton Mifflin, 1987).

——, *The Works, 1532: With Supplementary Material from the Editions of 1542, 1561, 1598, and 1602* (1968; London: Scolar Press, 1976).

Cheney, Patrick, "Introduction: Marlowe in the Twenty-First Century," in Patrick Cheney (ed.), *The Cambridge Companion to Christopher Marlowe* (Cambridge: Cambridge University Press, 2004), pp. 1–23.

——, *Marlowe's Counterfeit Profession: Ovid, Spenser, Counter-Nationhood* (Toronto: University of Toronto Press, 1997).

——, *Shakespeare, National Poet-Playwright* (Cambridge: Cambridge University Press, 2004).

Cicero, Marcus Tullius, *De inventione*, trans. H.M. Hubbell (London: Heinemann, 1949).

——, *Letters to Friends*, trans. and ed. D.R. Shackleton Bailey (3 vols, Cambridge: Harvard University Press, 2001).

——, *On Duties* (*De officiis*), eds M.T. Griffin and E.M. Atkins (Cambridge: Cambridge University Press, 1991).

Clark, A.C., *Fontes Prosæ Numerosæ* (Oxford: Clarendon Press, 1909).

Clarke, Danielle, *The Politics of Early Modern Women's Writing* (London: Longman, 2001).

Coghill, Neville, "Comic Form in *Measure for Measure*," *Shakespeare Survey*, 8 (1955): 14–27.

Coke, Edward, *The Fourth Part of the Institutes of the Laws of England* (4th edn, London, 1669).

Colie, Rosalie, *Paradoxia Epidemica: The Renaissance Tradition of Paradox* (Princeton: Princeton University Press, 1966).

Collinson, Patrick, "The Monarchical Republic of Queen Elizabeth I," in John Guy (ed.), *The Tudor Monarchy* (London: Arnold, 1997), pp. 110–34.

Cooper, Thompson, "Englefield, Sir Francis (d. 1596?), catholic exile," *Dictionary of National Biography* (London: Oxford University Press, 1917–), vol. 6, pp. 790–93.

Crockett, Bryan, *The Play of Paradox: Stage and Sermon in Renaisssance England* (Philadelphia: University of Pennsylvania Press, 1995).

D'Amico, Jack, *Shakespeare and Italy* (Gainesville: University Press of Florida, 2001).

Daniel, Samuel, *Selected Poetry and A Defense of Rhyme,* eds Geoffrey G. Hiller and Peter L. Groves (Asheville: Pegasus, 1998).

Daybell, James, "Women's Letters and Letter Writing in England, 1540–1603," diss., University of Reading, 1999.

——, "Women's Letters and Letter Writing in England, 1540–1603: An Introduction to the Issues of Authorship and Construction," *Shakespeare Studies*, 27 (1999): 161–86.

——, *Early Modern Women's Letter Writing, 1450–1700* (Basingstoke: Palgrave, 2001).

——, *Women Letter-Writers in Tudor England* (Oxford: Oxford University Press, 2005).

De la Mothe, G., *The French Alphabeth* (London, 1592).

Dempster, Germaine, "Chaucer at Work on the Complaint in the Franklin's Tale," *Modern Language Notes*, 52 (1973) 16–23.

Derrida, Jacques, *Dissemination*, trans. Barbara Johnson (Chicago: University of Chicago Press, 1981).

Desonay, Fernand, *Ronsard, pote de l'amour* (3 vols, Brussels: Palais des Académies, 1952).

Desportes, Philippe, *Les Amours d'Hippolyte*, ed. Victor E. Graham (Geneva: Droz, 1960).

Dickinson, J.W., "Renaissance Equity and *Measure for Measure*," *Shakespeare Quarterly*, 13 (1962): 287–97.

Diehl, Huston, "'Infinite Space': Representation and Reformation in *Measure for Measure*," *Shakespeare Quarterly*, 49 (1998): 393–410.

Dilke, O.A.W., "Lucan and English Literature," in D.R. Dudley (ed.), *Neronians and Flavians: Silver Latin I* (London: Routledge, 1972), pp. 83–112.

Dinshaw, Carolyn, *Chaucer's Sexual Poetics* (Madison: University of Wisconsin Press, 1989).

Dollimore, Jonathan, *Radical Tragedy: Religion, Ideology and Power in the Drama of Shakespeare and His Contemporaries* (Chicago: University of Chicago Press, 1984).

Donaldson, E. Talbot (ed.), *Chaucer's Poetry: An Anthology for the Modern Reader* (2nd edn, New York: Ronald Press, 1975).

Donawerth, Jane, "'As Becomes a Rational Woman to Speak': Madeleine de Scudéry's Rhetoric of Conversation," in Molly Meijer Wertheimer (ed.), *Listening to Their Voices: The Rhetorical Activities of Historical Women* (Columbia: University of South Carolina Press, 1997), pp. 305–19.

Donne, John, *The Divine Poems*, ed. Helen Gardner (1952, 1966; Oxford: Clarendon Press, 1978).

Downie, J.A. and Parnell, J.T. (eds), *Constructing Christopher Marlowe* (Cambridge: Cambridge University Press, 2000).

Dowriche, Anne, *French Historie* (London, 1589).

Du Bellay, Joachim, *Oeuvres poétiques*, eds Daniel Aris and Françoise Joukovsky (2 vols, Paris: Bordas, 1993–1996).

Dubrow, Heather, *Echoes of Desire: English Petrarchism and Its Counterdiscourses* (Ithaca: Cornell University Press, 1995).

Duby, George, *The Chivalrous Society*, trans. Cynthia Postan (Berkeley: University of California Press, 1977).

Duncan-Jones, Katherine, *Sir Philip Sidney, Courtier Poet* (Oxford: Oxford University Press, 1995).

——, *Ungentle Shakespeare: Scenes from His Life* (London: Arden Shakespeare, 2001).

Dunkel, Wilbur, "Law and Equity in *Measure for Measure*," *Shakespeare Quarterly*, 13 (1962): 275–85.

Dutton, Richard, *Licensing, Censorship and Authorship in Early Modern English: Buggeswords* (Basingstoke: Palgrave, 2000).

Eden, Kathy, *Hermeneutics and the Rhetorical Tradition: Chapters in the Ancient Legacy and Its Humanist Reception* (New Haven: Yale University Press, 1997).

——, *Poetic and Legal Fiction in the Aristotelian Tradition* (Princeton: Princeton University Press, 1985).

Eisenstein, Elizabeth, *The Printing Press as an Agent of Change: Communications and Cultural Transformations in Early-Modern Europe* (2 vols, Cambridge: Cambridge University Press, 1979).

Elam, Keir, *Shakespeare's Universe of Discourse: Language-Games in the Comedies* (Cambridge: Cambridge University Press, 1984).

Eliot, John, *Ortho-epia Gallica* (1593), ed. R.C. Alston (Menston: Scolar, 1968).

Elizabeth I, *Elizabeth 1: Collected Works*, eds Leah S. Marcus, Janel Mueller, and Mary Beth Rose (Chicago: University of Chicago Press, 2000).

Ellis, Henry, *Original Letters Illustrative of English History* (3 vols, London: Harding, Triphook, and Lepard, 1824).

——, *Original Letters Illustrative of English History* (4 vols, London: R. Bentley, 1846).

Elsky, Martin, *Authorizing Words: Speech, Writing, and Print in the English Renaissance* (Ithaca: Cornell University Press, 1989).

Elton, G.R., *England Under the Tudors* (London: Routledge, 1992).

Engle, Lars, "*Measure for Measure* and Modernity: The Problem of the Sceptic's Authority," in Hugh Grady (ed.), *Shakespeare and Modernity: Early Modern to Millenium* (London: Routledge, 2000), pp. 85–104.

Enterline, Lynn, *The Rhetoric of the Body from Ovid to Shakespeare* (Cambridge: Cambridge University Press, 2000).

Erasmus, Desiderius, *Collected Works of Erasmus*, trans. and ed. R.A.B. Mynors (Toronto: University of Toronto Press, 1989).

——, *Desiderii Erasmi Roterodami Opera Omnia*, ed. P. van der Aa (10 vols, Leiden: P. van der Aa, 1703–1706).

Erne, Lukas, *Shakespeare as Literary Dramatist* (Cambridge: Cambridge University Press, 2003).

Erondelle, Peter, *French Garden For English Ladyes and gentlewomen to walke in* (1605), ed. R.C. Alston (Menston: Scolar, 1969).

Euripides, *Medea*, trans. Paul Roche (New York: Norton, 1974).

Evans, Katherine and Cheevers, Sarah, *This Is A Short Relation of some of the Cruel Sufferings (for the Truths sake) of Katharine Evans & Sarah Chevers ...* (London, 1662).

Feeney, D.C., *The Gods in Epic: Poets and Critics of the Classical Tradition* (Oxford: Clarendon Press, 1991).

Fehrenback, R.J., and Leedham-Green, E.S., *Private Libraries in Renaissance England: A Collection and Catalogue of Tudor and Early Stuart Book Lists* (5 vols, Tempe: MRTS, 1992–98).

Fink, Zera S., *The Classical Republicans: An Essay in the Recovery of a Pattern of Thought in Seventeenth Century England* (Evanston: Northwestern University Press, 1945).

Finlay, Roger, *Population and Metropolis: The Demography of London, 1580–1650* (Cambridge: Cambridge University Press, 1981).

Fisken, Beth Wynne, "Mary Sidney's *Psalmes*: Education and Wisdom," in Margaret P. Hannay (ed.), *Silent but for the Word: Tudor Women as Patrons, Translators, and Writers of Religious Works* (Kent: Kent State University Press, 1985), p. 166–83.

Fleischer, Manfred, "The Success of Ursinus: A Triumph of Intellectual Friendship," in Derk Visser (ed.), *Controversy and Conciliation: The Reformation and the Palatinate 1559–1583* (Allison Park: Pickwick, 1986), pp. 101–15.

Fletcher, H. George, *In Praise of Aldus Manutius: A Quincentenary Exhibition* (New York: Pierpoint Morgan Library, 1995).

Fletcher, John Rory, *The Story of the English Bridgettines of Syon Abbey* (Devon: Burleigh, 1933).

Florio, John, *His First Fruites* (1578) (New York: Da Capo, 1969).

——, *Queen Anne's New World of Words* (1611), ed. R.C. Alston (Menston: Scolar, 1968).

——, *Second Fruites (*1591), ed. R.C. Simonini, Jr. (Gainesville: Scholars' Facsimiles & Reprints, 1953).

Foley, Henry (ed.), *Records of the English Province of the Society of Jesus: historic facts illustrative of the labours and sufferings of its members in the sixteenth and seventeenth centuries* (7 vols, London: Burns & Oates, 1877–1883).

Ford, David Nash, "Royal Berkshire History," http://www.berkshirehistory.com.

Fortier, Mark, "Equity and Ideas: Coke, Ellesmere, and James I," *Renaissance Quarterly*, 51 (1998): 1255–81.

Fox, Adam, *Oral and Literate Culture in England, 1500–1700* (Oxford: Clarendon Press, 2000).

—— and Woolf, Daniel (eds), *The Spoken Word: Oral Culture in Britain, 1500–1850* (New York: Manchester University Press, 2002).

Fox, Alistair, *The English Renaissance: Identity and Representation in Elizabethan England* (Oxford: Blackwell, 1997).

—— and Guy, John, *Reassessing the Henrician Age* (Oxford: Blackwell, 1986).

Frantz, David O., "Florio's Use of Contemporary Italian Literature in *A Worlde of Wordes*," *Dictionaries*, 1 (1979): 47–56.

Fraunce, Abraham, *The Arcadian Rhetorike*, ed. Ethel Seaton (Oxford: Blackwell, 1950).

Freccero, John, "The Fig Tree and the Laurel: Petrarch's Poetics," in Patricia Parker and David Quint (eds), *Literary Theory/Renaissance Texts* (1975; Baltimore: Johns Hopkins University Press, 1986), pp. 20–32.

Freer, Coburn, *Music for a King: George Herbert's Style and the Metrical Psalms* (Baltimore: Johns Hopkins University Press, 1972).

Freud, Sigmund, *The Interpretation of Dreams*, trans. James Strachey (New York: Avon, 1965).

Fumaroli, Marc, "Genèse de l'épistolographie classique: rhétorique humaniste de la lettre de Pétrarque à Juste Lipse," *Revue de l'histoire littéraire de la France* 78 (1978): 886–905.

Gadamer, Hans-Georg, *Truth and Method*, trans. Joel Weinsheimer and Donald G. Marshall (2nd edn, New York: Crossroad, 1989).

Gallagher, Lowell, *Medusa's Gaze: Casuistry and Conscience in the Renaissance* (Stanford: Stanford University Press, 1991).

Garber, Marjorie, *Shakespeare's Ghost Writers: Literature as Uncanny Causality* (New York: Methuen, 1987).

Gascoigne, George, *A Hundreth Sundrie Flowres*, ed. George W. Pigman III (Oxford: Clarendon Press, 2000).

Gaskell, Philip, *A New Introduction to Bibliography* (New York: Oxford University Press, 1972).

The Geneva Bible, a Facsimile of the 1560 Edition, ed. Lloyd E. Berry (Madison: University of Wisconsin Press, 1969).

The Geneva Bible: The Annotated New Testament, 1602 Edition, ed. Gerald T. Sheppard (Cleveland: Pilgrim, 1989).

Gill, Roma, "Marlowe, Lucan, and Sulpitius," *Review of English Studies*, 24 (1973): 401–13.

Gillow, Joseph, *Literary and Biographical History, or Bibliographical Dictionary of the English Catholics from the breach with Rome, in 1534, to the present time* (5 vols, 1885; New York: Burt Franklin, 1961).

Goldberg, Jonathan, *Writing Matter: From the Hands of the English Renaissance* (Stanford: Stanford University Press, 1990).

Gorges, Arthur, *The Poems*, ed. Helen Estabrook Sandeson (Oxford: Clarendon Press, 1953).

Goux, Jean-Joseph, *Oedipus, Philosopher* (Stanford: Stanford University Press, 1993).

Graves, Robert, *The Greek Myths: Volume I* (New York: George Braziller, 1957).

Green, Mary Anne Everett, *Letters of Royal and Illustrious Ladies of Great Britain* (3 vols, London: H. Colburn, 1846).

Greenblatt, Stephen J., *Renaissance Self-Fashioning: More to Shakespeare* (Chicago: University of Chicago Press, 1980).

——, *Shakespearean Negotiations: The Circulation of Social Energy in Renaissance England* (Berkeley: University of California Press, 1988).

——, *Will in the World* (New York: W.W. Norton, 2004).

Greene, Robert, *Greenes Groatsworth of Witte* (London, 1592).

——, *The Historie of Orlando Furioso* (London, 1599).

——, *The Scottish Historie of Iames the fourth* (London, 1593).

Greene, Roland, "Sir Philip Sidney's *Psalms*, the Sixteenth-Century Psalter, and the Nature of Lyric," *Studies in English Literature*, 30 (1990): 19–40.

——, *Post-Petrarchism: Origins and Innovations of the Western Lyric Sequence* (Princeton: Princeton University Press, 1991).

Greene, Thomas M., *The Light in Troy: Imitation and Discovery in Renaissance Poetry* (New Haven: Yale University Press, 1982).

Grell, Ole Peter, *Calvinist Exiles in Tudor and Stuart England* (Aldershot: Scolar, 1996).

Guazzo, Stephano, *The Civile Conuersation of M. Steeuen Guazzo*, trans. George Pettie (London, 1581).

——, *The Civile Conversation of M. Steeven Guazzo*, trans. George Pettie and Bartholomew Young (2 vols, London: Constable and Co. Ltd., 1925).

Guilday, Peter, *The English Catholic Refugees on the Continent, 1558–1795* (London: Longmans, Green, 1914).

Gusualdo, Giovanni Andrea, *Il Petrarcha, colla spositione di Misser Giovanni Andrea Gesualdo* (Venice, 1533).

Gwynn, Robin D., *Huguenot Heritage: The History and Contribution of the Huguenots in Britain* (2nd edn, Brighton: Sussex Academic Press, 2001).

Hadfield, Andrew, "Was Spenser a Republican?", *English*, 47 (1998): 169–82.

——, "Was Spenser Really a Republican After All? A Reply to David Scott Wilson-Okamura," *Spenser Studies*, 17 (2003): 275–90.

——, *Shakespeare and Renaissance Politics* (New York: Thomson Learning, 2003).

——, *Shakespeare and Republicanism* (Cambridge: Cambridge University Press, 2005).

Hake, Edward, *Epieikeia: A Dialogue on Equity in Three Parts*, ed. D.E.C. Yale (New Haven: Yale University Press, 1953).

Hamilton, Dom Adam, *The Chronicle of the English Augustinian Canonesses Regular of the Lateran, at St. Monica's in Louvain (now at St. Augustine's Priory, Newton Abbot, Devon)* (2 vols, London: Sands, 1904–1906).

Hamlin, Hannibal, *Psalm Culture and Early Modern English Literature* (Cambridge: Cambridge University Press, 2004).

Hammill, Graham, "'The thing / Which never was': Republicanism and *The Ruines of Time*," *Spenser Studies*, 18 (2003): 165–83.

Hanks, William F., "Notes on Semantics in Linguistic Practice," in Craig Calhoun, Edward LiPuma and Moishe Postone (eds), *Bourdieu: Critical Perspectives* (Cambridge: Polity Press, 1993), pp. 139–55.

Hannay, Margaret, "Incorporating Women Writers into the Survey Course: Mary Sidney's Psalm 73 and *Astrophil and Stella* 5," in Patrick Cheney and Anne Lake Prescott (eds), *Approaches to Teaching Shorter Elizabethan Poetry* (New York: MLA, 2000), pp. 133–8.

——, "The Countess of Pembroke as a Spenserian Poet," in Sigrid M. King (ed.), *Pilgrimage for Love: Essays in Early Modern Literature in Honor of Josephine A. Roberts* (Tempe: Arizona Center for Medieval and Renaissance Studies, 1999), pp. 41–62.

Hansen, Elaine Tuttle, *Chaucer and the Fictions of Gender* (Berkeley: University of California Press, 1992).

Hardie, Philip, *The Epic Successors of Virgil: A Study in the Dynamics of a Tradition* (Cambridge: Cambridge University Press, 1993).

Hardison, O.B., "Blank Verse before Milton," *Studies in Philology*, 81 (1984): 253–74.

Harrison, G.B. (ed.), *The Elizabethan Journals* (2 vols, Garden City: Anchor, 1965).

Hawkins, Harriet, *Measure for Measure: Harvester New Critical Introductions to Shakespeare* (Brighton: Harvester, 1987).

Hawkins, Peter, "From Mythography to Myth-making: Spenser and the *Magna Mater Cybele*," *Sixteenth-Century Journal*, 12 (1981): 51–64.

Haydn, Hiram, *The Counter-Renaissance* (New York: Scribner, 1950).

Hazeltine, H.D., "The Early History of English Equity," in Paul Vinogradoff (ed.), *Essays in Legal History* (London: Oxford University Press, 1913), pp. 261–85.

Healy, Thomas, *Christopher Marlowe* (Plymouth, Eng.: British Council, 1994).

Heitsch, Dorothea and Vallée, Jean-François (eds), *Printed Voices: The Renaissance Culture of Dialogue* (Toronto: University of Toronto Press, 2004).

Helgerson, Richard, "Barbarous Tongues: The Ideology of Poetic Form in Renaissance England," in Heather Dubrow and Richard Strier (eds), *The Historical Renaissance: New Essays on Tudor and Stuart Literature and Culture* (Chicago: University of Chicago Press, 1988), pp. 273–92.

——, *Forms of Nationhood: The Elizabethan Writing of England* (Chicago: University of Chicago Press, 1992)

——, *Self-Crowned Laureates: Spenser, Jonson, Milton and the Literary System* (Berkeley: University of California Press, 1983).

Henderson, John, "Lucan / The Word at War," in A.J. Boyle (ed.), *The Imperial Muse: Ramus Essays in Roman Literature of the Empire to Juvenal through Ovid* (Berwick, Australia: Aureal, 1988), pp. 122–64.

Herbert, George, *The Complete English Poems*, ed. John Tobin (New York: Penguin, 1991).

Hieatt, A. Kent, "The Genesis of *Shakespeare Sonnets* in Spenser's *Ruines of Rome*," *PMLA*, 98 (1983): 800–814.

Hoenselaars, A.J., *Images of Englishmen and Foreigners in the Drama of Shakespeare and His Contemporaries* (Rutherford: Fairleigh Dickinson University Press, 1992).

Holybande, Claudius, *French Littleton* (1576), ed. R.C. Alston (Menston: Scolar, 1970).

Hooker, Richard, *Of the Laws of Ecclesiastical Polity*, ed. W. Speed Hill (Cambridge: Belknap, 1977).

Houliston, Victor, "Persons [Parsons], Robert (1546–1610), Jesuit," *Oxford Dictionary of National Biography*, http://www.oxforddnb.com, article 21474.

Howard, Donald R., *The Idea of the Canterbury Tales* (Berkeley: University of California Press, 1976).

Hudson, Charles (ed.), *Red, White and Black: Symposium on Indians in the South* (Athens: Southern Anthropological Society, 1966).

Hulse, Clark, *Metamorphic Verse: The Elizabethan Minor Epic* (Princeton: Princeton University Press, 1981).

——, "Spenser, Bacon, and the Myth of Power," in Heather Dubrow and Richard Strier (eds), *The Historical Renaissance: New Essays on Tudor and Stuart Literature and Culture* (Chicago: University of Chicago Press, 1988), pp. 315–46.

Hume, Anthea, *Edmund Spenser: Protestant Poet* (Cambridge: Cambridge University Press, 1984).

Humiliata, Mary, "Standards of Taste Advocated for Feminine Letter Writing, 1640–1797," *HLQ*, 13 (1950): 261–77.

Hunter, G.K., *Dramatic Identities and Cultural Tradition* (Liverpool: Liverpool University Press, 1978).

——, *English Drama, 1586–1642* (Oxford: Clarendon Press, 1997).

——, *John Lyly: The Humanist as Courtier* (Cambridge: Harvard University Press, 1962).

Hutchison, Ann M., "Beyond the Margins: The Recusant Bridgettines," in *Studies in St. Birgitta and the Brigittine Order, 2, Analecta Cartusiana: Spiritualität Heute und Gestern*, 35: 19 (Salzburg: Institut für Anglilstik und Amerikanistik Universität Salzburg, 1993): 267–84.

——, "Eyes Cast Down, But Self Revealed: Letters of a Recusant Nun," in Bonnie Wheeler (ed.), *Representations of the Feminine in the Middle Ages* (Dallas: Academia, 1993), pp. 329–37.

——, "Mary Champney a Bridgittine nun under the rule of Queen Elizabeth I," *Birgittiana*, 13 (2002): 3–32.

——, "Three (Recusant) Sisters," in Anne Clark Bartlett et al. (eds), *Vox Mystica: Essays on Medieval Mysticism In Honor of Professor Valerie M. Lagorio* (Rochester: D.S. Brewer, 1995), pp. 147–58.

—— (ed.), "The life and good end of Sister Marie," *Birgittiana*, 13 (2002): 33–89.

Hutson, Lorna, "'Our Old Storehowse': Plowden's Commentaries and Political Consciousness in Shakespeare," *Shakespeare Yearbook*, 7 (1996): 249–73s.

——, *The Usurer's Daughter: Male Friendship and Fictions of Women in Sixteenth Century England* (London: Routledge, 1994).

James VI and I, *Political Writings*, ed. Johann P. Sommerville (Cambridge: Cambridge University Press, 1994).

James, Heather, "Ovid and the Question of Politics in Early Modern English," *ELH*, 70 (2003): 343–73.

Javitch, Daniel, "Rival Arts of Conduct in Elizabethan England: Guazzo's *Civile Conversation* and Castiglione's *Courtier*," *Yearbook of Italian Studies*, 1 (1971): 178–98.

Jodelle, Etienne, *Poètes du seizième siècle*, ed. Albert-Marie Schmidt (Paris: Gallimard, 1969).

Johnson, W.R., *Momentary Monsters: Lucan and His Heroes* (Ithaca: Cornell University Press, 1987).

Jones, Emrys, *The Origins of Shakespeare* (Oxford: Clarendon Press, 1977).

Jordan, Constance, *Shakespeare's Monarchies: Ruler and Subject in the Romances* (Ithaca: Cornell University Press, 1997).

Kastan, David Scott, *Shakespeare After Theory* (New York: Columbia University Press, 1999).

Keats, John, *The Letters of John Keats: 1814–1821*, ed. Hyder Edward Rollins (2 vols, Cambridge: Harvard University Press, 1958).

Kellogg, Alfred, *Chaucer, Langland, Arthur: Essays in Middle-English Literature* (New Brunswick: Rutgers University Press, 1972).

Kennedy, William J., *Authorizing Petrarch* (Ithaca: Cornell University Press, 1994).

——, *The Site of Petrarchism: Early Modern National Sentiment in Italy, France, and England* (Baltimore: Johns Hopkins University Press, 2003).

Kenny, Anthony, *Wittgenstein* (Harmondsworth: Penguin, 1973).

King, Helen, "Once Upon a Text: Hysteria from Hippocrates." in Sander L. Gilman et al. (eds), *Hysteria Beyond Freud* (Berkeley: University of California Press, 1993), pp. 3–90.

Kirkpatrick, Robin, *English and Italian Literature from Dante to Shakespeare* (New York: Longman, 1995).

Knight, G. Wilson, *The Wheel of Fire: Interpretation of Shakespeare's Tragedy* (1930; New York: Meridian, 1964).

Knight, Stephen, "Ideology in 'The Franklin's Tale'," *Parergon*, 28 (1980): 3–35.

Knight, W. Nicholas, "Equity, *The Merchant of Venice*, and William Lambarde," *Shakespeare Survey*, 27 (1974): 93–104.

Knox, John, *Works of John Knox*, ed. David Laing (6 vols, Edinburgh: James Thin, 1895).

Korsten, Frans, and Walker, Claire, *Elizabeth Evelinge, I* (Aldershot: Ashgate, 2002).

Krier, Theresa, *Birth Passages: Maternity & Nostalgia, Antiquity to Shakespeare* (Ithaca: Cornell University Press, 2001).

Kuin, Roger, *Chamber Music: Elizabethan Sonnet-Sequences and the Pleasure of Criticism* (Toronto: University of Toronto Press, 1998).

Kuriyama, Constance Brown, *Christopher Marlowe: A Renaissance Life* (Ithaca: Cornell University Press, 2002).

Lake, Peter with Questier, Michael, *The Antichrist's Lewd Hat: Protestants, Papists, & Players in Post-Reformation England* (New Haven: Yale University Press, 2001).

Lambley, Kathleen, *The Teaching and Cultivation of the French Language in England during Tudor and Stuart Times* (Manchester: Manchester University Press, 1920).

Languet, Hubert, *Huberti Langueti ... Epistolae Politicae et Historicae ad Philippum Sydnaeum* (Leiden, 1646).

——, *Huberti Langueti galli Epistolae ad Philippum Sydneium equitem anglum*, ed. David Dalrymple (Edinburgh: Murray and Cochran, 1776).

Latham, Agnes M.C., "Sir Walter Raleigh's *Instructions to his Son*," in *Elizabethan and Jacobean Studies Presented to Frank Percy Wilson in Honour of His Seventieth Birthday* (Oxford: Clarendon Press, 1959), pp. 199–218.

Law, Thomas Graves, "Parsons or Persons, Robert (1546–1610), jesuit missionary and controversialist," in *Dictionary of National Biography* (London: Oxford University Press, 1917–), vol. 15, pp. 411–18.

——, "Sanders or Sander, Nicholas (1530?–1581)," *Dictionary of National Biography* (London: Oxford University Press, 1917–), vol. 17, pp. 748–51.

Lee, Sidney, *The French Renaissance in England* (Oxford: Clarendon Press, 1910).

Leech, Clifford, *Christopher Marlowe: Poet for the Stage,* ed. Anne Lancashire (New York: AMS, 1986).

Leedham-Greene, E.S., *Books in Cambridge Inventories: Book Lists from the Vice-Chancellor's Court Probate Inventories in the Tudor and Stuart Periods* (2 vols, Cambridge: Cambridge University Press, 1986).

Lefebvre, Henri, *The Production of Space,* trans. Donald Nicholson-Smith (Oxford: Blackwell, 1991).

Leicester, H. Marshall, Jr., *The Disenchanted Self: Representing the Subject in the Canterbury Tales* (Berkeley: University of California Press, 1990).

Lemke, Jay, *Textual Politics: Discourse and Social Dynamics* (London: Taylor and Francis, 1995).

Lever, J.W., Introduction to William Shakespeare's *Measure for Measure* (1965; London: Methuen, 1987).

Levin, Harry, *The Overreacher: A Study of Christopher Marlowe* (Cambridge, MA: Harvard University Press, 1952).

Levith, Murray J., *Shakespeare's Italian Settings and Plays* (New York: St. Martin's, 1989).

Lewalski, Barbara, *Protestant Poetics and the Seventeenth-Century Religious Lyric* (Princeton: Princeton University Press, 1979).

Lewis, C.S., *English Literature of the Sixteenth Century, Excluding Drama* (1954; London: Oxford University Press, 1973).

Lindley, David, "The Stubbornness of Barnardine: Justice and Mercy in *Measure for Measure*," *Shakespeare Yearbook*, 7 (1996): 333–51.

Lipsius, Justus, *De recta pronunciacione Latinæ linguæ dialogus* (Leiden, 1586).

——, *Principles of Letter-Writing: A Bilingual Text of* Justi Lipsi Epistolica Institutio, trans and eds R.V. Young and Thomas Hester (Carbondale: Southern Illinois University Press, 1996).

Lock, Anne Vaughan, *The Collected Works of Anne Vaughan Lock*, ed. Susan M. Felch (Tempe: Arizona Center for Medieval and Renaissance Studies, 1999).

Lodge, Thomas, *The Complete Works of Thomas Lodge*, ed. Edmund Gosse (4 vols, Glasgow: Hunterian Club, 1883).

Loomie, A.J., "Englefield, Sir Francis (1522–1596), courtier and Roman Catholic exile," *Oxford Dictionary of National Biography*, <http://www.oxforddnb.com, article 8811>.

Lucan, *The Civil War, Books I–X*, trans. J.D. Duff (London: Heinemann, 1928).

——, *"De Bello Civili": Book II*, ed. Elaine Fantham (Cambridge: Cambridge University Press, 1992).

——, *"Pharsalia,"* trans. Jane Wilson Joyce (Ithaca: Cornell University Press, 1993).

Lupton, Julia Reinhard and Reinhard, Kenneth, *After Oedipus: Shakespeare in Psychoanalysis* (Ithaca: Cornell University Press, 1993).

Lyotard, Jean-François, *The Lyotard Reader*, ed. Andrew Benjamin (Oxford: Blackwell, 1989).

Machiavelli, Niccolò, *The Portable Machiavelli*, trans and eds Peter Bondanella and Mark Musa (New York: Penguin, 1979).

Mack, Peter, *Elizabethan Rhetoric: Theory and Practice* (Cambridge: Cambridge University Press, 2002).

MacLean, Gerald M., *Time's Witness: Historical Representation in English Poetry, 1603–1660* (Madison: University of Wisconsin Press, 1990).

Maclean, Ian, *Interpretation and Meaning in the Renaissance: The Case of Law* (Cambridge: Cambridge University Press, 1992).

Magnusson, Lynne, *Shakespeare and Social Dialogue: Dramatic Language and Elizabethan Letters* (Cambridge: Cambridge University Press, 1999).

Maitland, F.W., *Equity: A Course of Lectures* (2nd edn, Cambridge: Cambridge University Press, 1969).

Malloch, A.E., "John Donne and the Casuists," *Studies in English Literature*, 2 (1962): 57–76.

Marcus, Leah S., "Textual Indeterminacy and Ideological Difference: The Case of *Dr. Faustus*," *Renaissance Drama*, 20 (1989): 1–29.

Marlowe, Christopher, *The Complete Plays*, ed. Mark Thornton Burnett (London: Dent; Rutland, VT: Tuttle, 1999).

——, *The Complete Poems and Translations*, ed. Stephen Orgel (Harmondsworth: Penguin, 1971).

——, *Lucans First Booke* (1600).

——, *The Poems*, ed. Millar MacLure (London: Methuen, 1968).

Martin, Christopher, "Retrieving Jonson's Petrarch," *Shakespeare Quarterly*, 45 (1994): 89–92.

Martindale, Charles, "The Epic of Ideas: Lucan's *De Bello Civili* and *Paradise Lost*," *Comparative Criticism*, 3 (1981): 133–56.

——, *Redeeming the Text: Latin Poetry and the Hermeneutics of Reception* (Cambridge: Cambridge University Press, 1993).

Masten, Jeffrey, "Playwrighting: Authorship and Collaboration," in John D. Cox and David Scott Kastan (eds), *A New History of Early English Drama* (New York: Columbia University Press, 1997), pp. 357–82.

——, *Textual Intercourse: Collaboration, Authorship, and Sexualities in Renaissance Drama* (Cambridge: Cambridge University Press, 1997).

Masters, Jamie, *Poetry and Civil War in Lucan's "Bellum Civile"* (Cambridge: Cambridge University Press, 1992).

May, Steven, *The Elizabethan Courtier Poets: The Poems and Their Contexts* (Asheville, 1999).

Mayer, T.F., "Sander [Sanders], Nicholas (c. 1530–1581), religious controversialist," *Oxford Dictionary of National Biography*, <http://www.oxforddnb.com, article 24621>.

McConica, James, *The History of the University of Oxford: Vol. 3, The Collegiate University* (Oxford: Clarendon Press, 1986).

McCoy, Richard C., *The Rites of Knighthood: The Literature and Politics of Elizabethan Chivalry* (Berkeley: University of California Press, 1989).

McDonald, Christie V., "Choreographies: An Interview between Jacques Derrida and Christie V. McDonald," *Diacritics*, 12 (1982): 66–76.

McLuhan, Marshall, *The Gutenberg Galaxy* (Toronto: University of Toronto Press, 1962).

——, *Understanding Media: The Extensions of Man* (London: Sphere, 1973).

McNally, James Richard, "*Rector et Dux Populi*: Italian Humanists and the Relationship between Rhetoric and Logic," *Modern Philology*, 67 (1969): 168–76.

Miller, Robert P., "Chaucer's Pardoner, the Scriptural Eunuch, and the *Pardoner's Tale*," *Speculum*, 30 (1955): 180–99.

Minshull, Catherine, "Marlowe's 'Sound Machevill'," *Renaissance Drama*, 13 (1982): 35–53.

Montaigne, Michel de, *Essais* (Paris: Gallimard, 1953).

——, *The essayes ... of Lo: Michaell de Montaigne*, trans. John Florio (London, 1603).

Montrose, Louis A., "Professing the Renaissance: The Poetics and Politics of Culture," in H. Aram Veeser (ed.), *The New Historicism* (New York and London: Routledge, 1989), pp. 15–36.

Moorhouse, A.C., *The Triumph of the Alphabet* (New York: Schuman, 1953).

Morgan, Gerald, "A Defence of Dorigen's Complaint," *Medium Aevum*, 46 (1977): 77–97.

Morson, Gary Saul and Emerson, Caryl, *Mikhail Bakhtin: Creation of a Prosaics* (Stanford: Stanford University Press, 1990).

Murtaugh, Daniel S., "The Garden and the Sea: The Topography of *The Faerie Queene*, III," *ELH*, 40 (1973): 325–38.

Nelson, William, *The Poetry of Edmund Spenser: A Study* (New York: Columbia University Press, 1963).

Neville, Alexander, *The lamentable tragedie of Oedipus the sonne of Laius Kyng of Thebes out of Seneca* (London, 1563).

Nohrnberg, James, *The Analogy of "The Faerie Queene"* (Princeton: Princeton University Press, 1976).

Nolhac, Pierre de, *Pétrarque et l'humanisme* (2 vols, 2nd rev. edn, Paris: Champion, 1965).

Norbrook, David, *Writing the English Republic: Poetry, Rhetoric, and Politics, 1627–1660* (Cambridge: Cambridge University Press, 1999).

Ong, Walter J., *Orality and Literacy: The Technologizing of the Word* (New York: Methuen, 1982).

Ovid, *Ovid's Metamorphosis: The Arthur Golding Translation, 1567*, ed. John Frederick Nims (Philadelphia: Paul Dry, 2000).

Parker, M.D.H., *The Slave of Life: A Study of Shakespeare and the Idea of Justice* (London: Chatto and Windus, 1955).

Parker, Matthew, *The Whole Psalter Translated into English Metre* (London, 1567).

Parker, Patricia, *Literary Fat Ladies: Rhetoric, Gender, Property* (London: Methuen, 1987).

Peltonen, Markku, *Classical Humanism and Republicanism in English Political Thought, 1570–1640* (Cambridge: Cambridge University Press, 1995).

Pembroke, Mary Sidney Herbert, Countess of, *The Collected Works of Mary Sidney Herbert, Countess of Pembroke*, eds Margaret P. Hannay, Noel J. Kinnamon and Michael G. Brennan (2 vols, Oxford: Clarendon Press, 1998).

Perkins, William, *Epieikeia: or, A treatise of Christian Equitie and moderation …* (1604).

Persons, Robert, *Relacion de algunos martyrios, que de nueuo han hecho los hereges en Inglaterra, y de otras cosas tocantes a nuestra santa y Catolica religion. Traduzida de Ingles en Castellano, por el padre Roberto Personio* (Madrid, 1590).

Petrarca, Francesco, *Le Familiari, Libri I–IV,* ed. Ugo Dotti (Urbino: Argali, 1970).

——, *Petrarch's Lyric Poems: The "Rime sparse" and Other Lyrics*, trans. and ed. Robert M. Durling (1976; Cambridge: Harvard University Press, 1995).

A plaine pathway to the French tongue, Very profitable for Marchants and also all other, which desire the same (1571), ed. R.C. Alston (Menston: Scolar, 1968).

Plato, *The Collected Dialogues of Plato*, eds Elizabeth Hamilton and Huntington Cairns (Princeton: Princeton University Press, 1961).

——, *Statesman*, trans. Harold N. Fowler (London: Heinemann, 1925).

Platt, Peter G., "'The Meruailouse Site': Shakespeare, Venice, and Paradoxical Stages," *Renaissance Quarterly*, 54 (2001): 121–54.

Playfere, Thomas, *A Sermon preached at Saint Maryes Spittle in London on Tuesday in Easter weeke, 1595* (1596).

Plowden, Edmund, *The Commentaries, or Reports of Edmund Plowden* (London: E. Brooke, 1779).

Pocock, J.G.A., *The Machiavellian Moment: Florentine Political Thought and the Atlantic Republican Tradition* (Princeton: Princeton University Press, 1975).

—— (ed.), *The Political Works of James Harrington* (Cambridge: Cambridge University Press, 1977).

Pollard, A.F., "Sanders, Nicholas (c. 1530–1581)," *Encyclopaedia Britannica* (29 vols, 11th edn, Cambridge: Cambridge University Press, 1911), vol. 24, p. 138.

Pollen, J.H., "Nicholas Sander (Sanders)," *Catholic Encyclopedia Online*, <http://www.newadvent.org/cathen>.

——, "Robert Persons (also, but less correctly, Parsons)," *Catholic Encyclopedia Online*, <http://www.newadvent.org/cathen>.

—— (ed.), *Unpublished Documents Relating to the English Martyrs, I (1584–1603)*, Catholic Record Society Publications 5 (London: Privately Printed for the Society by J. Whitehead & Son, Leeds, 1908).

Pope, Elizabeth Marie, "The Renaissance Background of *Measure for Measure*," *Shakespeare Survey*, 2 (1949): 66–82.

Prall, Stuart E., "The Development of Equity in Tudor England," *The American Journal of Legal History*, 8 (1964): 1–19.

Praz, Mario, "Machiavelli and the Elizabethans," *Proceedings of the British Academy*, 14 (1928): 49–97.

Prescott, Anne Lake, "Divided State," *English Literary Renaissance*, 25 (1995): 445–57.

——, *French Poets and the English Renaissance* (New Haven: Yale University Press, 1978).

——, *Imagining Rabelais in Renaissance England* (New Haven: Yale University Press, 1998).

——, "King David as a 'Right Poet': Sidney and the Psalmist," *ELR*, 19 (1989): 131–51.

——, "Musical Strains: Marot's Double Role as Psalmist and Courtier," in Marie-Rose Logan and Peter Rudnytsky (eds), *Contending Kingdoms: Historical, Psychological, and Feminist Approaches to the Literature of Sixteenth-Century England and France* (Detroit: Wayne State University Press, 1990), pp. 42–68.

——, "Spenser (Re)Reading du Bellay: Chronology and Literary Response," in Judith H. Anderson, Donald Cheney, and David A. Richardson (eds), *Spenser's Life and the Subject of Biography* (Amherst: University of Massachusetts Press, 1996), pp. 131–45.

——, "The Laurel and the Myrtle: Spenser and Ronsard," in Patrick Cheney and Lauren Silberman (eds), *Worldmaking Spenser: Explorations in the Early Modern Age* (Lexington: University of Kentucky Press, 2000), pp. 63–78.

——, Hieatt, A. Kent and Hieatt, Charles W., "When Did Shakespeare Write Sonnets 1609?", *Studies in Philology*, 88 (1991): 69–109.

—— and Cheney, Patrick (eds), *Approaches to Teaching Shorter Elizabethan Poetry* (New York: MLA, 2000).

—— and Travistky, Betty S. (eds), *Female and Male Voices in Early Modern England: An Anthology of Renaissance Writing* (New York: Columbia University Press, 2000).

Prouty, Charles, *George Gascoigne: Elizabethan Courtier, Soldier, and Poet* (New York: Columbia University Press, 1942).

Quint, David, *Epic and Empire: Politics and Generic Form from Virgil to Milton* (Princeton: Princeton University Press, 1983).

Rabelais, François, *Gargantua and Pantagruel*, trans. J.M. Cohen (New York: Viking, 1955).

Radoff, M.L., "The Influence of French Farce in *Henry V* and *Merry Wives of Windsor*," *MLN*, 48 (1933): 427–35.

Returns of Aliens Dwelling in the City and Suburbs of London from the Reign of Henry VIII to That of James I, eds R.E.G. Kirk and Ernest F. Kirk (Aberdeen: Aberdeen University Press, 1902–1907).

Ribner, Irving, "Marlowe and Machiavelli," *Comparative Literature*, 6 (1954): 348–56.

Richards, Jennifer, *Rhetoric and Courtliness in Early Modern Literature* (Cambridge: Cambridge University Press, 2002).

Richmond, Hugh M., "Ronsard and the English Renaissance," *Comparative Literature Studies*, 7 (1970): 141–60.

Ricoeur, Paul, *Freud and Philosophy: An Essay on Interpretation*, trans. Denis Savage (New Haven: Yale University Press, 1970).

Ridley, Thomas, *A View of the Civile and Ecclesiastical Law* (London, 1607).

Rienstra, Debra K., "Mary Sidney, Countess of Pembroke, *Psalmes*," in Anita Pacheco (ed.), *A Companion to Early Modern Women's Writing* (Oxford: Blackwell, 2002).

—— and Kinnamon, Noel J., "Revisioning the Sacred Text," *Sidney Journal*, 17 (1999): 53–77.

Riggs, David, "The Killing of Christopher Marlowe," *Stanford Humanities Review*, 8 (2000): 239–51.

——, *The World of Christopher Marlowe* (London: Faber, 2004).

Roche, Thomas P., *Petrarch and the English Sonnet Sequences* (New York: AMS Press, 1989).

Rogers, D.M. (ed.), *Diego de Yepes Historia Particular de la Persecucion de Inglaterra Madrid 1599* (London: Gregg International, 1971).

Rollins, Hyder Edward, *A New Variorum Edition of Shakespeare: The Sonnets* (2 vols, Philadelphia: Lippincott, 1944).

Ronan, Clifford J., "*Pharsalia* 1.373–8: Roman Parricide and Marlowe's Editors," *Classical and Modern Literature*, 6 (1986): 305–9.

Ronsard, Pierre de, *Oeuvres complètes*, eds Jean Céard, Daniel Ménager, and Michel Simonin (2 vols, Paris: Gallimard, 1993–1994).

——, *Oeuvres complètes*, eds Paul Laumonier, Raymond Lebègue, and Isidore Silver (20 vols, Geneva: Droz, 1914–1974).

Rousseau, G.S., "'A Strange Pathology': Hysteria in the Early Modern World, 1500–1800," in Sander L. Gilman et al. (eds), *Hysteria Beyond Freud* (Berkeley: University of California Press, 1993), pp. 91–224.

Rummel, Erika, "Erasmus' Manual of Letter-writing: Tradition and Innovation," *Renaissance and Reformation* 25 (1989): 299–312.

Rusche, Harry, "Pride, Humility, and Grace in Book I of *The Faerie Queene*," *Studies in English Literature*, 7 (1967): 29–39.

Sackville, Thomas and Norton, Thomas, *Gorboduc*, ed. Irby B. Cauthen, Jr. (Lincoln: University of Nebraska Press, 1970).

Saint German, Christopher, *St. German's Doctor and Student*, eds T.F.T. Plucknett and J.L. Barton (London: Selden Society, 1974).

Sanders, Elizabeth, "The History of Syon (continued). Englefield Correspondence—English College Valladolid: The Coppy of S. Elizabethe Sanders Letter Unto Your Wor. of Her Being in England. The First Letter (Rouen 1587)," *Poor Soul's Friend and St. Joseph's Monitor* (January/February 1966): 11–22.

——, "The History of Syon (continued). Englefield Correspondence—English College Valladolid: Sister Elizabeth Saunders 'Second Letter' to Sir Francis Englefield," *Poor Soul's Friend and St. Joseph's Monitor* (March/April 1966): 43–54.

Schanzer, Ernest, *The Problem Plays of Shakespeare: A Study of Julius Caesar, Measure for Measure, Antony and Cleopatra* (New York: Schocken, 1963).

Schleiner, Louise, *Tudor and Stuart Women Writers* (Bloomington: Indiana University Press, 1994).

Schoenbaum, Samuel, *Shakespeare's Lives* (new edn, Oxford: Clarendon Press, 1991).

——, *William Shakespeare: A Compact Documentary Life* (New York: Oxford University Press, 1977).

Scott, Margaret, "Machiavelli and the Machiavel," *Renaissance Drama*, 15 (1984): 147–74.

Scott, Mary Augusta, "The Book of the Courtyer: A Possible Source of Benedick and Beatrice," *PMLA*, 16 (1901): 475–502.

Scouludi, Irene, "Alien Immigration into and Alien Communities in London, 1558–1640," *Proceedings of the Huguenot Society of London*, 16 (1937): 27–50.

——, "The Stranger Community in London," *Proceedings of the Huguenot Society of London*, 24 (1987): 434–42.

Scudéry, Madeleine de, *Selected Letters, Orations, and Rhetorical Dialogues*, eds Jane Donawerth and Julie Strongson (Chicago: University of Chicago Press, 2004).

Selden, John, *Table Talk* (1689), ed. S.W. Singer (1855; Freeport: Books for Libraries, 1972).

Sellstrom, A. Donald, "*La Mort de Pompée*: Roman History and Tasso's Theory of Christian Epic," *PMLA*, 97 (1982): 830–43.

Seneca, *Four Tragedies and Octavia,* trans. E.F. Watling (New York: Penguin, 1966).

——, *Tragedies*, ed. and trans. John G. Fitch (2 vols, Cambridge: Harvard University Press, 2004).

Shaheen, Naseeb, "Shakespeare's Knowledge of Italian," *Shakespeare Survey*, 47 (1994): 161–70.

Shakespeare, Wiliam, *The Norton Shakespeare*, eds Stephen Greenblatt et al. (New York: Norton, 1997).

——, *The Riverside Shakespeare*, eds G. Blakemore Evans et al. (Boston: Houghton, 1997)

Shannon, Laurie, *Sovereign Amity: Figures of Friendship in Shakespearean Contexts* (Chicago: University of Chicago Press, 2002).

Shapiro, James, "'Metre meete to furnish Lucans style': Reconsidering Marlowe's *Lucan*," in Kenneth Friedenreich, Roma Gill, and Constance B. Kuriyama (eds), "*A Poet and a filthy Play-maker*": *New Essays on Christopher Marlowe* (New York: AMS, 1988), pp. 315–25.

——, *Rival Playwrights: Marlowe, Jonson, Shakespeare* (New York: Columbia University Press, 1991).

——, *A Year in the Life of William Shakespeare* (New York: HarperCollins, 2005).

Shifflett, Andrew, "'By *Lucan* Driv'n About': A Jonsonian Marvell's Lucanic Milton," *Renaissance Quarterly*, 59 (1996): 803–23.

Shuger, Debora Kuller, *Political Theologies in Shakespeare's England: The Sacred and the State in* Measure for Measure (New York: Palgrave, 2002).

——, *The Renaissance Bible: Scholarship, Sacrifice, and Subjectivity* (Berkeley: University of California Press, 1994).

Sidney, Philip, *The Poems of Sir Philip Sidney*, ed. W.A. Ringler (Oxford: Clarendon Press, 1962).

——, *Sir Philip Sidney, Selected Works*, ed. Katherine Duncan-Jones (Oxford: Oxford University Press, 1989).

——, and Pembroke, Mary Sidney Herbert, Countess of, *The Psalms of Sir Philip Sidney and the Countess of Pembroke*, ed. J.C.A. Rathmell (New York: New York University Press, 1963).

Simon, Joan, *Education and Society in Tudor England* (Cambridge: Cambridge University Press, 1966).

Skinner, Quentin, "Classical Liberty and the Coming of the English Civil War," in Martin van Gelderen and Quentin Skinner (eds), *Republicanism: A Shared European Heritage* (2 vols, Cambridge: Cambridge University Press, 2002), vol. 2, pp. 9–28.

——, *Liberty before Liberalism* (Cambridge: Cambridge University Press, 1998).

Skulsky, Harold, "Pain, Law, and Conscience in *Measure for Measure*," *Journal of the History of Ideas*, 25 (1964): 147–68.

Slights, Camille Wells, *The Casuistical Tradition in Shakespeare, Donne, Herbert, and Milton* (Princeton: Princeton University Press, 1981).

Smarr, Janet Levarie, "Anacreontics," in A.C. Hamilton et al. (eds), *The Spenser Encyclopedia* (Toronto: University of Toronto Press, 1990).

Smith, Nigel, *Literature and Revolution in England 1640–1660* (New Haven: Yale University Press, 1994).

Snyder, Susan, "The Left Hand of God: Despair in Medieval and Renaissance Tradition," *Studies in the Renaissance*, 12 (1965): 18–59.

Sommerville, Johann P., "English and European Political Ideas in the Early Seventeenth Century: Revisionism and the Case of Absolutism," *Journal of British Studies*, 35 (1996): 168–94.

Soowthern, John, *Pandora* (1584), ed. George B. Parks (New York: Columbia University Press, 1938).

Spenser, Edmund, *The Faerie Queene*, eds A.C. Hamilton et al. (rev. edn, Harlow: Pearson Education, 2001).

——, *The Faerie Queene*, ed. Thomas P. Roche, Jr. (New York: Penguin, 1978).

——, *The Works of Edmund Spenser*, eds Edwin Greenlaw et al. (11 vols, Baltimore: Johns Hopkins University Press, 1932–57).

Steane, J.B., *Marlowe: A Critical Study* (Cambridge: Cambridge University Press, 1964).

Stephens, Dorothy, "'Newes of devils': Feminine Sprights in Masculine Minds in *The Faerie Queene*," *ELR*, 23 (1993): 363–81.

Stern, Virginia, *Gabriel Harvey: A Study of His Life, Marginalia, and Library* (Oxford: Clarendon Press, 1979).

Stow, John, *The Annales, or a generall chronicle of England, begun first by Iohn Stow* (London, 1615).

Sypher, Wylie, "Shakespeare as Casuist: *Measure for Measure*," *Sewanee Review*, 58 (1950): 262–80.

Thomas, Keith, *Religion and the Decline of Magic* (New York: Scribner's, 1971).

Thomas, William, *Principal Rules of the Italian Grammar, with a Dictionarie for the better understanding of Boccace, Petrarke, and Dante* (1550), ed. R.C. Alston (Menston: Scolar, 1968).

Tilley, M.P., *A Dictionary of the Proverbs in England in the Sixteenth and Seventeenth Centuries: A Collection of the Proverbs Found in English Literature and the Dictionaries of the Period* (Ann Arbor: University of Michigan Press, 1950).

Tonkin, Humphrey, *The Faerie Queene* (London: Unwin Hyman, 1989).

Trill, Suzanne, "Sixteenth-Century Women's Writing: Mary Sidney's *Psalmes* and the 'Femininity' of Translation," in William Zunder and Suzanne Trill (eds), *Writing and the English Renaissance* (London: Longman, 1996).

Trimpi, Wesley, *Muses of One Mind* (Princeton: Princeton University Press, 1983).

Turner, R.W., *The Equity of Redemption* (Cambridge: Cambridge University Press, 1931).

Van Buren, Jane Silverman, *Modernist Madonna: Semiotics of the Maternal Metaphor* (Bloomington: Indiana University Press, 1989).

van Dorsten, Jan A., *Poets, Patrons, and Professors: Sir Philip Sidney, Daniel Rogers, and the Leiden Humanists* (Oxford: Oxford University Press, 1962).

Van Dyke, Carolynn, *The Fiction of Truth: Structures of Meaning in Narrative and Dramatic Allegory* (Ithaca: Cornell University Press, 1985).

Venant, Jean-Pierre and Vidal-Niquet, Pierre, *Myth and Tragedy in Ancient Greece*, trans. Janet Loyd (New York: Zone, 1990).

Vives, Juan Luis, *A very fruitfull and pleasant booke, called the Instruction of a Christian Woman* (London, 1585).

Vološinov, V.N., *Marxism and the Philosophy of Language*, trans. Ladislav Matejka and I.R. Titunik (Cambridge: Harvard University Press, 1986).

Walker, Claire, *Gender and Politics in Early Modern Europe: English Convents in France and the Low Countries* (Hampshire: Palgrave Macmillan, 2003).

Wall, Wendy, "Authorship and the Material Conditions of Writing," in Arthur F. Kinney (ed.), *The Cambridge Companion to English Literature 1500–1600* (Cambridge: Cambridge University Press, 2000), pp. 64–89

——, *The Imprint of Gender: Authorship and Publication in the English Renaissance* (Ithaca: Cornell University Press, 1993).

Waller, Gary, *Mary Sidney, Countess of Pembroke: A Critical Study of Her Writings and Literary Milieu* (Salzburg: Institut für Anglistik und Amerikanistik, Universität Salzburg, 1979).

Warner, Marina, "Why do Ogres Eat Babies? Monstrous Paternity in Myth and Fairy Tales," in Lieve Spaas and Trista Selous (eds), *Paternity and Fatherhood: Myths and Realities* (London: Palgrave, 1998), pp. 195–203.

Warrington, John (ed.), *Aristotle's Poetics, Demetrius on Style, Longinus on the Sublime* (London: Dent, 1963).

Watt, Tessa, *Cheap Print and Popular Piety, 1550–1640* (Cambridge: Cambridge University Press, 1991).

West, William, *Symboleography* (London, 1594).

Wetherbee, Winthrop, "Dante, Lucan, and Virgil," in Robert von Hallberg (ed.), *Canons* (Chicago: University of Chicago Press, 1984), pp. 131–48.

The Whole Booke of Psalmes Collected into English Meter by Thomas Sternhold, J. Hopkins and Others (London, 1562).

Wilcox, Helen, "'Whom the Lord with Love Affecteth': Gender and the Religious Poet, 1590–1633," in Danielle Clarke and Elizabeth Clarke (eds), *"This Double Voice": Gendered Writing in Early Modern England* (New York: St. Martin's Press, 2000).

Willen, Diane, "Comment on Women's Education in Elizabethan England," *Topic*, 36 (1982): 66–73.

Wilson, Richard, *Will Power: Essays on Shakespearean Authority* (London: Harvester Wheatsheaf, 1993).

Wilson, Robert, *The Three Ladies of London*, ed. H.S.D. Mithal (New York: Garland, 1988).

Wilson-Okamura, David Scott, "Republicanism, Nostalgia, and the Crowd," *Spenser Studies*, 17 (2003): 253–73.

Wofford, Susanne Lindgren, "Britomart's Petrarchan Lament: Allegory and Narrative in *The Faerie Queene* III.iv," *Comparative Literature*, 39 (1987): 28–57.

Woodbridge, Linda, "Patchwork: Piecing the Early Modern Mind In England's First Century of Print Culture," *ELR*, 23 (1993): 5–45.

Woods, Susanne, *Natural Emphasis: English Versification from Chaucer to Dryden* (San Marino: Huntington Library, 1985).

Worden, Blair, "Republicanism, Regicide, and Republic: The English Experience," in Martin van Gelderen and Quentin Skinner (eds), *Republicanism: A Shared European Heritage* (2 vols, Cambridge: Cambridge University Press, 2002), vol. 1, pp. 307–27.

Wyatt, Thomas, "Aliens in England before the Huguenots," *Proceedings of the Huguenot Society of London*, 19 (1953): 74–94.

Yates, Frances A., *John Florio: The Life of an Italian in Shakespeare's England* (Cambridge: Cambridge University Press, 1934).

Yepes, Diego de, *Historia particular de la persecucion de Inglaterra, y de los martirios que en ella ha auido, desde el año del Señor, 1570* (Madrid, 1599).

Yungblut, Laura Hunt, *Strangers Here Amongst Us: Policies, Perceptions, and the Presence of Aliens in Elizabethan England* (London: Routledge, 1996).

Zim, Rivkah, English Metrical Psalms: Poetry as Praise and Prayer, 1535–1601 (Cambridge: Cambridge University Press, 1987).

Index

31.